SO-BAS-209

SPOTLESS

Experiencing the Everlasting Covenant
through Righteousness by Faith

Shelley Quinn

3ABN
books

Title: Spotless—Experiencing the Everlasting Covenant through Righteousness by Faith

Author: Shelley Quinn
Copyright © by Shelly Quinn

Produced by Safeliz for 3ABN

Editors: Joel Iparraguirre and Tompaul Wheeler
Internal layout: Sara Calado
Cover: AoliaB
Cover photo: dreamstime.com

Pradillo, 6 · Pol. Ind. La Mina
E-28770 · Colmenar Viejo, Madrid, Spain
Tel.: [+34] 91 845 98 77
contact@safeliz.com · www.safeliz.com

First edition, August 2023

ISBN: 978-84-19752-00-0

PRINTED IN CHINA
IMP12

All Rights Reserved

◯3ABN | books

3ABN Books is dedicated to bringing you the best in published materials consistent with the mission of Three Angels Broadcasting Network, Inc. Our goal is to uplift Jesus through books, video, and audio materials by our family of 3ABN presenters. Our in-depth Bible study guides, devotionals, biographies, and lifestyle materials promote the whole person in health and the mending of broken people. For more information, call 618-627-4651 or visit 3ABN's Website: 3ABN.tv

Unless otherwise noted, Scripture quotations are taken from THE HOLY BIBLE, NEW KING JAMES VERSION. Copyright © 1982 by Thomas Nelson. Used by permission. All rights reserved.

Scriptures marked NIV are taken from The Holy Bible, New International Version® NIV® Copyright © 1973, 1978, 1984, 2011 by Biblica, Inc.™ Used by permission. All rights reserved worldwide.

Scriptures marked NASB are taken from the NEW AMERICAN STANDARD BIBLE®, Copyright © 1960, 1962, 1963, 1971, 1972, 1973, 1975, 1977, 1995 by The Lockman Foundation. Used by permission.

All rights reserved. No part of this book may be transmitted or reproduced in any form or by any means, electronic or mechanical, including photocopying and recording, or by any information storage and retrieval system, without permission in writing from the publisher.

Shelley Quinn

SPOTLESS

Experiencing the Everlasting Covenant
through Righteousness by Faith

Contents

THE WONDER OF IT ALL

Prologue

I believe the Bible is the inspired Word of God—a self-revelation of our Creator, who loves us and makes Himself known to us. God demonstrates His love by His actions. We learn who He is through the record of His interactions with humanity over a period of approximately 4,000 years of world history in the Old Testament, and about 100 years in the New.

The unifying theme of Scripture is God's everlasting covenant of *righteousness by faith* to redeem humanity from sin. Determined by the Godhead before Creation, and announced in the Garden of Eden, this covenant is disclosed in three thoughts: the Person of Jesus Christ is "the Lamb slain from the foundation of the world" (Revelation 13:8); His blood shed on Calvary is "the blood of the everlasting covenant" (Hebrews 13:20); and the goal of His covenant is the great exchange—"For He made Him who knew no sin to be sin for us, that we might become the righteousness of God in Him" (2 Corinthians 5:21, emphasis added).

What can you expect in this book? Written in a narrative style for easier reading—with a sentence structure that is intentionally simple and direct—the content is largely a paraphrase of Scripture, providing an explanation that holds true to its meaning. Scripture references are included in parentheses, to allow easy verification of biblical accuracy. There is nothing more important in our lives than to become like the noble Bereans (Acts 17:10–12), who searched the Scriptures daily to find out whether what they were taught lined up with God's Word. You will also find occasional *sidebar-inserts* of historical information, included to magnify your overall understanding of Scripture. Any of my personal conjectures are clearly pointed out as such.

This book provides a panoramic, bird's eye view of the central story of the Bible—the Messiah. It offers a fresh revelation of the Person of Jesus Christ, and an intimate understanding of God's amazing, self-sacrificing love. It begins in Genesis, the first book written by Moses, because Jesus said, "For if you believed Moses, you would believe Me; for he wrote about Me. But if you do not believe his writings, how will you believe My words?" (John 5:46–47). It is only through the covenant language and terms that God first identified in Moses' writings that we get the key to unlock the true identity of Christ. The wonder of it all will fill your heart with awe.

This is the story of righteousness by faith—a relational term that defines how God relates to His people, and how He expects them to relate to Him. As we follow the interactions between God and the ancients, Scripture will teach us that the Lord seeks reciprocal love and loyalty from those who enter into covenant relationship with Him.

Of special importance to us is how God and Abraham related to each other. Abraham is called the spiritual "father of us all" (Romans 4:16). The covenant of *righteousness by faith* that God signed, sealed, and delivered to him is the foundation of both the *Old Covenant* and the *New Covenant*. Contrary to popular opinion, God has never made a contract with humanity. His covenants are His expressed will—He makes all the promises, and He keeps all the promises.

Why is this book worth your time? No matter your level of biblical understanding, you will find deep insights that reveal essential scriptural truths for eternal life. For over 20 years I have searched the Scriptures on the topic of God's covenants. As I wrote, I prayed for the Lord to show me things that had been "fenced in and hidden" from my understanding (Jeremiah 33:3). He did—opening my eyes to little details that made a big difference. To my surprise, the Lord led me through the story of the Patriarchs in great detail, revealing new insights through their stories.

Time is life. How you invest your time is how you invest your life. This book can be read by dedicating just one hour a day for the next two weeks. Isn't it worth the exchange of a few hours of study to know God's plan for your life?

Since we must live in an intimate covenant relationship with Him to be saved, it is critical to understand what God expects of us. Jesus said—

Not everyone who says to Me, "Lord, Lord," shall enter the kingdom of heaven, but he who does the will of My Father in heaven. Many will say to Me in that day, "Lord, Lord, have we not prophesied in Your name, cast out demons in Your name, and done many wonders in Your name?" And then I will declare to them, "I never knew you; depart from Me, you who practice lawlessness!" (Matthew 7:21–23).

Jesus also said, "Man shall not live by bread alone, but by every word that proceeds from the mouth of God" (Matthew 4:4, quoting Deuteronomy 8:3). His word provides us with the spiritual nutrition that develops our stamina to withstand the trials and tribulations of life.

I invite you to join me on the journey of a lifetime. Let's take a closer look at God's everlasting covenant of *righteousness by faith*. Understanding God's plan changed my life. He put my feet on His path of life, where the fullness of joy is found in His Presence.

SLOW OF HEART

Chapter One

"**B**rood of vipers! Who warned you to flee from the wrath to come?" (Matthew 3:7) John the Baptist vehemently denounced the open shame of the religious leaders.

Four hundred years of silence had passed since the prophet Malachi wrote the last book of the Old Testament, prophesying that Elijah would come to turn the hearts of humanity around (Malachi 4:5–6). Now the greatest of prophets had arrived, ministering in the spirit and power of Elijah, baptizing people to turn their hearts to God. Coming from a priestly family, he was commissioned by God as the last Old Covenant prophet—the "Elijah-to-come"—to herald humanity's coming Redeemer, and to make a straight path for the Messiah's mission (Matthew 11:7–11; 17:9–13).

What a scene in contrast it was that day at the Jordan River. Dressed in a rugged camel-haired garment, and filled with the Holy Spirit from the time he was in his mother's womb (Luke 1:15), John preached with passion. He lifted his eyes and saw Pharisees and Sadducees approaching, leaders of the two predominant sects of the Jewish religion that had originated during the 400 years of silence. They hadn't come to repent. They didn't fear God's coming wrath, mistakenly trusting in their physical descent from Abraham as assurance of salvation.

Pharisees—meaning "separated"—controlled the synagogues. Most of the scribes who interpreted Jewish law were Pharisees. They looked down on anything or anyone non-Jewish. Believing salvation came by works, they imposed intricate ceremonial rituals for purity. Their man-made traditions served only to contradict the Word of God in the Old Testament, and to camouflage the inner wickedness of human hearts. Of course, not all Pharisees could be described so harshly. Some were honest-hearted, but honestly wrong.

Sadducees—which may have meant "righteous ones"—controlled the temple services and operations in Jerusalem. They believed only in the Law of Moses (the first five books of the Bible), and sought to preserve practices from Moses' day. Sadducees rejected anything supernatural, such as angels, demons, or the resurrection of the dead. Most were descendants of high-priestly families or wealthy aristocrats. Quick to compromise, they tended to seek cordial relations with the Roman empire.

Both Pharisees and Sadducees looked to the coming Messiah as a political-military Deliverer who would free Israel from Roman rule.

Then He showed up.

Humble. Morally pure. Filled with passion for the Lord's will. Loving. Compassionate. Non-judgmental. This was no ordinary man. He had a charisma about Him that drew rugged men and delicate women alike to His side. He taught with authority. The people believed a great prophet was among them. Eventually, some placed their hope in this Person—Jesus Christ of Nazareth—as the Messiah.

The Pharisees became jealous of Jesus' popularity and incensed that He condemned their oral traditions. The Sadducees feared His teachings would destroy their political power and be their financial ruin. The two opposing sects finally united in one cause—to crucify the Person of Jesus Christ on the Friday of the Passover.

THE SAVIOR PROVIDES POST-RESURRECTION STUDIES

Little is known about the two obscure, ordinary disciples who walked the road to Emmaus and encountered Jesus on the day of His resurrection. Their story is found in Luke 24:13–32. We can assume that they had arrived in Jerusalem a week earlier for the Feast of Passover, along with the Feast of Unleavened Bread. They had likely arrived in the Holy City with great anticipation. What would Jesus do during this special Festival? Would He reveal Himself to all as Israel's King, and assume His reign on the throne of David?

The Sunday after the crucifixion they started their seven-mile journey home. Descending the rocky road, despair and confusion clouded their thoughts. Stunned, they couldn't shake the image of Jesus' bruised and broken body.

As they walked, they reasoned between themselves in hushed tones. No record of their conversation is included in the Bible, but I can imagine they discussed the horror of the event and lamented their continuing political situation. Perhaps part of their conversation went something like the following:

"I was certain He was Messiah. When He fed the thousands, it was reminiscent of the miracle of the manna in the desert. He was unique. He taught such things about the kingdom of God as I never imagined. I can't believe that compassionate, powerful man is dead."

"Of course," the one whose name was Cleopas (Luke 24:18) may have responded. "We both believed He was the Deliverer who would free our nation from Rome's stranglehold. Now our wait continues. How long will God allow Rome to occupy the Promised Land and enslave His people?"

"But how do you understand the women's report?" the inquiring companion may have asked. "Did you find it convincing, or was it just hysteria? Friday when the men removed Jesus' body and placed it in a tomb, those women were anxious to prepare spices and go anoint His dead body. They rested on the Sabbath, but I doubt they slept last night. Someone said the women went out to the tomb at the breaking of dawn today, and were stunned to see His body was gone. They worried about who could be responsible for taking it away. Perhaps, in their anguish, they just imagined angels then appeared to announce Jesus had risen."

"It's certainly puzzling," Cleopas may have added. "Who would unwrap a dead body to remove it, and leave the linen burial cloths folded inside the tomb?" (John 20:6–7).

Whatever their conversation was, they thought it was private. No one was within earshot. However, there was One who heard.

Suddenly, Jesus drew near—but God prevented them from recognizing Him. He asked,

> What kind of conversation is this that you have with one another as you walk and are sad? (Luke 24:17).

With pent-up frustration, Cleopas may have responded with more force than he intended. He was astonished that this stranger did not know about Jesus—everyone in Jerusalem was talking about it.

Cleopas unfolded the dramatic account of a mighty Prophet—the One they hoped would be the Redeemer of Israel—who had been condemned to death by the chief priests and rulers, crucified by the Romans, and entombed. Besides which, certain women of their company said they found His tomb empty, and related an incredible story of a vision of angels who told them He was alive. To top it all off, certain men of their company ran to the tomb and found only His burial cloths, just as the women had said. Yet, when Cleopas and his companion had departed Jerusalem, there was no report of anyone having seen Him.

> Then Jesus spoke to them, saying, "O foolish ones, and slow of heart to believe in all that the prophets have spoken! Ought not the Christ to have suffered these things and to enter into His glory?" (Luke 24:25–26).

> And beginning at Moses and all the Prophets, He expounded to them in all the Scriptures the things concerning Himself (Luke 24:27).

"Slow of heart"—dull of hearing and not quick to perceive. "Foolish"–not understanding the prophecies. His reproach could have been received as an insult, but His manner of delivery came across as an invitation to understand greater truths. Jesus declared that they had no hope of understanding the Messiah's mission until they understood what was written about Him from Genesis to Malachi.

Launching into a Bible study, Jesus provided evidences of His identity from the Holy Scriptures. Enthralled, the two walked with Jesus, listening intently to the *proof texts* from the Old Testament, which contained the prophecies that testified of Him, and explained the everlasting covenant of God.

In the late afternoon they arrived at their home, and, still not recognizing Him, invited Jesus to a meal. Jesus sat at their table, took the bread, blessed and broke it, and handed a portion to each of them. Then God removed the veil from the eyes—and they recognized Jesus. And as suddenly as He had appeared, He vanished from their sight.

In wide-eyed amazement they asked each other, "Did not our heart burn within us while He talked with us on the road, and while He opened the Scriptures to us?" (v. 32). Revived by truth, they rushed out the door with hearts ablaze, and sprinted back to Jerusalem to share the good news with the other disciples. They found them behind closed doors—for fear of the Jewish leaders (John 20:19)—but already rejoicing because the Lord had appeared first to Mary Magdalene, out of whom He had cast seven demons, and to Simon Peter (Mark 16:9; Luke 24:34).

As the two disciples from Emmaus recounted their walk with the Lord, Jesus suddenly stood in the midst of the room. In all His goodness, He turned His face toward them, shined His countenance upon them, and said, "Peace to you" (v. 36).

Jesus' message of peace had rich meaning for Jewish believers. The corresponding word in Hebrew is "shalom." It means much more than tranquility. *Shalom* is a covenant word, layered with meanings of salvation. It embodies the idea of wholeness that is derived through all of God's blessings on His faithful people. Christ's greeting echoed the covenant blessing—

The LORD bless you and keep you;
The LORD make His face shine upon you, and be gracious to you;
The LORD lift up His countenance upon you, and give you peace (Numbers 6:24–26).

The disciples were securely locked in when Christ suddenly and unexpectedly appeared in their midst. Still reeling from the chaotic events they'd just endured, their initial reaction was one of trembling fear.

Jesus patiently calmed them, showing His wounded hands and feet, and eating broiled fish and honeycomb in their presence to prove He was not a ghost. "Then He said to them,

> 'These are the words which I spoke to you while I was still with you, that all things must be fulfilled which were written in the Law of Moses and the Prophets and the Psalms concerning Me.' And He opened their understanding, that they might comprehend the Scriptures" (Luke 24:44–45).

Christ presented essentially the same Old Testament study He had given on the road to Emmaus. As He pointed out prophecies that testified of Him and explained the everlasting covenant of God, a heavenly peace washed over them.

IS THE OLD TESTAMENT STILL RELEVANT TODAY?

Christians rightfully celebrate the *gospel* of the New Testament—the *good news* of Christ's life, death, and resurrection, that foretells His coming kingdom. However, what we often overlook is that this same gospel is the fulfillment of Old Testament prophecies. Do you realize the Old Testament contains what is written in the New, and the New Testament explains what is written in the Old? When Jesus referred to "the Law of Moses and the Prophets and the Psalms," He used the accepted Jewish description of the entire Old Testament. Beginning in Genesis and culminating in Revelation, the Bible is the progressive unfolding of God's everlasting covenant to save humanity.

Moses wrote the first five books of the Bible—which, as a collective work, are referred to as "the Law of Moses," and are also known in Hebrew as the *Torah*, and in Greek as the *Pentateuch*. The fifth book of Moses, Deuteronomy, is known as "the Book of the Law." It included the ceremonial and civil regulations of the Old Covenant that were abolished at Calvary's cross.

The Apostle Paul, a writer of the New Testament, uses the term "the law" in a way that confuses many who do not carefully consider his context. Paul liberally uses the term the law in reference to four things: 1) the collective five books written by Moses—known as the *Law of Moses*; 2) the book of Deuteronomy—known as the *Book of the Law*; 3) the moral law of God—known as the *Ten Commandments*; and finally, 4) the ingrained tendency of human nature—as in Romans 8:2, where he describes "*the law of sin and death*." Our determination of which law Paul is referring to requires careful consideration of his context—his discussion immediately preceding and following what he writes within the chapter, or the entire epistle (letter).

The Apostle Peter said that God had given Paul great wisdom, but admitted some things Paul wrote were "hard to understand, which untaught and unstable people twist to their own destruction, as they do also the rest of the Scriptures" (2 Peter 3:15–16). Some who read Paul's writings mistakenly assume that he refers to the entire Old Testament as "the law," and that the Old Testament was abolished at the cross. Paul certainly did not think so.

Paul frequently taught from God's divine revelation in the Old Testament, saying, "For whatever things were written before were written for our learning, that we through the patience and comfort of the Scriptures might have hope" (Romans 15:4). Another spiritual benefit of Old Testament texts that Paul pointed out is that they forewarn us of God's judgments on His disobedient people—serving as "examples" and "admonition" for us today (1 Corinthians 10:6, 11).

Not only are Old Testament teachings relevant to Christians, but they are also critical to our understanding of the New Covenant, which is a continuation of God's everlasting covenant—His oath-bound promises for salvation—that He planned before He created the world, announced in the Garden of Eden, revealed in a progressive manner in the Old Testament, and radically renewed through Christ. The golden thread of His love story is woven into Scripture from Genesis to Revelation.

As we journey together through "His Story," I will occasionally provide historical information, mention accepted practices for accurate Bible interpretation, and define words from the original languages in which Scripture was written. These inserts are crucial to clarify the Word of God. I promise not to overwhelm you with technical information, but I pray you will consider these inserts seriously.

Here is the first such insert. New Testament books are not ordered by the dates they were written. The book of James is considered the first written—around AD 44–49, most likely before the first council of the New Testament church was held in Jerusalem. Paul's letter to the Galatians is likely the second written, around AD 49. Of the 27 New Testament books, Paul authored at least 13 (possibly 14, as many scholars recognize him as the unnamed author of Hebrews). A few decades later, John wrote his gospel, his three epistles, and the last book of the New Testament. Looking into the history of Roman rulers during John's era helps narrow the date he wrote Revelation to about AD 94–96—the last decade of the first century.

So why is that important to us? Virtually all scholars believe the date of Jesus' crucifixion was from AD 27–33. If the first book of the New Testament wasn't written until another 16 to 22 years later, what Scriptures did the early church study?

Paul longed to visit the church in Rome, but was providentially delayed, which prompted him (around AD 57–58) to write the epistle of Romans, with its overarching theme of *righteousness by faith*. Not long afterwards, Paul finally traveled to Rome as a prisoner for his faith. Placed on house arrest, he was allowed to rent a cottage where he was guarded 24/7 by a Roman soldier. From that small house he freely taught God's gospel of grace for two years, receiving all visitors who would come to him (Acts 28:30–31). He invited a large group of Jews to visit, to try to persuade them from Old Testament texts that Jesus was the Messiah:

> So when they had appointed him a day, many came to him at his lodging, to whom he explained and solemnly testified of the kingdom of God, persuading them concerning Jesus from both the Law of Moses and the Prophets, from morning till evening (Acts 28:23).

Did you realize that Paul wrote many of his books during this first Roman imprisonment? He wrote Colossians, Ephesians,

Philippians, and Philemon while chained under house arrest. Later, during his much harsher second imprisonment in Rome, from AD 64–67, Paul wrote his last letter, a final farewell to Timothy, before he died for his faith (probably in AD 67). In his goodbye, he reminded Timothy that all who live godly lives will suffer persecution, and that he should carefully avoid deception (2 Timothy 3:12–14). Then Paul added this advice—

> But you must continue in the things which you have learned and been assured of, knowing from whom you have learned them, and that from childhood you have known the Holy Scriptures, which are able to make you wise for salvation through faith which is in Christ Jesus. All Scripture is given by inspiration of God, and is profitable for doctrine, for reproof, for correction, for instruction in righteousness (2 Timothy 3:14–16).

To which holy writings was Paul referring? He spoke of the Old Testament, and by implication included New Testament writings that were circulating and already considered sacred Scriptures, although they were not yet a collected work (1 Timothy 5:18; 2 Peter 3:15–16). Paul wrote that Jews had an advantage because "to them were committed the oracles of God" (Romans 3:2). "Oracles"—direct revelations from the Lord Himself—were recorded in the Old Testament. Paul frequently used these earlier writings to explain the gospel. Only his two shortest books, Titus and Philemon, do not contain references to Moses, the Prophets, and the Psalms.

Don't miss this point. The central theme of the Old Testament is the everlasting covenant of God and the coming Messiah. These Scriptures pointed to Jesus Christ, who would impart life to His people. Jesus told the Jews, "You search the Scriptures, for in them you think you have eternal life; and these are they which testify of Me" (John 5:39).

The gospel is the fulfillment of Old Testament prophecies that proclaimed Jesus as Messiah. The ministry of Jesus confirmed these prophecies, and shined God's brilliant light into a dark world (2 Peter 1:19–21). Without knowledge of the Old Testament, we can never understand God's everlasting covenant of salvation by grace through faith in Christ Jesus.

What We "Think" We Know

As we see a progression of the acceptance of truth in the disciples' lives, it is interesting to note the increased faith that accompanies it. At first, they received Jesus as a great teacher, then a prophet, and finally as the One who fulfilled the office of Christ. *Christ* is the Greek title that corresponds to the Hebrew title *Messiah*. Both mean the *Anointed One* (meaning chosen by the Lord to serve in a particular office). The Christ-Messiah was the anointed Person chosen by God to fulfill His everlasting covenant of redemption for the world.

The disciples had progressed in thought until they hit the wall of *preconceived opinion*, beyond which they could not advance in truth until Jesus was resurrected. The disciples could not see past the prevailing understanding of the Messiah as a political and military leader—a conquering king who would be their Deliverer from Roman bondage.

On several occasions, Jesus bluntly told His disciples He would be betrayed, tortured, and killed, and rise on the third day. It happened first near Mount Hermon, in a city called Caesarea Philippi. Jesus asked His disciples, "Who do men think I am?" Some people thought He was John the Baptist, back from the dead, after Herod had him beheaded (Matthew 14:10). Some thought He was Elijah reappearing. Others thought He was one of the prophets.

Then He asked, "But who do you say that I am?" (Mark 8:29).

Peter, speaking with inspiration from God, responded without hesitation, "You are the Christ." The *Messiah*. The *Anointed One*. The disciples had finally seen the light. Or had they? Right there at Caesarea Philippi—at that moment—Jesus first announced His true Messianic mission to earth.

He began to teach them that the Son of Man must suffer many things, and be rejected by the elders and chief priests and scribes, and be killed, and after three days rise again (Mark 8:31).

What? This did not fit with the disciples' beliefs. Peter—ever the impulsive spokesman for the group—took Jesus aside and expressed their sharp disapproval of such an idea. Jesus knew who was fostering this attitude among the group. He turned to look at His disciples, then rebuked Peter, saying—

Get behind Me, Satan! For you are not mindful of the things of God, but the things of men (Mark 8:33).

Still, the disciples had a preconceived notion about the Messiah as a political and military Deliverer. The words of Jesus didn't register with them. Error insulated their minds against truth.

On another occasion, several months before His crucifixion, as they passed through Galilee on the way to Capernaum, Jesus again presented His upcoming fate of death and resurrection. But His meaning was "hidden from them" (Mark 9:31–32). Truth contradicted their cherished beliefs. Reluctant to ask for an explanation, they rejected His words.

Months later, Jesus set His face like flint to journey for a final time to Jerusalem. His disciples realized the religious leaders wanted to silence Jesus, and they followed anxiously behind Him in absolute amazement of His determination. Pausing His pace, Jesus took the twelve aside to provide His third and final warning of the upcoming events.

Behold, we are going up to Jerusalem, and the Son of Man will be betrayed to the chief priests and to the scribes; and they will condemn Him to death and deliver Him to the Gentiles; and they will mock Him, and scourge Him, and spit on Him, and kill Him. And the third day He will rise again (Mark 10:33–34).

With each of His three predictions about His suffering and death, He included the hope of His resurrection. Blatantly ignoring His words, the disciples refused to recognize truth because it differed from what they had been taught since childhood. In fact, on this third occasion, James and John, blinded by self-absorbed ambition, responded by getting Jesus off to themselves, selfishly asking for places of prominence in His supposed soon-coming kingdom on earth (vv. 35–38).

Three times Jesus told His disciples of His coming suffering, death, and resurrection.

Three times they dismissed His words from their minds, because His truth didn't agree with their preconceived notions.

Slow of heart? It is difficult for us to comprehend the dull-hearted disciples. They walked with Jesus for three and a half years, yet these foolish ones never understood His teaching about the Messiah's mission before He was resurrected. Wasn't it prophesied in the Old Testament? Yes. Jesus tried to teach them during His ministry on earth, but His words simply didn't register with them. They were called to be witnesses for the Lord, but had heard the story of the Messiah all wrong. His words of truth rolled right past their wall of human reasoning.

What If We Are Telling the Story of Jesus All Wrong?

What if today's Christians are telling the story of Jesus all wrong?

Telling His story inaccurately could account for the lack of faith in the world today.

Who is Jesus? How do we define His mission to earth? Called to be witnesses for Christ, are believers in Him simply going through the motions of religion, repeating hearsay theories that have been twisted together as a result of dull understanding? Something is wrong in our approach to God's truth, or there wouldn't be so many walled-in denominations of the Christian church. If His story is told right, nations will come to His light.

Jesus had a divine purpose in His post-resurrection teachings. He didn't want His disciples to be *confused* by truth, or to be found *contradicting* truth. His desire was that they would be *convinced* by truth. He led His disciples in a study of Old Testament Scriptures to reveal the progressive unfolding of His covenant identity; His covenant purpose; His covenant mission on earth completed. We must understand the Old Testament *history* of God's covenant of redemption to understand *His Story*. How fortunate we are today to have the advantage of His further revelation found in the New Testament to help explain the Old. Prophecies are only fully understood as they are fulfilled.

It is critical that we understand *His Story* as it is revealed in both the Old and New Testaments. As we journey through Scripture together, you will come to understand that the Person of Jesus Christ is—and has always been—the everlasting covenant promise of God for salvation. More importantly, you will see the beauty and vital necessity of living in a New Covenant relationship with Him.

The unifying theme of Scripture is that our God is a covenant-making, covenant-keeping God. How do we rightly interpret the word "covenant"? How do we enter into a covenant with God? This book clearly and progressively unfolds scriptural answers.

Before our world was created, God—the Father, Son, and Holy Spirit—made a covenant among themselves, establishing their plan of salvation for humanity with oath-bound promises. All three Persons of the Godhead are active in this plan, and God makes and keeps all the promises for the salvation of humanity! To display the immeasurable riches of their love, mercy, and grace, they agreed to offer the gift of salvation to those who would enter into covenant loyalty by faith—trusting in God to restore their righteousness by faith and to empower them to walk in obedience to the faith, motivated by love.

The Holy Spirit changed my life through this study on God's everlasting covenant of redemption. I saw God in a whole new light, and came to understand how trustworthy and faithful He is. My eyes were opened to God's most tender, self-sacrificing love—a love that cannot be measured. That love stirred a deep longing to belong to Him, and I could not help but love Him with my whole heart. I understood, for the first time, what it really meant to be humble, to be saved by grace and made righteous by faith in Christ Jesus. This gave me a sense of security in Him. He converted me from being one who was "slow of heart" to one who is ablaze—burning with love and enormous appreciation for our all-loving, covenant-making, covenant-keeping God.

I'm praying for you right now. As we search the Scriptures together, I pray our Lord will clear away all confusion that contradicts His truth, and convince you of His most incredible truth of who the Person of Jesus Christ is, and what He will accomplish in your life when you open your heart to Him.

May He reveal Himself to you in a way that will make you stand in awe of Him. Amen!

SUMMARY OF "HIS" STORY
Chapter One

- Four hundred years elapsed between the last Old Testament book of the Bible and the birth of the Messiah. This is called the *intertestamental* period.

- John the Baptist was the "Elijah-to-come," heralding the coming of the Messiah.

- Pharisees and Sadducees were leaders of two prominent sects of the Jewish religion during the time of Christ. Both sects originated during the intertestamental period.

- These sects mistakenly taught that the Messiah would be a political-military leader, who would deliver the nation of Israel from Roman rule.

- The Hebrew title "Messiah" corresponds with the Greek title "Christ." Both mean the "Anointed One"—the Person who will fulfill God's everlasting covenant of redemption.

- "Preconceived opinions"—an opinion formed before having adequate evidence—often insulate our minds against God's truths. These assumptions make us "slow of heart" (dull of hearing, and not quick to perceive). Our example in this chapter: Jesus predicted His death and resurrection three times to His disciples. Their preconceived notion of the Messiah's mission closed their minds. They couldn't accept Christ's words.

- To open their minds to truth, Jesus gave two Bible studies on the day of His resurrection. Both Old Testament studies brought forth evidence of who He was and why He came to earth, convincing His disciples He was the Messiah-Christ.

- The unifying theme of Scripture is that God is a covenant-making, covenant-keeping God.

- God—the Father, Son, and Holy Spirit—are all active in the plan of salvation. Before our world was created they made a covenant among themselves to offer the gift of salvation to those who would enter into covenant loyalty by faith in the Person of Jesus Christ.

- The simplified definition of covenant is God's oath-bound promises that are legally binding.

- We can't understand the Person of Jesus Christ or His mission if we don't recognize Old Testament truths.
- "The Law of Moses" refers to his collective writings of the Bible's first five books.
- "The Book of the Law" singles out Deuteronomy as the book of the Old Covenant, which prescribed civil and ceremonial laws that were abolished at the cross.
- The Apostle Paul frequently used the Old Testament to prove Jesus was the Messiah, and to explain the Kingdom of God, pronouncing those Scriptures were a warning and admonition to New Testament believers.
- Paul liberally applies the term "the law" in his writings, sometimes referring to: 1) the Law of Moses—the first 5 books of the Bible; or 2) the Book of the Law—the book of Deuteronomy; 3) the Ten Commandments—God's law of love; or 4) the ingrained tendency of human nature.
- We must carefully consider the context of Paul's writings to understand to which law he referred.
- *Shalom* (peace) is covenant language, meaning more than tranquility. Layered with the concepts of God's covenant redemption, and covenant blessings that bring completeness to our lives, it is the peace Christ brings to His covenant people.

THE INFINITY FOCUS

Chapter Two

Have you ever traveled to the Grand Canyon? In the year 2000, as my sister and I set out on a 1,500-mile road trip, we decided to "swing by" that national park. Actually, it wasn't my idea. I was apathetic because it added another 1,000 miles to our journey. Satisfied with the documentaries and award-winning photos of the location that I had seen over the years, it seemed no big deal to me to see it for myself—but my perspective changed when we finally arrived.

Edging our way to the rim of the steepest side of the Canyon, the grandeur our eyes beheld was soul-stirring. We instinctively whispered in hushed tones. Overwhelmed by the presence of God, our sense of wonder and awe gave rise to worship. The panoramic vista we saw with our own eyes no photo could have captured.

The Lord used that experience to stir a longing in my heart to understand the story of the Bible. Although I knew a lot of Scripture promises, I relied heavily on traditional beliefs that had been handed down to me by my family. I was brought up in a "New Testament" church that believed the Old Testament was no longer relevant for Christians. I had studied my way out of that belief system after my college years, but the fragmented portions of the Bible familiar to me were still positioned in such a way that they reflected a disjointed view of God. It was as if I was looking at God through a kaleidoscope.

Whether we realize it or not, our picture of God is interpreted through the lens of our perspective with which we approach Scripture, and the focus of our *viewfinder*. My perspective was fogged over by preconceived opinions. I believed that the God presented in the Old Testament was a wrathful Person who differed from the God of love in the New. My focus was far too narrow to comprehend God's declarations in both Testaments that He never changes.

God had to give me a clear "infinity focus" to provide a panoramic view of His consistent grace and everlasting covenant with humanity.

Are you familiar with the term *infinity focus*? Cameras, telescopes, and microscopes have what's called an "objective lens." This lens gathers light rays from the object being observed. When the focus is dialed in correctly by widening the depth of field, all the rays of light converge to produce an authentic image. This is called an *infinity focus*, and it is difficult for amateur photographers to achieve.

God impressed me to forget what I thought I knew, and start over by approaching Scripture with a new *objective lens*, looking through the perspective of His infinite love. He further changed my viewfinder, widening it to the writings of Moses, the Psalms, and the Prophets. As I gathered rays from the "Father of lights, with whom there is no variation or shadow of turning" (James 1:17), I learned that God never changes—He is the same yesterday, today, and forever (Malachi 3:6; Hebrews 13:8). He is consistent. That makes Him trustworthy.

Understanding God's plan of *righteousness by faith* for the human race demands an *infinity focus*—a depth of field that widens our view from eternity past to eternity future. As amateurs in the realm of infinity, we need the Holy Spirit's illumination, because the Bible is filled with spiritual words that can only be spiritually discerned (1 Corinthians 2:14).

The purpose of our journey through Scripture is to provide you with a panoramic view of God's plan of salvation by grace, His everlasting covenant of *righteousness by faith*. You will see for yourself that the Bible is the progressive unfolding of a single story, revealed by the God of grace, mercy, and judgment, whose interactions with humanity are the same in both Testaments.

This is the story of Jesus. *His Story* is woven throughout Scripture, from the first book of the Bible to the last. The risen Savior shared Old Testament stories with His disciples to increase their understanding of His mission as the Messiah. We will walk through these stories, and advance to His Story in the New Testament to see how He fulfilled this mission. This book will provide you with a bird's eye view of the Bible, and an intimate view of our Lord.

To see the beauty of the story of salvation, we must first dial in an infinity focus to get an authentic image of the nature of God. This chapter is dense with Scripture, and will not be the easiest read. Nonetheless, it can open your eyes to the identity of Christ and the reason for His death, enlarging your appreciation of God's immeasurable love for you.

UNDERSTANDING THE GODHEAD

The Bible declares that "God is love" (1 John 4:8, 16). That is not a description of His feelings, but of the very essence of His being. Love is His nature. How can we define His love? Infinite. Self-sacrificing. Immeasurable. Inexhaustible. His nature of unselfish love—a love that does not seek personal gain—sets Him apart from sin, which makes Him holy. *Holiness* simply means to be *separated from sin*. Because the essence of God's nature is unselfish love, He cannot sin. Love does no harm. God demonstrates love by His actions, revealing Himself to us as He continues to do what is best for humanity's eternal benefit.

The word employed in the New Testament to describe His divine nature is "Godhead," which reveals three distinct Divine Persons: the Father, Son, and Holy Spirit (e.g. Matthew 28:19; 2 Corinthians 13:14; 1 Peter 1:2; Revelation 1:4–6). Yet, these three Persons are One God, sharing the same essential qualities, purpose, and plan. In perfect unity, and with divine humility, these three Persons do not seek for superior authority within their circle of love.

Scholars label this identity as the "Trinity"—a word not used in the Bible, but which accurately describes the multifaceted, Three-in-One nature of God implied in the Old Testament and fully revealed in the New. It's crucial to understand the Godhead, or we will never understand who the Person of Jesus Christ is. Jesus said—

The first of all the commandments is: "Hear, O Israel, the LORD our God, the LORD is one. And you shall love the LORD your God with all your heart, with all your soul, with all your mind, and with all your strength." This is the first commandment (Mark 12:29–30).

Jesus is quoting from Deuteronomy 6:4. The Hebrew word there for one is *echad*, which can indicate a *compound unity* of more than one. The Apostle Paul clearly describes "one God," including the plural Persons of the Godhead: one Spirit, one Lord, one Father (Ephesians 4:4–6).

I recall in 2005 trying to explain the Trinity to a Muslim scholar who had called 3ABN, a worldwide Christian network where I serve in ministry. Living in a closed Muslim country, she began watching our network to improve her English, and became drawn to my explanation of God. Still, she couldn't get beyond her preconceived notion that Christians worshiped three Gods. I tried every concept of the Trinity I knew to explain that we believe in only one God. None of my babbling descriptions opened her understanding. Thankfully, she eventually became a devoted Christian, and we remain friends today.

Sometime later, as I contemplated the dimensions of two places which represent God's presence—the Most Holy Place within the Temple, and the New Jerusalem that will descend from Heaven when God creates a new earth—I recognized that both were cubes. The dimensions of their width, height, and length were equal (1 Kings 6:20; Revelation 21:16). God's presence is in the cube.

How do you calculate a cube? When you multiply three instances of the same value of a number, it equals a cube. Could multiplication be the answer? Is it that simple to explain that three Persons of the Godhead equal One?

The dimensions of God's nature are equal—interchangeable—Three Persons of the same perfect value as the others. If we multiply three instances of One, what's our convincing result? $1 \times 1 \times 1 = 1$. That result is also expressed as 1^3 (one to the *third power*, or one *cubed*). The nature of God is One to the third power!

It makes perfect sense. One is the only number that can be multiplied—or divided—by itself and the result equals the same number with which you started. Does God use the multiplication formula to define more than one person as a *single being*? Yes, He does. He declares that a man and a woman joined in marriage become "one" (Genesis 2:24; Matthew 19:5–6). Do you see the rationale?

Love isn't love until you offer it as a gift. The God of love desired to have children on whom He could lavish His love, and who would love Him in return. In anticipation of having children, He first created a paradise into which He could place them.

On the sixth day of Creation, God said, "Let Us make man in Our image, according to Our likeness" (Genesis 1:26). He created Adam and Eve in His perfect image, with His moral code of love imprinted in their hearts, and bestowed upon them the sacred gift of *free will— the right to determine their own actions.* They were His children born of His love. The genealogy of Adam lists him as "the son of God" (Luke 3:38). By implication, Eve would be God's daughter.

In the following two chapters, we will review the *beginning of time* for a fresh revelation of God's love. How did sin and death enter into the perfect paradise God originally created? In short, God placed only one restriction on the first couple, a boundary He established out of loving concern for their wellbeing. Warning them that a certain tree must be avoided, He declared that a violation of this boundary would result in death.

It was not Adam and Eve's destiny to sin. They made wrong choices, abusing their free will. God's image within them was marred by sin, and humanity's spiritual innocence was lost. Once lost, it couldn't be restored by human effort.

Through Adam, the *first representative* of humanity, sin gained entrance into the world (Romans 5:12). The children of Adam and Eve were born in *their likeness* (Genesis 5:3). All the nations of the earth were created by God from one man's blood— Adam's (Acts 17:26), and the fallen state of human nature was passed down.

WHO IS THE PERSON OF JESUS CHRIST?

"The wages of sin is death." If humans had to pay their own penalty for sin, they would utterly perish. Although the Lord did not predestine humans to fall into sin, the outcome did not catch the all-knowing God by surprise. In eternity past, He determined to offer the free gift of eternal life, "in Christ Jesus our Lord" (Romans 6:23).

Motivated by unselfish love, the Father, Son, and Holy Spirit would all participate in the plan of salvation. One of them would come down to become the Substitute sacrifice for the sins of humanity—He was the "Lamb slain from the foundation of the world" (Revelation 13:8). That is God's everlasting covenant, planned before He ever created our world. The One who came down to be embodied in human flesh—to become the Person of Jesus Christ—is sometimes described by Christians as "the Second Person of the Godhead." (Not intending to mean second in His authority, but rather second in the full revelation of His Person.)

We have arrived at the ridge of God's great revelation. Here's where we need to dial in an infinity focus, with the aid of the Holy Spirit.

> Christ Jesus, who, although He existed in the form of God, did not regard equality with God a thing to be grasped, but emptied Himself, taking the form of a bondservant, and being made in the likeness of men. And being found in appearance as a man, He humbled Himself by becoming obedient to the point of death, even death on a cross (Philippians 2:5–8, NASB).

The Lord of glory stepped out of heaven to become one of us, so that He could qualify as the Substitute human representative in death, and become the new representative of humanity to take Adam's place (1 Corinthians 15:45–49). Scholars call this the "Incarnation"—God becoming flesh in the Person of Jesus Christ, dwelling on Earth in the perfect union of divinity and humanity. God becoming human to die. *Incarnation* is another term that is not found in Scripture, but it perfectly describes the process of God becoming embodied in flesh.

What a demonstration of unselfish love! Let's get out our binoculars to take a closer look. It is crucial that we comprehend the significance of these four verses.

Philippians 2:5 announces "Christ Jesus." The One who was incarnated in flesh to become the Person of Jesus Christ is described elsewhere in Scripture as none other than our Creator God.

In the beginning was the Word, and the Word was with God, and the Word was God. He was in the beginning with God. All things were made through Him, and without Him nothing was made that was made. And the Word became flesh and dwelt among us, and we beheld His glory, the glory as of the only begotten of the Father, full of grace and truth. (John 1:1–3, 14).

God . . . has in these last days spoken to us by His Son, whom He has appointed heir of all things, through whom also He made the worlds; who being the brightness of His glory and the express image of His person, and upholding all things by the word of His power, when He had by Himself purged our sins, sat down at the right hand of the Majesty on high (Hebrews 1:1–3).

Philippians 2:6 states that Jesus, "although He existed in the form of God, did not regard equality with God a thing to be grasped" (emphasis added). This is an outright declaration of Christ's Deity. The Greek word Paul used for "form" means the *essence* or *continuous state* of Deity. It is used only in the New Testament of Christ. Paul declared that the Second Person of the Godhead existed throughout eternity in the essential, unchanging nature and character of God. He existed as One with the Father, and was equal to the Father God (John 10:30).

The New Testament clearly identifies Christ as God (John 1:1; Romans 9:5; Colossians 2:9; Titus 2:13; Hebrews 1:8; 2 Peter 1:1; 1 John 5:20). Jesus Himself claimed to be God (John 5:18; 8:58; 10:33, 38; 14:9, 20:28).

Philippians 2:7 continues, "but emptied Himself, taking the form of a bondservant, and being born in the likeness of men" (emphasis added). What was it He emptied? He certainly didn't empty Himself of His Deity—He was fully man, yet still fully God. The Apostle Paul explains it by saying in the Man Jesus there still "dwells all the fullness of the Godhead bodily" (Colossians 2:9). How is that possible? Because when One is divided by One, it still equals its same value of One.

Our Creator God didn't cling to His divine rights and privileges. He emptied Himself of His glory—the honors of Deity. At the end of

His ministry on earth, Jesus prayed, "And now, O Father, glorify Me together with Yourself, with the glory which I had with You before the world was" (John 17:5).

From Heaven Jesus came to Earth, and was born as a helpless human baby in Bethlehem—becoming like us. "Inasmuch then as the children have partaken of flesh and blood, He Himself likewise shared in the same, that through death He might destroy him who had the power of death, that is, the devil . . . . Therefore, in all things He had to be made like His brethren" (Hebrews 2:14, 17). While on earth, Jesus didn't call on His own divine powers as God, but operated in His human nature by relying on the Holy Spirit—just as we must. We'll look further into this in Chapter Twelve.

What manner of love was this? Unfathomable. To think our Creator loved us so much that He would condescend to become one of us forever—in the Person of Jesus Christ—surpasses our comprehension. The risen Christ ascended to Heaven in glorified human flesh. His nature was permanently changed to embody perfect divinity and perfect humanity. His act was beyond humility. Bible scholars call it His "humiliation."

Philippians 2:8 states, "And being found in appearance as a man, He humbled Himself by becoming obedient to the point of death, even death on a cross" (emphasis added). He became human to take our sin burden on Himself and pay our penalty of death to satisfy God's righteous justice. At the cross, sin was exposed in all its hatefulness as it collided with God's truth, mercy, and lovingkindness. At the cross, He kissed His created beings with righteousness and peace (Psalm 85:10). The goal of His everlasting covenant has always been this great exchange—

> For He made Him who knew no sin to be sin for us, that we might become the righteousness of God in Him (2 Corinthians 5:21).

God placed our sins on the Person of Jesus Christ, and poured out His wrath against sin—the punishment we deserved—on our spotless, sinless Substitute as He hung on the cross to pay our sin penalty. In the great exchange, He credits us with the spotless record of Christ's perfectly righteous human life. His lifeblood—the blood of the everlasting covenant—was the ransom price He paid to redeem us from evil.

Knowing that you were not redeemed with corruptible things, like silver or gold, from your aimless conduct received by tradition from your fathers, but with the precious blood of Christ, as of a lamb without blemish and without spot (1 Peter 1:18–19).

Now may the God of peace who brought up our Lord Jesus from the dead, that great Shepherd of the sheep, *through the blood of the everlasting covenant,* make you complete in every good work to do His will, working in you what is well pleasing in His sight, through Jesus Christ, to whom be glory forever and ever. Amen (Hebrews 13:20–21; emphasis added).

The disciple Thomas knew Jesus as a Man, and doubted the resurrection. The risen Christ appeared to him and had Thomas touch His pierced hands, and put his hand in the hole in Christ's wounded side that had been thrust through with a spear (John 19:34). Thomas touched Him, and believed. Overwhelmed with awe, Thomas declared, "My Lord and my God!" (John 20:27–28).

Daily, I am overcome by the same awe as I consider my Savior. Recognizing God's act of humiliation has filled me with inexpressible gratitude. I praise my Lord for His overwhelming demonstration of love without measure, which fills me with holy wonder!

The mission of the Messiah was to prove the justice, mercy, and grace of the Godhead.

THE JUSTICE AND MERCY OF GOD

God governs by the power of love. He has established boundaries for human behavior—laws and principles that protect the rights of all humans and uphold His rights as our Sovereign Creator. To ignore His boundaries is to act in a lawless manner—as though He has no law. The Apostle John provides a God-inspired definition of sin, declaring in 1 John 3:4, "Sin is lawlessness." Sin is contrary and incompatible to God's government of love. Since sin violates His authority, all sin is ultimately against God (Genesis 39:9; Psalm 51:4).

The Lord hates sin, because sin is the absence of love. Prideful. Selfish. Rebellious. Perverse. Self-harming. Sin never takes place in a vacuum—the consequences of one person's sin always harms another, violating their rights. When someone sins against us, one of our loved ones, or another vulnerable person, our sense of fair play cries out for justice, doesn't it?

Justice is important to God, because He is "just"—meaning He is absolutely good, virtuous, impartial, fair-minded, honest, incorruptible, trustworthy, and righteous. In performing His justice, He consistently does all things in accordance with what is perfectly right. God's system of justice demonstrates His incredible love for humanity, and is the foundation of His everlasting covenant. As we define His amazing system, it may seem somewhat technical, but this segment is important to His Story—it explains why Christ died for us.

Justice requires judgment—a legal transaction that demands our Heavenly Judge levies one of two possible verdicts:

- Either to **condemn** the accused person, declaring them **guilty** and worthy of punishment,
- Or to **justify** the person, pronouncing an acquittal of the charges, and making an official declaration that the accused is **innocent**.

God's holiness demands justice. He declared a death penalty for sin in the beginning, and it still applies today (Genesis 2:17; Romans 6:23). However, His supreme desire is that everyone on earth will come to the knowledge of His truth and be saved (1 Timothy 2:3–4). He doesn't show favoritism—there is no partiality with God (Romans 2:11). Hear the loving cry from God's heart—

I have no pleasure in the death of the wicked, but that the wicked turn from his way and live. Turn, turn from your evil ways! For why should you die . . . ? (Ezekiel 33:11).

God's love demands mercy and grace. Cathleen Falsani, an American journalist and author, has a quotable quote:

- **JUSTICE** is getting what you deserve.
- **MERCY** is NOT getting what you deserve.

• **GRACE** is getting what you absolutely DON'T deserve.

How could a holy and just God—a God who cannot lie—remit the death penalty He had declared for sin? The whole human race is guilty of sin, and deserving of the penalty, but to pay our own penalty of death meant we would perish (Romans 6:23). To remain just, God would either be required to abolish His moral code of love or mete out justly deserved punishment.

Couldn't He just sweep our sins under the rug, pardoning us because He loves us so? No. That would not satisfy justice in a manner that remained consistent with His perfect nature. All along He had a plan to usher in grace the moment sin occurred by introducing His solution of substitutionary sacrifice. In unfailing love, God planned to pay our sin penalty for us.

God—in Christ—sacrificed Himself to satisfy His own justice. He suffered and died to uphold His righteous law of love. As our Substitute, He removed our guilt for breaking His law— making it possible for God to be "just and the justifier of the one who has faith in Jesus" (Romans 3:26). When we enter into a covenant relationship with Him, His precious blood covers the record of our sins, and God declares us "justified"—*not guilty*. We are then in right standing with our Creator, because Christ's righteousness is credited to us by our faith in Him.

All have sinned and fall short of the glory of God, being justified freely by His grace through the redemption that is in Christ Jesus (Romans 3:23–24).

Much more then, having now been justified by His blood, we shall be saved from wrath through Him (Romans 5:9).

To be *justified by faith* is one aspect of being made *righteous by faith*. We need a clear understanding of what this means, so together we will more closely examine this beautiful truth. Scripture will prove that God's gift of righteousness does not give us a license to sin. Christ didn't suffer and die for us so that we could live like the devil.

Righteousness by faith in Christ is God's system of justice, and the very foundation of God's everlasting covenant of redemption.

In the Old Testament, this justice was initiated through a repetitious substitutionary sacrificial system that pointed forward in faith to Christ. In the New Testament, Christ fulfilled that sacrificial system, standing in as humanity's Substitute, offering up His life "once for all" (Romans 6:10; Hebrews 7:27; 10:10). And this plan was in place from eternity past. Let's dial in the infinity focus.

THE GRACE OF GOD

The Person of Jesus Christ and His death on the cross was "foreordained before the foundation of the world" (1 Peter 1:20). The marvelous truth is "grace was given to us in Christ before the beginning of time" (2 Timothy 1:9).

> For God so loved the world that He gave His only begotten Son, that whoever believes in Him should not perish but have everlasting life (John 3:16).

> But God demonstrates His own love toward us, in that while we were still sinners, Christ died for us (Romans 5:8).

Grace is the basis of all God's dealings with the human race—from the beginning of time—and is the underpinning of His everlasting covenant of salvation. It might surprise you to learn that God introduced what I call the "Calvary Plan" in the Garden of Eden. Our review of Scripture will prove that His remedy for sin has always been *righteousness by faith*—a gift of His grace that you will come to understand with greater clarity on our journey together.

"Grace" is a covenant word, an English translation of a Greek word in New Testament texts. It essentially represents God's marvelous favor by which He freely bestows gifts on the human race. Gifts that are undeserved, and cannot be earned by works.

God's grace was active in the Old Testament. "Hesed" is my favorite covenant word that is equivalent to grace—plus so much more. *Hesed* is like a multifaceted diamond that shines with brilliance and clarity to describe God's unchanging nature of love. It is used over 240 times in the original Hebrew language of Old Testament texts, and is so rich in meaning that no single English word can encapsulate it. *Love, loving, loving-kindness, mercy, grace, steadfastness, covenant faithfulness,* and *loyalty* are all integrated in its meaning.

Bible translators have a difficult time expressing the concept of hesed. It describes the actions of God toward His people.

Salvation by *grace/hesed* is the everlasting covenant of God with humanity.

God demonstrated His love and grace to undeserving people in the Old Testament. Looking *forward* in faith to salvation by the promised Messiah-Redeemer, Old Testament believers *were* saved by grace.

The same plan of salvation exists for undeserving New Testament believers. Looking back to Christ's death at Calvary—and *up* to Heaven where He continues His priestly ministry for salvation—New Testament believers *were* and *are now* saved by grace (Hebrews 6:20; 7:24–25).

THE PROGRESSIVE UNFOLDING OF GOD'S SELF-REVELATION

You are the object of God's love. All the holy Scriptures were inspired by God who wants to reveal Himself to you, and give you the wisdom to receive the salvation that comes through Jesus Christ.

All Scripture is given by inspiration of God, and is profitable for doctrine, for reproof, for correction, for instruction in righteousness, that the man of God may be complete, thoroughly equipped for every good work (2 Timothy 3:16).

Prophecy never came by the will of man, but holy men of God spoke as they were moved by the Holy Spirit (2 Peter 1:21).

From the first verse of the Bible to the last, our promise-making, promise-keeping God reveals His personality, power, presence, patience, and passion for righteousness in an unfolding, progressive manner. Step-by-step, little-by-little, the perfect heavenly Father teaches us His everlasting covenant in a manner we can comprehend.

The fallen nature of humanity is truly "slow of heart" (Luke 24:25). Truth finally sinks in, and we see His infinite plan for humanity and recognize His inexhaustible love.

The resurrected Christ explained who He was by taking His disciples through Old Testament prophecies that testified of Him before His incarnation. As we review prophecies that He likely included in the studies He gave, we will come to understand what the Lord offered the human race.

When we glimpse His grace and see the experience He offers, we cannot help but fall to our knees and invite Him into our lives. Through Christ, we can be spiritually born-again. God promises to make us partakers of His divine nature (John 3:3; 1 Peter 1:23; 2 Peter 1:3–4). By His power, He recreates us in His image—with His moral code of love again imprinted upon our hearts—and we become new creations (2 Corinthians 5:17). All this is a result of Christ laying His life down for us.

Christ's ministry for us did not end at the cross. An important result of His incarnation as the "Son of Man" is that He became the "last Adam" (1 Corinthians 15:45). From this one Man's blood, God is creating a new nation of people who are destined to become like Him (Romans 8:29). As the last Adam, He is now seated on the heavenly throne (Mark 16:19; Romans 8:34, Hebrews 1:3), ministering as the new Representative of mankind and our High priest. He intercedes for us in Heaven, and He is able to save to the uttermost (Hebrews 7:25). He invites us to "come boldly to the throne of grace, that we may obtain mercy and find grace to help in time of need" (Hebrews 4:16).

Paul declared that God saved us, "not according to our works but according to His own purpose and grace which was given to us in Christ Jesus before time began" (2 Timothy 1:9).

Grace— God's unmerited favor that cannot be earned by works.

Before time began—before God created the cosmos and laid the foundation of our world, He planned to save all by grace.

With that infinity focus, we proceed to the Old Testament's testimony of Christ.

SUMMARY OF "HIS" STORY
Chapter Two

- An "infinity focus" captures all the rays of God's light from eternity past to now, to understand the grace He provided for us before time began.

- God is changeless. Both the Old Testament and New Testament represent His infinite nature of love, as well as His righteous anger against sin. His nature of unselfish love separates Him from sin.

- Christianity is monotheistic. Christians believe in one God.

- Scripture describes the Godhead (the essential nature of God) as being shared in three distinct Persons, God—the Father, Son, and Holy Spirit—who are One. $1 \times 1 \times 1 = \mathbf{1^3}$. One is the only number that can be multiplied or divided by itself and still equal one.

- Scripture explains that the Creator God stepped out of Heaven, was incarnated as the Person of Christ Jesus, and died as our Substitute to pay our sin penalty.

- Before the foundation of the world, God had the Calvary Plan in place. In anticipation of His substitutionary death, Christ was "the Lamb slain from the foundation of the world."

- God's everlasting covenant of redemption—"Salvation by grace" and "righteousness by faith"—has always been God's offer to redeem humanity from all ages.

- Adam was the first representative of humanity. Created in God's image, Adam had God's moral code of love imprinted on his heart. Humankind was not destined to sin.

- Sin marred the image of God in us, and humanity lost its spiritual innocence. It can never be regained by works.

- From Adam's blood, all nations were created, and the fallen nature was passed from generation to generation. All have sinned.

- Because of His foreknowledge, sin didn't catch God by surprise.

- God's justice declared a penalty for sin—death. If we had to pay the penalty ourselves, we would perish. God's system of justice was satisfied by a system of substitutionary sacrifice.

- God—in Christ—sacrificed Himself to satisfy His own justice.

- The goal of His everlasting covenant was the great exchange—Christ bore our sins, and credits us with His righteousness.

- His death on the Cross made it possible for God to justify us—to declare that we are not guilty.
- *Justification by faith* is the foundation of God's everlasting covenant.
- Christ became the Last Adam. From His blood, God is creating a new nation of people who are destined to become like Christ, imprinting His moral code of love upon their hearts.
- When we enter into covenant relationship, we partake of Jesus' divine nature and become new creations in Christ. We receive God's promise of the gift of eternal life.
- Christ continues to minister for us in Heaven, seated at the throne of God as the new representative of humanity.
- Christ intercedes for us continually, and is able to save us completely. We are invited to come boldly to His throne to receive grace and help in our time of need.
- *Hesed* is covenant language—a Hebrew word that integrates the qualities of *love, loving, loving-kindness, mercy, grace, steadfastness, covenant faithfulness,* and *loyalty* in one word.
- Grace is covenant language—a Greek word for God's unearned, undeserved favor.

IN THE BEGINNING

Chapter Three

To open His disciples' understanding, the resurrected Christ started with the writings of Moses. He often affirmed Moses as the author of the Bible's first five books—the "Law of Moses" (e.g. Luke 24:44), and had warned the Jewish leaders of His day—

> If you believed Moses, you would believe Me; for he wrote about Me. But if you do not believe his writings, how will you believe My words? (John 5:46–47).

This implies that we will never understand Jesus' words recorded in the New Testament if we do not understand Moses' writings. The first three chapters of Genesis serve as a prologue to all of Moses' writings. If we do not understand the beginning of time, Christ's story remains veiled.

GOD REVEALS HIMSELF TO US THROUGH HIS WORD

Scripture reveals to us that the second Person of the Godhead took on human flesh to become the Person of Jesus Christ, and was sent by God into the world to preach the good news of His coming kingdom. On the night of His betrayal, Jesus was tried before the Sanhedrin court of the Jews. He had avoided the title of "Christ" until that moment. Mark's Gospel offers us a short transcript of the trial.

The high priest asked Jesus, "Are You the Christ, the Son of the Blessed?" Jesus answered, "I am. And you will see the Son of Man sitting at the right hand of the Power, and coming with the clouds of heaven." Tearing his clothes, the high priest accused Jesus of blasphemy, and the religious leaders condemned Him to die (Mark 14:61–64). "Blasphemy" is claiming to be God (John 10:30–33).

Earlier on that same night, Jesus had prayed His longest recorded prayer, found in John 17:1–26. He interceded for Himself, His disciples, and for future generations who would believe on Him for eternal life. Moved by deep emotion, He said to the Father, "This is eternal life, that they may know You, the only true God, and Jesus Christ whom You have sent" (John 17:3). The fundamental requirement for eternal life is a knowledge of our Lord.

Do you think these words of Jesus referred to intellectual knowledge? Many scholars possess an academic knowledge of Scripture, but have no personal experience with the Creator. Inexperienced in His love, some approach Scripture using the wrong lens for understanding, and become "slow of heart." Jesus was speaking of the kind of knowing that comes only from heart-to-heart communication. If we ask, God will give us a heart to know Him (Jeremiah 24:7).

God wants us to know Him intimately. Created in His image, our deep-down desire to be known, understood, and loved is merely a reflection of God's own desire. God progressively revealed Himself to us by inspiring over forty authors—living on two or three continents—to write 66 books over a period of approximately 1,500 years. The result? A single, unified self-revelation of God we call "the Bible."

To see the full revelation of God's everlasting covenant and loving interactions with humanity requires understanding His Story in both Testaments. The *Old Testament* covers four thousand years of earth's history, and the *New Testament* covers approximately the first hundred years of the Christian faith.

These ancient writings are never outdated, because the Word of God contains His creative power of life and sanctification—*the power to set us apart from sin for His holy purpose.*

For the word of God is living and powerful (Hebrews 4:12).

The words that I speak to you are spirit, and they are life (John 6:63).

The word of our God stands forever (Isaiah 40:8).

Sanctify them by Your truth. Your word is truth (John 17:17).

And you shall know the truth, and the truth shall make you free (John 8:32).

Receive . . . the implanted word, which is able to save your souls (James 1:21).

It is written, *"Man shall not live by bread alone, but by every word that proceeds from the mouth of God."* (Matthew 4:4; compare Deuteronomy 8:3; emphases added).

All Scripture is inspired by God. As we read His Word, it is the voice of God speaking to our hearts and minds to reveal His personality, to explain His historical interactions with humanity, and to share His plans for our future. He speaks words of love to encourage us, to correct us, and to instruct us in righteousness (2 Timothy 3:16; 2 Peter 1:21).

Good and upright is the LORD; therefore He teaches sinners in the way. The humble He guides in justice, and the humble He teaches His way. All the paths of the LORD are mercy and truth, to such as keep His covenant and His testimonies (Psalm 25:8–10).

God is faithful. He is consistent (Malachi 3:6; Hebrews 13:8; James 1:17). His character is *constant*, and His commitment to His everlasting covenant is unswerving. *His Story* must be read through the lens of His infinite love, and with appreciation of His reliability.

THE BOOK OF BEGINNINGS

Genesis is the book of "beginnings" of all things. Creation. Humanity. Sin. Redemption. The substitutionary sacrificial system. It details the beginning of God's revelation of His everlasting covenant—which He first announced in the Garden after sin entered His paradise, and later confirmed with Abraham and his sons.

Genesis covers approximately 2,300 years of world history. This is a greater time period than all the remaining books of the Bible combined. Everything God inspired Moses to record in Genesis happened before Moses' lifetime. Until Moses started recording Scripture, God's Word was handed down orally from generation to generation.

Now this is *crucial* to recognize—the first 11 chapters of Genesis are merely a "highlight reel" of the first 2,000 years after Creation, and are provided as a backdrop for our understanding of the rest of our world's history. Two thousand years—compressed into just eleven action-packed chapters! Four epic events are highlighted: 1) the Creation; 2) the Fall; 3) the Flood; and 4) the Dispersion. The remaining 39 chapters cover approximately 300 years, providing the history of Abraham, Isaac, Jacob, and Joseph—all covenant-keeping people.

An infinity focus is required to correctly interpret the first three chapters of Genesis. Why? God inspired these opening chapters as a prologue—an introduction that is essential to understanding the rest of Moses' writings. And what did Jesus say? If we don't believe *His Story* as Moses recorded it, it is doubtful we will ever believe the rest of *His Story* as recorded in the New Testament. To set the stage for our remaining study, let's look to the very beginning.

THE FIRST ACCOUNT OF CREATION

God's revelation starts with the words, "In the beginning God" (Genesis 1:1). God did not find it necessary to explain His existence. Instead, He directed Moses to record two separate accounts of Creation that reveal two distinct dimensions of His omnipresence (His divine ability to be everywhere at the same time.)

The first account of Creation reveals God's realm of infinite existence—outside the time and space of His created universe. This is called the *transcendence* of God. His existence at this level is beyond human comprehension, because everything we know has a beginning and an end, and we can only occupy the space in which we are at any one given time.

In this narrative of Genesis 1, God defines His acts of Creation as occurring in six literal 24-hour periods. "The evening and the morning were the first day" . . . "So the evening and the morning were the second day" . . . and so on for the third . . . fourth . . . fifth . . . and sixth days (Genesis 1:5, 8, 13, 19, 23, 31). Speaking our world into existence, God's creative act is described by the Hebrew word *bārā'*. It means to create something out of nothing. Significantly, that word is never ascribed to human action. *Bārā'* is used of God alone.

God spoke to create everything until the sixth day, when He created a human, saying, "Let Us make man in Our image, according to Our likeness" (Genesis 1:26). His use of the plural pronouns *Our* and *Us*, suggests there are multiple members of the Godhead. Scripture from Genesis to Revelation convinces me that there are three Persons of the Godhead who are perfectly united as One in nature, thought, and purpose.

The opening chapter of Genesis simply ends with God surveying all that He had created on the first six days and considering it "very good" (Genesis 1:31). God's creation of Adam is not explained until the second Creation account.

THE SECOND ACCOUNT OF CREATION

In Genesis 2 we find a second narrative of Creation. This time, God inspired Moses to reiterate the story with emphasis on the more intimate details that reveal He is an "up-close-and-personal" God who listens, speaks, and acts for the benefit of His creatures. This describes God's *immanence*—His presence inside His created time and space—a presence that permeates the whole realm of Earth. He is nearby, fully present to, and actively involved with all of His creation.

This second account shows God's personal touch on the creation of humanity. God did not stand at some distance to speak man into existence. Rather, as a heavenly Potter, He stooped low to the ground to fashion man from the dirt with His own hands. Then the loving Potter placed His face close to that formed lump of clay, and breathed the breath of life—His vital energy of life—into its nostrils. Man became a *living being* or, as the King James Version translates it, "man became a living soul" (Genesis 2:7). Can you imagine when Adam first opened his eyes, blinking at the brightness of God's countenance, and saw the loving gaze of his up-close-and-personal Creator staring back?

In His own image God created Adam and Eve (Genesis 1:27), imprinting His own divine moral code of love and righteousness on their hearts, and instilling intelligence in their minds to rule over this world. As the rightful owner of the earth (Psalm 24:1, 1 Corinthians 10:26), God delivered to humanity the privilege and position of custodial care for His entire creation. The couple received dominion from God, with absolute authority to rule over all the operations and jurisprudence of the planet (Genesis 1:26; Psalm 115:16). Take note of this transaction—it becomes an integral part of the rest of *His Story*.

The first couple were not created as infants, but as fully mature adults with the capacity to reason and rule, as well as to procreate life. God's law of life demands reproduction. Before Eve was created as a comparable mate for Adam, the Lord brought all the beasts of the field and the birds of the air before the man—His created son—giving Adam the privilege and responsibility to name the creatures (Genesis 2:19–20).

Prior to creating the first human couple, the Lord had planted a lush garden—the Garden of Eden (*Eden* means *pleasure* or *delight*). The pleasure in store for Adam and Eve included fully-grown trees that yielded tasty food, lush vegetation, exotic flowers to perfume the air, and refreshing rivers (Genesis 2:8–14). All creation was fully mature. (My conviction is that geologists will never determine the age of the earth because God created it with apparent age.)

There was never to be a rainy day—a mist came up from the earth to water the ground (Genesis 2:6). There was no death in the beginning—the ugliness of death was not known until sin entered our world. Nothing withered. Nothing died. No creature was trying to eat another, as He created humans and animals alike as vegetarians. To the couple, God appointed a diet from all the seed-bearing fruit trees (Genesis 1:29). To the animals and birds, God gave every green herb for food (v. 30).

Does a vegetarian lion sound fanciful to you? Check out the modern book by Georges Westbeau, available online, titled *"Little Tyke:*

The True Story of a Gentle Vegetarian Lioness." Refusing all meat from the time she was a cub, Little Tyke grew to become a healthy and huge lioness, who interacted with children and nuzzled with lambs.

God placed the couple into this idyllic garden. Adam and Eve lived in purity and wonder, time spent without tears or sorrow. Tending the garden was not heavy toil. I can imagine they found it pleasurable and satisfying. Created in God's image, they had His work ethic within them. Can you picture the couple romping playfully with the beasts of the fields, and the lion and the lamb sleeping cuddled together? Surely it was like this in the beginning.

GOD ESTABLISHES TWO INSTITUTIONS OF INTIMACY

Genesis' second chapter reveals that our up-close-and-personal Creator established two institutions of intimacy in the Garden. The first was *marriage and conjugal bliss*: "Therefore a man shall leave his father and mother and be joined to his wife, and they shall become one flesh. And they were both naked, the man and his wife, and were not ashamed" (Genesis 2:24–25). Jesus affirmed the institution of marriage—

> Have you not read that He who made them at the begin-ning *"made them male and female,"* and said, *"For this reason a man shall leave his father and mother and be joined to his wife, and the two shall become one flesh"*? So then, they are no lon-ger two but one flesh (Matthew 19:4–6; emphasis added).

The second institution was a temple in time. On the seventh day of Creation, God established the weekly cycle by setting aside a 24-hour period of time for humanity's physical and spiritual refresh-ment. God Himself paused and rested on the occasion, and crowned the day with His special blessing. He sanctified the seventh day, set-ting it apart for holy purposes.

> Thus the heavens and the earth, and all the host of them, were finished. And on the seventh day God ended His work which He had done, and He rested on the seventh day from all His

work which He had done. Then God blessed the seventh day and sanctified it, because in it He rested from all His work which God had created and made (Genesis 2:1–3).

It is interesting to note that the seventh day of Creation week—when the Lord created a special 24-*hour-period of time*—is not included in the first account of Genesis 1, which lists a daily reckoning of His creative works for the other six days. That used to strike me as odd, because I knew the original Bible texts were not written with chapter and verse divisions; they simply did not exist until scholars added them. So why did scholars separate this event from the others? Then it dawned on me—they thought it was better placed at the beginning of the second account in Genesis 2, which emphasizes the intimacy of God's presence in Creation.

Scholars evidently recognized this special creation of *time* to be the Lord's crowning act of intimate concern for His creatures. The loving heavenly Father wanted to protect one day each week to provide His children rest from their usual employment of working in the Garden, so that Adam and Eve could spend special uninterrupted family time with Him and with each other. This creation of a special day served as the perfect pivot point for Moses' introduction of the Lord's up-close-and-personal Presence in the second account of Creation.

The inspired writings of Paul speak of God's purpose and grace given to us in Christ Jesus "before time began" (2 Timothy 1:9; Titus 1:2), indicating that time didn't exist as we know it until God built it into His creation. In Heaven, if time is measured it is done so differently. The Apostle Peter tells us a thousand years on earth is only like a day to the Lord (2 Peter 3:8).

For humanity, God created a solar cycle to establish the time of a year, setting the sun in the middle of our solar system and putting our planet on a rotational path around it. We determine our yearly cycle by the time it takes the earth to revolve around the sun once.

God created a lunar cycle to establish the time of a month, setting the moon into orbit around the earth. We measure our months by the basic time it takes our moon to make one full orbit.

God created our bodies for a 24-hour cycle, so He caused the earth to revolve on its axis, to provide us with periods of productive light and of restful darkness. We measure our days by one complete rotation of the Earth on its axis.

God created scientific cycles to make these periods of time easily recognized by all of humanity. But how do we understand why we measure a week by seven days? The only reason is a divine cycle of time established by our Creator God. Common sense and history tell us the seventh day has continued as the identifying mark of the Lord's authority to establish Earth's periods of time.

The seventh day was God's special pleasure made for the benefit of humanity. Scripture later identifies this day as the "Sabbath." Because the Lord blessed and sanctified the day He laid special claim to it, calling it "My holy day" (Isaiah 58:13). Seeing this now will provide increased understanding of our later review of Exodus. Jesus affirmed the institution of the Sabbath, saying—

The Sabbath was made for man, and not man for the Sabbath. Therefore the Son of Man is also Lord of the Sabbath (Mark 2:27–28).

Who but the Creator could have known humans and beasts would need one out of every seven days to be physically and spiritually refreshed? Some world governments have tried tampering with the length of the divinely established time, trying shorter or longer weekly cycles. When their experiments failed miserably, they wisely reverted to God's original plan of seven days for the duration of a week.

Did God rest on the seventh day of Creation because He was tired? The Bible tells us otherwise. Isaiah wrote, "Have you not known? Have you not heard? The everlasting God, the LORD, the Creator of the ends of the earth, neither faints nor is weary" (Isaiah 40:28). His watch care is constant—He never slumbers or sleeps (Psalm 121:3–5).

Did God enter a permanent rest mode after that first Sabbath day—as some suggest—withdrawing His personal presence from the earth, leaving the human race to figure out their own destiny? Jesus told us otherwise, and proved God's compassionate actions toward us are constant. Of the many miracles He worked, seven were on different Sabbath days.

One Sabbath at the pool of Bethesda, Christ took pity on a man who had been lame for 38 years. Approaching that poor soul, Jesus asked, "Do you want to be made well?" When the man confessed his frustration at his helpless situation, Jesus spoke with the same creative authority as He had to bring our world into existence. He told the man, "Rise, take up your bed and walk" (John 5:6–8). Instantly healed, the man picked up his mat, and carried it—an unlawful Sabbath activity according to Jewish tradition. Incensed Pharisees confronted Jesus about His work on Sabbath.

> But Jesus answered them, "My Father has been working until now, and I have been working." Therefore the Jews sought all the more to kill Him, because He not only broke the Sabbath, but also said that God was His Father, making Himself equal with God (John 5:17–18).

I need to make a sidebar insert of information here. An explanation is required for the crucial distinction between the *weekly Sabbath* that the Bible refers to as belonging to God and established with permanence, and the *annual sabbaths* referred to as Old Covenant ceremonial feasts belonging to the nation of Israel that were intended to be temporary. This is out of order for our study, but necessary.

Under the terms of the Old Covenant given to Moses, God appointed festivals—which included special *annual sabbaths*—to commemorate His continued provision and protection for national Israel. Feasts were scheduled to begin on specific monthly dates, so the *annual sabbaths* of the festivals could fall on any day of the week. For example, God established the Feast of Trumpets, calling for a "sabbath-rest, a memorial of blowing of trumpets, a holy convocation" that began on the first day of the seventh month each year (Leviticus 23:24). If that day landed on a Tuesday, it was still considered a *sabbath*.

Just as your birthday doesn't change, but the date falls on different days of the week from year to year, annual sabbaths sometimes landed on the weekly *seventh-day Sabbath*. Many Jews regarded such a day to be twice as holy, and deemed the occasion a *high day*. The Apostle John records that the day after Christ's crucifixion was a "high day" (John 19:31). Jesus spent that Sabbath in the grave.

All the Feasts of the Old Covenant were merely a foreshadowing of Christ's ministry (Colossians 2:17; Hebrews 10:1). Scripture concludes that these ceremonial feasts were abolished at Jesus' death, and New Covenant Christians are not obligated to keep them. Hebrews 8:13 explains that the New Covenant made the Old Covenant obsolete.

A COVENANT OF LIFE

Now, in the center of the Garden of Eden were two trees—the tree of life, and the tree of the knowledge of good and evil (Genesis 2:8–9). These trees symbolically represented a moral choice that will prove central to the life of every human being.

To His beloved creatures of the human race, God bestowed the sacred gift of *free will*—the capacity to freely determine our own course of actions. Why? For the sake of love He could do nothing less. Love is not controlling. Love cannot be coerced, or it is not love. Without *free will*, humans would be nothing but robots—machines programmed with certain intelligence to perform routine tasks. Experiencing a heart-to-heart relationship by choice was the only way to share true love, joy, and peace with Him, so to God it was worth the risk of humanity's response.

Our Creator desired us to learn to trust that His intentions are always for our best interests, so that we would be willingly motivated by love for the Lord, and walk in loyalty to Him. Of course, we see those who refuse to let God love them, rejecting Him and His Word. With the gift of *choice*, came the responsibility for—and consequences of—our actions.

Because it was God's eternal plan to be humanity's Provider, He graciously and abundantly provided for Adam and Eve. They could depend on their loving Heavenly Father. In the Garden, they walked with Him (Genesis 3:8), and He lavished His love on them. The Lord surely taught them about the goodness of life and how to be faithful stewards over the Earth and every creature on it. He placed only one restriction on the righteous couple—

> And the LORD God commanded the man, saying, "Of every tree of the garden you may freely eat; but of the tree of the knowledge of good and evil you shall not eat, for in the day that you eat of it you shall surely die" (Genesis 2:16–17).

"You shall die" is literally translated as "dying you shall die." Crossing this boundary would result in God restricting their access to the Tree of Life. The dying process would begin. Adam and Eve were not created immortal. Scripture clearly states that God alone has immortality (1 Timothy 6:16). He is the self-existent, eternal God who has no beginning or end. Mentioning the human *soul* or *spirit* over 1,600 times, the Bible never once associates it with immortality. God did not create humans as immortal beings.

Speaking to New Testament Christians at Corinth, Paul explains Christ will deliver the promised gift of immortality to believers in Him at His Second Coming.

> Behold, I tell you a mystery: We shall not all sleep, but we shall all be changed in a moment, in the twinkling of an eye, at the last trumpet. For the trumpet will sound, and the dead will be raised incorruptible, and we shall be changed. For this corruptible must put on incorruption, and this mortal must put on immortality. So when this corruptible has put on incorruption, and this mortal has put on immortality, then shall be brought to pass the saying that is written: *"Death is swallowed up in victory"* (1 Corinthians 15:51–54; emphasis added).

The continuance of ongoing life for Adam and Eve depended on their access to the Tree of Life, and was conditioned on their loyalty to the Lord's revealed will. God's earnest warning to avoid the prohibited tree—with the warning of death for disobedience—was directed to Adam when he was first created and without a mate (Genesis 2:16–17). No doubt, the loving Heavenly Father repeated this warning to His daughter, Eve. It becomes apparent she was fully aware of this condition for continued life (Genesis 3:2–3).

Any oath-bound promise of God indicates a covenant. Some scholars describe Genesis 2:16–17 as a "covenant of works" that demanded perfect obedience. That terminology—"covenant of works"—is never used in Scripture, and I vigorously oppose it. Scholars who juxtapose that idea with God's "covenant of grace" often imply that God no longer requires obedience. The New Testament adamantly speaks to the contrary:

Not everyone who says to Me, "Lord, Lord," shall enter the kingdom of heaven, but he who does the will of My Father in heaven (Matthew 7:21).

Do you not know that to whom you present yourselves slaves to obey, you are that one's slaves whom you obey, whether of sin leading to death, or of obedience leading to righteousness? (Romans 6:16).

For the wages of sin is death . . . . (Romans 6:23).

He [Jesus] became the author of eternal salvation to all who obey Him (Hebrews 5:9).

Thoughtful consideration of God's first covenant with Adam and Eve finds a more appropriate definition to be a "covenant of life." A loving Father had created the couple with free will, generously giving them authority to rule over His creation. By instituting a single prohibition to avoid only one of possibly hundreds of trees in the Garden, He wanted them to respect His boundary of love—placed there for their protection. They needed to trust His Word of warning to enjoy His covenant promise of life. Adam and Eve knew they must practice His will to live, and understood the consequence of death if they rejected His counsel. Either way, it was their choice.

Was God's one prohibition a test of their loyalty? As I look through the infinity lens of His love, I believe God was compelled to offer the couple a choice of principles to allow the exercise of free will. They declared their independence from God's instruction—a choice that abused God's intention for the sacred gift of free will. In our next chapter, we will see God's ready plan to redeem them when He immediately announced His everlasting covenant of righteousness by faith.

The evidence of Scripture will clearly show us that God still requires obedience to His revealed will for those who enter into covenant with Him. As our Creator and Sovereign Lord, God has never forfeited His right to establish and enforce laws of love to protect the righteousness of His sovereign kingdom. When humans willfully reject His love and rebel against His law of love, the inevitable end is the forfeiture of eternal life.

ALL THAT IS WITHIN HIS POWER OF LOVE

It was not Adam and Eve's destiny to die. God knew in advance of Creation what their eventual choice would be, but I'm convinced He did all that is within His power of love to help them make the right choice.

The Lord declared that He never changes. Although He won't force His love on anyone, His interaction with humanity throughout history proves His benevolent actions are consistent, and He persistently admonishes humans to choose His right way of living. This persuades me that God constantly works to influence all by His love. Let's leave the Garden of Eden for a moment and look to that night in history when Christ was betrayed.

On the night before His crucifixion, Christ ate a final meal with His disciples. Christians commonly call this meal "The Last Supper." All four gospel writers of the New Testament recorded this event. I will paraphrase a few points found in John 13:1–10.

Jesus was aware that Judas Iscariot planned to hand Him over to the religious leaders, who would condemn Him to death. Seated at the table for the Last Supper, Judas harbored treachery and duplicity in his heart. For three and a half years, this greedy man had followed Jesus, but his character was not influenced by Christ's love, and he never changed.

In an act of divine love, Jesus arose and prepared to wash the disciples' feet. His humility startled them. Washing away dirt and dung collected on sandal-clad feet—feet that had trodden streets crowded with people and livestock—was a service relegated to the lowliest of servants. Customarily, foot washing was performed before reclining at the table to eat, but there had been no servants in their midst, and no volunteers from the group to perform the task. It wasn't that they had not noticed, but that the disciples felt it was beneath their dignity. Yet, to demonstrate servant-leadership, the Lord lovingly insisted on washing all.

As Christ stooped before Judas to caress his caked and unclean feet, the Lord's heart surely pitied this lost soul. God desires for no one to perish (Ezekiel 33:11; 1 Timothy 2:4; 2 Peter 3:9). Did Jesus perhaps linger a bit longer with Judas, gazing intently into his eyes while He towel-dried his feet? In pretense, did Judas smile at the Lord? His brazen heart was certainly experienced at camouflaging his true motives.

The ever-compassionate heart of the Lord was revealed in His conversation at the Supper. His comments seemed to be a veiled pleading, an invitation to Judas to turn to Him in repentance. When Jesus announced that one of them would betray Him, all the disciples searched their hearts—all, but Judas. The Lord called out His betrayer aloud, but not by name. He further proclaimed that not all the disciples were clean (pure), but His strongest warning is recorded in Matthew's account:

> The Son of Man indeed goes just as it is written of Him, but woe to that man by whom the Son of Man is betrayed! It would have been good for that man if he had not been born (Matthew 26:24).

Handing Judas a choice morsel of bread—a Jewish custom of special honor and friendship—Jesus identified Judas as the betrayer. Only Jesus and Judas understood the interaction at the time. The other disciples were clueless.

Judas was not born to betray the Lord. Yes, by omniscience, God had prophesied the event, and knew in advance that Judas would ignore the loving appeals of Christ. Still, Jesus provided Judas with ample opportunity to turn away from the devious bargain he had already struck with religious leaders. God did not predestine Judas' life to end on such a tragic note. Ignoring the Lord's attempts to convert him, Judas conceded to the will of Satan, and finally—right there at the table—Satan entered his hardened heart. Rising from the table, Judas walked into the night air, turning his back on the only one who could save him.

The Lord God is the same yesterday, today, and forever. He does all that's within His power of love to save all. The true power of love is choice, and for the sake of love, the Lord created us with free will. From the beginning, He placed a sacred boundary around our right to choose our own destiny. His righteousness and the power of His love make it impossible for Him to violate that promised boundary.

He has a plan for our lives that is better than the one we are living. With loving patience, He calls us into His kingdom of light. Yet, the decision is ours to make.

Just as it was for Adam and Eve in the beginning.

SUMMARY OF "HIS" STORY
Chapter Three

- Jesus said that if we don't believe Moses' writings, we cannot believe His words.
- God reveals Himself through a progressive manner from the Old Testament to the New Testament.
- Jesus claimed to be God, the long-awaited Messiah—the Christ.
- Jesus said eternal life is found by knowing God.
- We know God through His Word, which contains His creative power of life.
- The Bible contains 66 books, written by the inspiration of the Holy Spirit to over 40 authors, in a period of approximately 1,500 years.
- The Old Testament covers 4,000 years of God's interaction with His people.
- The New Testament covers approximately the first 100 years from the birth of Christ.
- God inspired Moses to write Genesis to provide us with a backdrop of the history of beginnings.

- Genesis chapters 1–11 cover a highlight reel of the first 2,000 years after Creation, recording four epic events: 1) the Creation; 2) the Fall; 3) the Flood; and 4) the Dispersion.
- Genesis chapters 12–50 cover approximately 300 years of the patriarchal history of four great men: Abraham, Isaac, Jacob, and Joseph.
- God inspired Moses to include two back-to-back accounts of Creation to describe His attribute of *omnipresence*—He exists everywhere at the same time.
- The first account of Creation reveals God's *transcendence*—His eternal existence everywhere outside the physical realm of Creation.
- God's inspired Word proclaims literal 24-hour-periods of Creation.
- God created the world and its creatures out of nothing—speaking all into existence, until it came to the creation of Adam.
- God created Adam and Eve in His image to share His love with children.
- God gave the couple the privilege and responsibility to rule the earth.
- The second account of Creation reveals God's *immanence*—His existence everywhere *inside* creation. He is an up-close-and-personal God, who listens, speaks, and acts.
- God formed Adam from the dirt, and breathed the breath of life into his nostrils.
- God established two institutions of intimacy—marriage, and the seventh-day Sabbath.
- God established scientific cycles to mark the time of a year/month/day—observable by sight.
- God established the weekly, seven-day cycle as a mark of His authority—observed by faith.
- Common sense and history tell us the seventh day has continued to mark our weekly cycle.
- God bestowed the gift of free will to humans, desiring a reciprocal relationship of love.
- God established a boundary for the first couple's protection, prohibiting one tree from their diet.
- This prohibition was an oath-bound promise, which makes it a covenant. God explained the consequences for rejecting this covenant would result in death—"dying they would die."
- The couple rejected the covenant, fracturing their relationship with God.
- God pronounced them guilty, and the dying process began.

- God had a plan ready to resolve their problem.
- God self-imposed a boundary around His gift of free will—He will not cross it.
- He never forces us, but He does all within His power of love to help us make the right choice.

GOD ANNOUNCES HIS COVENANT IN THE GARDEN

Chapter four

How long did Adam and Eve live blissfully in Paradise before they sinned? The timeline is not recorded in the sweeping review of 2,000 years of world history given in the first eleven chapters of Genesis. Scripture describes the Heavenly Father walking with them in the Garden (Genesis 3:8). Since He had delivered custodial care of the world to the couple, He surely taught them about the wonder of plant and animal life, and how to maintain the natural order of Creation.

Did God warn the couple about the war of words that had broken out in Heaven? Did He tell them a high-ranking angel named Lucifer had trafficked lies about the Lord, led a rebellion against God's government, and garnered the sympathies of a third of the angels who followed him and fell into sin? (Revelation 12:3, 4, 7–9). I am convinced He did. It is only fitting with God's righteous and just nature to have shared this vital information with them.

HOW DID SIN ORIGINATE?

The ideas many people have heard about angels are mostly folklore, and are far from what the Bible describes. Because the fallen angel Lucifer plays the principal role in the history of sin, it is important to clarify who he is and how God originally created him.

Contrary to popular opinion, the word *angel* does not describe the nature of a being, but the position of that being's service as a messenger of God. The Hebrew word for angel *(mal'āk)*, as well as the New Testament Greek word for angel *(angelos)*, are translated into English as either *messenger* or *angel*. Both words are used to refer to ordinary human messengers, as well as God's prophets and priests (e.g. 1 Samuel 11:3; Haggai 1:13; Luke 7:27, 9:52; Malachi 2:7). Both words also refer to heavenly messengers.

The Bible does identify an order of created beings that fits our typical understanding of *angels*, describing them as *cherubim* and *seraphim*. Like us, they were not created immortal, and do not share God's attribute of omnipresence—they can be only in one place at one time. God created them to help accomplish His will and be heavenly messengers for His kingdom. These ministering spirits have different ranks in dignity and power.

Only two created angels are named in Scripture, and both held the highest ranking among the cherubim as the two covering cherubs at the heavenly throne of God. The first is Gabriel, who stood in the presence of God (Luke 1:19), and is mentioned by name only twice in Daniel and twice in Luke. The second "anointed cherub who covers" was "perfect" from the day God created him, until "iniquity" entered his heart (Ezekiel 28:11–15). His name was Lucifer.

Lucifer was not an archangel, as some suppose. The word *archangel* means *Captain* or *Chief* of the angels, who possesses ultimate authority over the celestial beings, and it is used only twice in the Bible (1 Thessalonians 4:16; Jude 1:9). Michael is named as the only archangel. Many scholars—like the beloved Bible commentator Matthew Henry— believe "Michael the Archangel" is another of Christ's many titles. Christ served as the Divine Messenger of God and "the Lord of hosts"—the Commander-in-Chief of all the heavenly hosts (1 Kings 22:19).

Standing in the presence of God, sin originated when pride and envy erupted in Lucifer's heart. He was not satisfied to be God's messenger. He wanted to be exalted and become equal to God (Isaiah 14:13–14). When iniquity flared within him, he was changed—becoming the first and chief of all narcissists. Lucifer longed to be worshiped. It is forbidden for created beings to be worshiped—only God, the Creator, is worthy of worship (Matthew 4:10; Colossians 2:18; Revelation 22:8–9).

Becoming an accuser against God, a lying deceiver, and a masterful manipulator, Lucifer is eventually revealed in Scripture as the "great dragon," and "that serpent of old, called the Devil and Satan, who deceives the whole world" (Revelation 12:9). Jesus described Satan's character by saying he "does not stand in the truth, because there is no truth in him. When he speaks a lie, he speaks from his own resources, for he is a liar and the father of it" (John 8:44).

Do you wonder why God did not destroy Lucifer as soon as he sinned? Think about that for a moment. Had He taken immediate action, Lucifer's accusations against Him would have been supported, and the host of angels who remained faithful to God would have been confused. The Lord had to prove Himself faithful and loving to all the onlookers in the Universe.

Although God does not need counsel from anyone to approve His decisions, Scripture indicates He graciously allows some of His created beings to come into His presence, and suggest input to accomplish His will (Job 1:6; 1 Kings 22:19; Daniel 4:17). God is not the authoritarian dictator many accuse Him of being. It is quite plausible this council of beings had input on allowing Satan a short time on Earth to prove or disprove his accusations (Revelation 12:12).

THE SEDUCTION OF THE SERPENT

Among the many beautiful fruit trees, God placed two trees in the center of the Garden—the tree of life, and the tree of the knowledge of good and evil. God declared a boundary around the latter, warning Adam and Eve to avoid eating from it. He clearly explained that partaking of its fruit would result in death (Genesis 2:16–17).

This was the Lord's only prohibition to the righteous couple. His intention was to protect them from an experiential knowledge of evil with all of its pain, guilt, and shame. Further, because their knowledge was inferior to His, He did not want them to independently decide what would be good or evil for their lives. Adam and Eve could exercise their free will to eat from either. If they avoided the fruit of that tree, they would continue life in paradise—that was God's *covenant of life* with them.

In Genesis 3:1, the storyline sweeps past their early time of life in the Garden, fast forwarding to the day Eve encountered a serpent at the prohibited tree. Accustomed to this creature, she would not have been alarmed. God did not initially create the serpent in a snake-like form that we see today. Not until after the Fall—when God pronounced a curse on the creature—did it have to slither on the ground for its remaining existence (Genesis 3:14).

What Eve could not have known at first was that the serpent had been possessed by Satan, who used it as a medium. Satan transformed himself to masquerade as a messenger of light (2 Corinthians 11:14). Reflecting the dazzling beauty with which God had originally created Lucifer, the creature in the tree captured her attention. When he spoke with soothing charm, her curiosity was captivated. A talking serpent?

Without Adam by her side, Eve was vulnerable to Satan's seduction. The great deceiver knew what God had warned the couple, but subtly twisted and distorted God's words as he attempted to engage her in conversation. Are you aware of Satan's modus operandi? He twists the truth just enough to make his lies seem credible. In his cunning fashion, he asked if God had really said, "You shall not eat of **every** tree of the garden?" (Genesis 3:1; emphasis added).

Eve enthusiastically defended the great liberty God had given the couple, declaring the fruit from this particular tree was the only thing He had prohibited, warning that its consumption would bring death. What was Eve's mistake? She engaged in conversation with the devil. This emboldened him. Now he directly contradicted God with his great lie, "You shall not surely die" (Genesis 3:4).

Coercing her to eat, he claimed she would become like God. Eve was deceived. She ate the fruit, thinking it was the right thing to do, and went to find her husband working nearby in the Garden to share the tasty treat. The New Testament clearly explains a difference between her deception and Adam's reaction.

Adam was not deceived, but the woman being deceived, fell into transgression (1 Timothy 2:14; compare 2 Corinthians 11:3).

Her sin was unintentional; his was not. He knew this was forbidden fruit. If Adam was not deceived, why would he eat? Was it that he recognized Eve's impending penalty, and could not bear a separation from her? We don't know for certain, but he consciously made the decision to declare his independence from God through a willing transgression.

THE CONSEQUENCES OF SIN

When Adam sinned by deliberate disobedience, the first representative of humanity broke covenant with His Creator. Now human nature was corrupted, and the human race doomed.

Therefore, just as through one man sin entered the world, and death through sin, and thus death spread to all men, because all sinned (Romans 5:12).

Adam did more than betray his Creator, he delivered dominion of the world to Satan. Elected by God to govern the world in His image and by His righteous standards, the couple surrendered control to the enemy. Through deception, Eve was naively disqualified to rule. When Adam willingly submitted to Satan's rule, he consciously handed in his resignation as Earth's governor to be enslaved by Satan—who held the power of death (Hebrews 2:14). Today we are faced with the same choice, and warned in Romans 6:16, "Do you not know that to whom you present yourselves slaves to obey, you are that one's slaves whom you obey, whether of sin leading to death, or of obedience leading to righteousness?"

The couple forfeited their right, and Satan seized absolute authority to rule over all the operations and jurisprudence of the planet.

Rather than operating through the power of love as the Lord does, Satan would rule through the love of power and control.

Thousands of years later, Jesus' ministry began with forty days in the wilderness being tempted by the devil. When Satan asserted he had authority over Earth, Jesus did not dispute his claim. Just listen to the devil's boasting, as he tried to bait the Lord to bow before him:

> Then the devil, taking Him up on a high mountain, showed Him all the kingdoms of the world in a moment of time. And the devil said to Him, "All this authority I will give You, and their glory; for this has been delivered to me, and I give it to whomever I wish. Therefore, if You will worship before me, all will be Yours" (Luke 4:5–7).

In the Garden, the couple experienced the bitter fruit of unrighteousness, and their eyes were opened to the truth of sin. Suddenly they lost the covering of God's light—His righteousness. They felt inadequate. Sullied. Naked. Ashamed. Guilty before God. The two quickly fashioned together garments of fig leaves—not realizing the futility of human effort to restore righteousness (Isaiah 64:6).

Aware of their fall, God took the initiative—as He always does—to search out the sinners. The guilt-ridden couple hid from His presence when they heard Him walking in the Garden (Genesis 3:8). Unfortunately, trying to hide from God when we sin has become an inherited tendency of the human race.

The Lord asked them investigative questions, and the consequences of their decisions became apparent. Eve justified her actions and tried to shift the blame to the serpent. Adam blamed God. After all, God was the one who had given him the woman who had handed him the fruit. Of course, the man did not confess his deliberate choice. How much we resemble Adam and Eve with all of our blame-shifting, justifying, and denying of the sin that has penetrated our hearts.

Now here's a critical point. Have you ever heard of "the curse of sin"? Most people seem to think God cursed Adam and Eve, and humanity in general. But, He did not. In the Old Testament, several different Hebrew words are translated as "curse," and these words have varying degrees of bitterness.

Because the serpent had allowed Satan to use it as a medium to deceive the woman, God cursed its form—changing it to a creature without legs or wings which would be confined to slither on its belly in the dust of the ground for the rest of its days (Genesis 3:14). Obviously, God's curse on Satan—the deceiving spiritual serpent—likewise held no offer of hope for reversal. But hope for humanity came shining through in the middle of this curse passage.

In my mind, I hear trumpets blasting to accompany the Lord's announcement.

THE LORD ANNOUNCES HIS EVERLASTING COVENANT

The first prophetic announcement of the everlasting covenant—the everlasting good news of righteousness by faith—is the message of hope to fallen humanity. Speaking to the serpent, the Lord said:

> And I will put enmity between you and the woman, and between your seed and her Seed; He shall bruise your head, and you shall bruise His heel (Genesis 3:15).

In less than thirty words, the Lord unveils His everlasting covenant and outlines the end of the cosmic conflict. The conclusion of the spiritual controversy that began in heaven between God and Satan—between good and evil—is here announced. Looking through our objective lens of God's infinite love, and with our infinity focus expanded to a panoramic view, let's unpack the rich meaning of His prophetic words:

- **"I will"**—this is covenant language. When our covenant-making, covenant-keeping Lord says, "I will," it is His covenant promise.
- **"put enmity"**—*enmity* means *hostility*. Through the convicting power of the Holy Spirit, the Lord strives to place a hatred of sin into each human heart. He works to motivate people to accept the everlasting covenant of His saving grace.

- **"between you and the woman"**—the Lord prophesied an ongoing battle between the devil and the human race. Satan's hatred for humanity was already apparent, but the cosmic conflict would intensify. The "woman" in this phrase refers to Eve, and her offspring. Within the context of this event, Eve is dubbed "the mother of all living" (Genesis 3:20). The *church* is also referred to as a woman within Bible prophecy.

- **"and between your seed"**—Those who follow Satan are his offspring, described as "children of the devil" and identified by their refusal to "practice righteousness" (1 John 3:10). Mocking the Lord's righteous requirements and ignoring His authority, Satan and his unholy alliance of fallen angels and human followers are hostile toward Him.

- **"and her Seed"**—*Seed* is here covenant language. As soon as sin marred the Lord's created sphere of righteousness, He announced the good news of a promised Seed—Jesus Christ. He declared the Deliverer would be the descendant of a woman (not of a man), which He became through incarnation in a virgin birth. This emphasizes the full humanity of God in the Person of Jesus Christ (Philippians 2:5–10).

We will follow the story of the *Seed* as it progressively unfolds throughout Scripture. Jesus is the Seed of Abraham (Galatians 3:16), the Seed promised to King David, who will sit on the throne to rule God's kingdom forever—without end (Luke 1:31–33). He would become the "Last Adam" who would take back dominion from Satan (1 Corinthians 15:45).

Through Jesus, God would provide a new beginning—a new genesis—for the human race. When humans enter into the everlasting covenant of Christ, we are "born again" with new spiritual DNA as we partake of the divine nature, and we do not live a life of habitual sin because Christ's seed remains in us (John 3:3; 1 Peter 1:23; 2 Peter 1:3, 4; 1 John 3:9). Given new hearts converted by grace, we are repulsed by sin and hate evil as He does.

- **"He shall bruise your head"** prophesies the final overthrow of Satan. The singular "Seed" would crush the head of the Serpent, dealing Satan a fatal blow at the cross. Christ came to "destroy the works of the devil" and to set Satan's captives free (1 John 3:8; Luke 4:18–21). He triumphed over Satan, destroying the devil's power of death (Colossians 2:15; Hebrews 2:14). At the first resurrection of life when Christ returns to deliver His promised gift of immortality, death will be "swallowed up in victory" (John 5:28–29; 1 Corinthians 15:53–55).
"The God of peace will crush Satan under your feet shortly" (Romans 16:20). The devil's final destruction comes at the end of the millennium when Satan is cast into the lake of fire and is destroyed (Revelation 20:10). When God creates the new earth, there will be no more curse (Revelation 22:3).
- **"and you shall bruise His heel."** This is the first prophetic announcement of the cross of Calvary. Prophecies continue to mount throughout the Old Testament to explain the agony and suffering with which the devil bruised Christ, and Satan's vicious efforts to kill the Lord of glory. When Jesus died on the cross and was buried in a tomb, Satan thought the battle he had begun in heaven and continued on earth had been won. His glee was extinguished early that Sunday morning when our Lord resurrected in conquering power as the true Victor.

God's curse on both the serpent and Satan explicitly denied reversal, but the announcement of the everlasting covenant brought glorious hope to the devastated couple. That hope extended to all their descendants. Shining His brilliant light into their dismal darkness, the Lord gave them a present hope of a future Deliverer.

A careful examination of this curse passage in Genesis 3:14–19 reveals God did not curse the couple, but He did bring judgment upon their sin. His righteous judgments support His claim to absolute obedience, and have varying degrees of severity.

The consequences for Eve allowing herself to be seduced into sin were such that the woman would experience pain when she brought forth children, and be ruled by her husband (Genesis 3:16). Because

Adam deliberately sinned, God cursed the ground, increasing the toil of humanity from that point forward (v. 17). The curse of sin caused death; the dying process began. God declared that at their demise humans would "return to the ground, for out of it you were taken; for dust you are, and to dust you shall return" (v. 19).

The highly-compressed version of this story does not provide details of their reactions. With an infinity focus, allow me to share what likely occurred. Although the curse of sin would affect them deeply in the future, they probably did not see His judgments as being too harsh.

Eve likely understood the Lord's judgment upon her from a positive perspective of salvation. She expected the Deliverer would come through her. Thinking his wife would bring forth this Child, Adam looked upon her with new appreciation. In the joy of the moment, he named his wife "Eve" because he recognized she was to be "the mother of all living" (v. 20). His heart overflowed with hope, as he realized the couple would bring forth children, and have a family to celebrate. Adam accepted the consequences of his sin, knowing they would bring suffering, misery, and death, but he must have been grateful for God's grace in extending his life. Having expected to die immediately, hard work probably sounded good to him.

The one consequence they had not anticipated happened next.

> Also for Adam and his wife the LORD God made tunics of skin, and clothed them (Genesis 3:21).

Adam had expected to be the first to die for his sin. Instead, the Lord made a sin offering for him and his wife, sacrificing the life of an innocent animal to cover their nakedness. Fig-leaf aprons of human devising wouldn't do. Realizing it was on account of their sin that a spotless lamb had to die must have sent a chill up their spine. Never before had they seen death.

Did God explain to them that this act foreshadowed the ministry of the coming Seed—"the Lamb slain from the foundation of the world" (Revelation 13:8)—who would die as the Substitute to cover all humanity's sins? Did they understand that their Redeemer would provide humans with His robe of righteousness by faith, and one day resurrect

His righteous ones to clothe them with immortality? (1 Corinthians 15:53–54). We will consider how this is revealed in Scripture.

A bitter consequence of their sin was being banished from the Garden (Genesis 3:23). In merciful grace, the Lord drove them away from the tree of life to prevent them from eating its fruit and continuing to live on forever in their pitiful plight. The children of Adam and Eve were born in their likeness—with the nature of fallen humanity (Genesis 5:3).

GOD'S SACRIFICIAL SYSTEM OPENS A PATHWAY TO RIGHTEOUSNESS BY FAITH

The penalty of sin is death, but God already had a plan in place to satisfy His perfect justice and demonstrate His self-sacrificing love. Our Creator would become a human, stand in as our Substitute, and shed His precious blood on Calvary to settle our sin debt. Salvation by grace would be offered freely to the human race, but at a great personal cost to Him.

To impress upon humanity's conscience the awfulness of sin, God instituted a substitutionary sacrificial system that pointed forward to the ministry of the coming Messiah, and the high price He would pay to redeem humanity. The design of this system demonstrated that the lifeblood of another would have to be sacrificed as a sin-substitute. Blood is vital to life, and is used as a biblical symbol to represent life. The Bible teaches that life is in the blood (Genesis 9:4, Leviticus 17:14). God designed the bloody sacrificial system to increase awareness of the appalling cost of the remedy for sin.

Under this Old Testament system, those who transgressed God's moral code of love symbolically transferred their sins to innocent creatures that they had to put to death—a death the guilty sinners deserved. In an exchange, the creature's spotless innocence was credited to them. This showed that the coming Messiah-Christ would take humanity's sins upon Himself and credit us with His righteousness (2 Corinthians 5:21).

By this demonstration of His grace, as soon as sin appeared God immediately opened a pathway for humans to be made righteous by faith in Him. Entering into this sacrificial practice established worship of the one true God, and declared faith in the expected

Seed whom God promised in the Garden. The Lord declared "not guilty" all who looked forward in faith, believing that the sacrifices represented salvation through their coming Redeemer, restoring their relationship with Him.

How can we be certain of this? According to Scripture, there is no way humans can restore their spiritual innocence. The Bible makes it clear that righteousness by faith is the only kind of righteousness. Our best human attempts at *righteousness* are nothing more than "filthy rags" before the Lord (Isaiah 64:6).

Yet in Genesis, men are declared righteous again. In fact, we see that God revealed Himself to these ancient people as their "Redeemer." And resurrection from the grave was already an established heavenly principle before Abraham's day. Let's examine Scripture that backs up these claims.

THE LINE OF GOD-FOLLOWERS FROM THE GARDEN FORWARD

Adam and Eve looked forward to the coming Seed—the coming Messiah—in faith of His plan of redemption. Certainly, God taught the couple about substitutionary sacrifice which was established as a common practice in Genesis. Although the abbreviated account does not record it, the couple obviously taught their children the requirements of God's substitutionary plan for righteousness.

Their son Abel had faith in God's divine plan. He brought a little lamb to sacrifice as his substitute. God respected Abel and his offering (Genesis 4:4). The New Testament affirms, "By faith Abel offered to God a more excellent sacrifice than Cain, through which he obtained witness that he was righteous" (Hebrews 11:4). By Christ's own testimony, this son of Adam and Eve was made righteous. He spoke of "the blood of righteous Abel" (Matthew 23:35).

Disregarding divine instruction, their other son—Cain, a farmer—had brought to the Lord an offering of his own works from the fruit of the ground. God rejected Cain's offering (Genesis 4:5). God shows no partiality (Romans 2:11), so this rejection was not arbitrary, but affirmed the divine truth that no one can be made righteous by self-effort. Trying to correct Cain, the up-close-and-personal

God instructed him, "If you do well, will you not be accepted? And if you do not do well, sin lies at the door. And its desire is for you, but you should rule over it" (Genesis 4:7). Listen to the New Testament echo of this warning: "Be sober, be vigilant; because your adversary the devil walks about like a roaring lion, seeking whom he may devour" (1 Peter 5:8). Crouching at the door of Cain's heart, sin pounced. Cain killed his righteous brother (Genesis 4:8).

Eve understood God's promise of the "Seed" of the woman—who would crush Satan's head—to mean that this Deliverer would come directly from her womb. When she gave birth to Seth, she exclaimed, "God has appointed another seed for me instead of Abel, whom Cain killed" (Genesis 4:25). While Seth was not *the* Seed, he was a righteous seed. After he came into the world we learn, "Then men began to call on the name of the LORD" (v. 26).

What does it mean *to call on the name of the Lord*? In a desire to repair their fractured relationship with their loving Creator, men cried out for His mercy and grace, and restoration of righteousness. God's plan of salvation has never changed. In the New Testament, Paul affirms, "whoever calls on the name of the LORD shall be saved" (Romans 10:13), and King David said—

> The LORD is near . . . to all who call upon Him in truth. He will fulfill the desire of those who fear Him; He also will hear their cry and save them. The LORD preserves all who love Him, but all the wicked He will destroy (Psalm 145:18–20).

Consider Enoch, who lived before the Flood. "Enoch walked with God; and he was not, for God took him" (Genesis 5:24). His faith made him righteous before the Lord, and God translated Enoch into heaven—without experiencing death. The New Testament affirms, "By faith Enoch was taken away so that he did not see death, *'and was not found, because God had taken him'*; for before he was taken he had this testimony, that he pleased God" (Hebrews 11:5; emphasis added). He is a symbolic "type" of the righteous who will be alive when Christ returns and will not experience death (1 Corinthians 15:51–54; 1 Thessalonians 4:16–17).

Now let's look at Noah. "Noah was a just man, perfect in his generations. Noah walked with God" (Genesis 6:9). By the time of Noah's life, sin had metastasized like a cancer. Violence filled the earth and evil reigned continually in the hearts of humanity (Genesis 6:5, 11). Yet Noah's walk with the Lord was consistent, and "Noah found grace in the eyes of the Lord" (v. 8). God warned Noah that He planned to cleanse the earth of its rampant sin through a flood, and gave him instructions to build an ark (v. 14).

Noah had never seen rain before. Earth's subterranean waters—the "fountains of the great deep"—had never broken open before (Genesis 7:11, 8:2). Taking God at His word, "By faith Noah, being divinely warned of things not yet seen, moved with godly fear, prepared an ark for the saving of his household . . . and became heir of the righteousness which is according to faith" (Hebrews 11:7).

Noah obeyed God's distinction of clean and unclean animals, introduced hundreds of years before the Levitical system (Leviticus 11). *Clean* means that God has *sanctified* something, setting it apart for His purposes, and it is acceptable to Him. *Unclean* means *unholy and unacceptable* to God. The Lord sent two each of *unclean* animals into the ark, but He directed seven pairs (fourteen creatures in total) of each *clean* animal into the shelter from the storm (Genesis 7:1–5). More were needed. Only clean animals could be sacrificed to God and were permitted by Him to be consumed for food after the Flood. When the waters receded, the first thing Noah did was worship God with a grateful heart for His salvation from the destruction. "Then Noah built an altar to the LORD, and took of every clean animal and of every clean bird, and offered burnt offerings on the altar" (Genesis 8:20).

Now on to the Patriarch Job. The book of Job is presented in the genre of wisdom literature in the Bible, rather than the order in which his life occurred. For our purposes, it is important to realize that Job lived sometime around the time of Abraham, and was not a Hebrew. He lived before the establishment of the formal priesthood, which occurred after the Exodus. Job functioned as the priest for his family, a practice common during the patriarchal period of Genesis 12–50. He regularly officiated burnt offerings to sanctify his children, in case they had sinned (Job 1:5).

God declared His servant Job was "a blameless and upright man, one who fears God and shuns evil" (Job 1:8). In a malevolent attempt to shatter Job's faith, Satan afflicted him with intense emotional and physical suffering. Job endured his sufferings patiently—for the most part—with an attitude that he had accepted God's many blessings, and should likewise willingly accept adversity (Job 1:21; 2:10). Mistakenly believing that God was afflicting him, Job confirmed his ongoing faith in the righteousness of God, saying, "Though He slay me, yet will I trust Him" (Job 13:15). Job already knew about, and was counting on, the resurrection. His great faith caused him to proclaim, "For I know that my Redeemer lives, and He shall stand at last on the earth; and after my skin is destroyed, this I know, that in my flesh I shall see God" (Job 19:25–26).

The sacrificial system initiated in the Garden opened a pathway for humans to become heirs of righteousness by faith. The accounts of Genesis show that God's people understood that the sacrifices typified (represented) their coming Redeemer, who would become their Substitute.

God's grace was active among the ancients. Understanding that the Redeemer would one day resurrect them, they believed in the promise of a new genesis—a future promise of a new beginning of the world, paradise restored. Like other descendants of righteousness, they rejoiced being among those "who are kept by the power of God through faith for salvation ready to be revealed in the last time" (1 Peter 1:5). Abel, Enoch, and Noah looked forward to the promised salvation that would be accomplished by Christ, and are listed among the famous heroes of faith in Hebrews 11—

And all these, having obtained a good testimony through faith, did not receive the promise, God having provided something better for us, that they should not be made perfect apart from us (Hebrews 11:39–40).

A holy and just God cannot ignore sin. He declared death as the penalty for sin. Yet, a merciful and loving God knew we could not pay that penalty without perishing. He paid the penalty for us. To become our Substitute, the Lord had to become a member of the human race who could rightfully represent us. Only a spotless human unsullied by sin could qualify. Only the blood of the Creator was worthy to satisfy the cost of all humanity's sin. The Bible urges us to live,

> Knowing that you were not redeemed with corruptible things, like silver or gold, from your aimless conduct received by tradition from your fathers, but with the precious blood of Christ, as of a lamb without blemish and without spot (1 Peter 1:18-19).

You are worth nothing less to Him than the price He paid for you, with His own precious blood shed on Calvary's cross. He created you uniquely—you are special to Him—and there is no one else like you. Your life is precious to the Lord. He wants to adopt you as His child and make you righteous so you can live with Him throughout eternity in the new Earth, when there will be no more death, sorrow, crying, or pain (Revelation 21:1–4).

Righteousness by faith has always been God's plan of salvation.

It is His everlasting covenant with the human race, first announced in the Garden.

He invites you now to enter into an intimate covenant relationship with Him.

SUMMARY OF "HIS" STORY
Chapter Four

- In the original Bible languages, the word *angel* defines a position of authority and service as a messenger. The term is used to identify ordinary human messengers and God's prophets and priests, as well as messengers from Heaven.
- God created an order of beings called *cherubim* and *seraphim* to be ministering spirits.
- Lucifer was a high-ranking cherub—one of two who covered the heavenly throne of God—created in perfection and beauty.

- Sin originated in Lucifer's heart when he wanted to receive the worship due only to God.
- Lucifer began a war of words in Heaven, defaming God's character and His government.
- Lucifer is identified as the "great dragon" and "that serpent of old, called the Devil and Satan, who deceives the whole world" (Revelation 12:9).
- Satan deceived Eve. Appearing as a messenger of light, he convinced her to eat from the prohibited tree. She believed she was doing the right thing, and found her husband in the Garden to share the tasty fruit.
- "Adam was not deceived" (1 Timothy 2:14). He knew it was wrong to eat the fruit.
- Sin entered the world through Adam. All have sinned.
- The couple forfeited their right to rule the world, delivering it to Satan.
- Satan seized control of the planet, claiming control. Jesus did not dispute the devil's claim.
- The couple tried to cover their sin with aprons of fig leaves, and to hide from God's presence.
- God always takes the initiative to find sinners.
- God announced His everlasting covenant in less than 30 words, giving the distraught couple hope of salvation through a Deliverer, and pronouncing the Devil's destruction.
- The "Seed"—Jesus Christ—would be born of a woman through a virgin birth.
- The Devil would cause Jesus to suffer, but Christ would destroy the works of the Devil, crushing his head.
- God cursed sin, but did not curse human beings. Rather, He passed judgments upon them.
- God pronounced the death sentence, and the process of dying began.
- God lovingly banished the couple from the Garden, but with hope in their hearts of continuing life and having a family.
- God immediately opened the pathway to restore righteousness by faith in the coming Redeemer, accomplished through the substitutionary sacrificial system God established in the Garden.
- Humans could do nothing to restore righteousness, but God declared them so again in Genesis.
- Abel followed God's plan and was declared righteous.

- After Seth fathered Enosh, men began calling on the name of the Lord.
- Righteous Enoch walked so close to God that the Lord translated him to Heaven without dying.
- Noah was righteous and found grace in God's eyes. Noah sacrificed to God.
- Noah obeyed God. He "became heir of the righteousness which is according to faith" (Hebrews 11:7).
- The patriarch Job was declared righteous, trusted God, and believed he would be resurrected to see His Redeemer. He served as the priest of his family, sacrificing to God for the sanctification of his children.
- "I will" is covenant language, indicating God's covenant promises.
- "Seed" is covenant language, pointing to Christ.

ABRAHAM—THE FATHER OF US ALL

Chapter five

The Apostle Paul tells us that God chose Abraham to be the "father of us all" (Romans 4:16). Why did God choose a man from the pagan city of Ur to serve in a position of such preeminence in the family of all believers for all generations? Abraham was the father not only of the biological Jews who were his *physical* descendants; he is the father of all who are his *spiritual* descendants.

The covenant of righteousness by faith God made with Abraham is the expression of God's everlasting covenant, and it is the underpinning—the solid foundation—of both the Old and New Covenants (Exodus 2:24; Luke 1:54, 55, 72–73). As this truth is unfolded in Scripture, it will cement in our minds forever that the Lord does not change, and His everlasting covenant determined in eternity past has never changed.

"If you are Christ's, then you are Abraham's seed, and heirs according to the promise" (Galatians 3:29). It is important that we review God's interactions with Abraham and his seed, because it is relevant to our understanding of the Lord's clear expectations of those who are in covenant relationship with Him.

GOD'S COVENANT INTERACTIONS

The word *covenant* describes a legally binding agreement. God makes two kinds of oath-bound covenants with humanity: 1) unilateral, meaning it is not conditioned upon human response; and 2) bilateral, meaning a human must choose to enter into the terms of His covenant. In both cases, God is the one who makes and keeps all the promises. His covenants differ from the contract form of agreement between humans, which we will consider in detail in chapter eleven.

Examples of God's unilateral covenants include the covenant He introduced to Noah, with the sign of a rainbow to assure humans He would not again destroy the earth with water (Genesis 9:12–17). Another example is when God extended His everlasting covenant with loyal King David by promising his Seed would sit on the throne forever (1 Chronicles 17:11–14). It's interesting to note that God would have extended this covenant promise to King Saul had Saul faithfully kept His commandments, but after Saul's failure the Lord sought out David—a man after His own heart (1 Samuel 13:13–14).

What about God's everlasting covenant of *righteousness by faith*—is it unilateral or bilateral? Certainly, it expresses God's divine will of salvation by grace, determined among the Godhead before our world was created. While God the Father, Son, and Spirit all take part in the process of salvation, one of them agreed to humble Himself to become a human, and die as our Substitute on Calvary's cross. He would bear the penalty for our sins, and—in the great exchange— would credit us with His righteousness by our faith in Him. This covenant is bilateral. It is conditioned upon the human response of faith. God's covenant blessings of righteousness by faith are provided only to those who *choose* to enter into covenant with God and willingly walk in His righteous ways, relying on His saving power.

In our last chapter, we considered the line of God-followers after the Fall of humanity. God opened the pathway for righteousness to be restored by faith in the coming Messiah. We saw Adam, Eve, and their son Abel restored to relationship with God. Then we considered how Seth, Enoch, Noah, and Job followed the one true God and became heirs of righteousness by faith. The Bible traces Abraham's genealogy all the way back to Seth, the son Eve thought would be the deliverer (1 Chronicles 1:1–27). As we follow the story of the *seed*, we see that Abraham was most definitely in the line of God-followers who would be the ancestors of Jesus.

Serving as Moses' pivot point from 2,000 years of history in the first eleven chapters of Genesis to the story of Abraham's life, Genesis 11 traces his ancestry only as far back as the Flood, beginning with his relative Shem. That arrested my attention. Did Shem serve a crucial role in Abraham's life? Let's see.

TRACING GOD'S COVENANT BLESSINGS THROUGH SHEM

Shem was one of Noah's three sons who entered the ark with their wives, and was among the eight survivors of the Flood (Genesis 6:10, 7:13). Soon after the family departed the ark, "God blessed Noah and his sons, and said to them: 'Be fruitful and multiply, and fill the earth'" (Gen 9:1). Making a unilateral covenant with humanity, God promised to never again destroy the earth by a flood. The sign of His covenant was the rainbow (vv. 8–17).

Shem was a "young" 98 years-old when he exited the ark. He fathered a child two years afterward at the age of 100, then lived another 500 years (Genesis 11:10, 11). He was still living during the lifetime of Abraham. The generations born before the Flood had far superior life spans. God severely shortened the cycle of life after the Flood, which is apparent when we compare the 600 years of Shem's life to Abraham's mere 175 years.

A fascinating backstory to Noah's sons is found in Genesis 9:20–27, showing us that God knew in advance how each would exercise their free will. The story also lays bare the failure of righteous Noah after the Flood. God's Word makes no attempt to cover up the dark events in the history of His righteous covenant people.

Upon exiting the ark, Noah planted a vineyard, drank of the wine, and became drunk. His son, Ham—and plausibly his grandson, Canaan—saw him lying naked in his tent, and gawked at his nakedness. In disrespect of Noah, they exposed his shame by reporting the incident to his other sons. Those sons—Shem and Japheth—refused to participate in the cruel mocking. Following God's moral code of love to honor your parents, they entered backward into Noah's tent without looking upon him, and covered him with a garment.

When Noah awoke, he spoke prophetically—guided by God, who declares the end from the beginning (Isaiah 46:10). He pronounced a curse on Ham's son Canaan (strongly implying that Noah's grandson either instigated or was complicit in the event). Canaan, Noah prophesied, would be the servant of Shem. Turning to Japheth, Noah blessed this other son, saying, "May God enlarge Japheth."

Then Noah turned to his son Shem and pronounced God's richest blessing over him, declaring that Shem's descendants would have preeminence over Canaan's. *Preeminence*—a distinction of superior status—is a *covenant blessing*, and the land of Canaan becomes an integral part of the history of Shem's descendants. The most unforgettable moment of Noah's blessing over Shem is when Noah declared the Lord to be "The God of Shem" (Genesis 9:26).

Shem carried God's covenant blessing and became the progenitor of the Israelites, a nation that would be formed generations later and become God's chosen people. Shem's descendants were known as *Semites*, from which the term *Semitic* is derived. Among his descendants, we find listed the Patriarch Eber, from which the term "Hebrew" may derive (Genesis 11:14–16). Abraham was a Hebrew (Genesis 14:13), and all of his biological descendants were Hebrews. The New Testament traces Jesus' genealogy to Abraham, Eber, Shem, Noah, Enoch, Seth, and all the way to the beginning of His bloodline in Adam, "the son of God" (Luke 3:34–38).

THE GOD-REJECTING NATIONS

From Noah's three sons came all the nations: the descendants of godly Shem became the people of God after the Flood, but the descendants of Ham and Japheth rejected God.

Ham's descendants became the Cushites, Egyptians, and Canaanites; Japheth's offspring became the Indo-European nations. These nations migrated and formed other nations. A trait they all shared was their refusal to worship the one true God. Lacking discernment, they invented and worshiped idols, which originated the system of pagan religion. In reality, these nations were worshiping demons, rather than their Creator (Deuteronomy 32:16–17; 1 Corinthians 10:20–22).

Many of Noah's descendants refused to obey God's command to fill the earth. With independent pride and arrogance, they built the Tower of Babel to glorify themselves by reaching the heavens of God's domain, saying, "Come, let us build ourselves a city, and a tower whose top is in the heavens; let us make a name for ourselves, lest we be scattered abroad over the face of the whole earth" (Genesis 11:4). God came down to confuse their language and disperse the people, separating them into different language groups that scattered over a wide geographical area (vv. 5–9).

DYSFUNCTION WITHIN ABRAHAM'S FAMILY

As Moses concluded the world history of the first eleven chapters of Genesis, and prepared to record the patriarchal life sketches in Genesis 12–50, the Lord inspired him to transition between these two major divisions of the book by tagging on an account of Abraham's family ancestry from Shem to Terah (Abraham's father). Before we investigate Shem's role in Abraham's story, let's take a brief look at the life of Terah and his children.

At the age of seventy, by one wife, Terah had three sons—"Abram," Nahor, and Haran (Genesis 11:26). Ten years later, by another wife, he had a daughter named "Sarai." The story of God's covenant couple begins using their given names of "Abram" and "Sarai." It was God who later changed their names (Genesis 17:5, 15). For the sake of clarity, from this point forward I will use their covenant names "Abraham" and "Sarah."

Apparently a well-to-do man, Terah reared his family in Ur of Chaldees—a city in a fertile area of the northern plateau of Mesopotamia near the Euphrates River. Ur was part of a cultured and sophisticated civilization where the practice of polytheism prevailed. We assume Terah's children were well educated, but they were sadly exposed to pagan worship within their own home. Terah did not walk in Shem's footsteps following the one true Creator God. He seemed to have an appreciation of the Lord, but fell into the practice of polytheism and worshiped idols (Joshua 24:2). His pagan practices were passed down to his son Nahor and his children. These generations continued the practice of idol worship—expressly forbidden by God's moral code of reciprocal love and loyalty from humanity to Him (Genesis 31:19; 35:2–4).

During the Patriarchal period God had not yet forbidden intermarriage between close family members, as He did several generations later (Levitus 18; 20). Marrying a close relative was a common and accepted custom at the time. Terah's sons certainly followed suit. One of them, Haran, had a son named Lot and a daughter named Milcah. Haran died before his father in the city of Ur (Genesis 11:28), leaving his children as orphans. But his daughter Milcah had married one of Terah's three sons, her uncle Nahor, and bore him eight sons (vv. 29; 22:20–23).

Abraham married his half-sister Sarah, who was sadly barren (Genesis 11:30; 20:12). Sarah's emotional despair over her infertility was surely intensified by seeing her sister-in-law's robust fertility.

WHY DID GOD CHOOSE ABRAHAM?

The Jewish people did not exist as a distinct ethnic group or nation during Abraham's lifetime. The term comes from the tribe of his great-grandson *Judah*, and the Israelite kingdom that bore his name. Eventually, this term was applied to all of Jacob's descendants, and the Jewish nation used the word *gentile* to identify anyone who was not Jewish.

Abraham came from a pagan nation. Although he witnessed idol worship within his own home, Abraham was a true believer in the Creator God. He followed God with all his heart, and God knew it. The Lord had divine confidence in Abraham—He trusted Abraham, and designated him as a loyal *friend* (2 Chronicles 20:7).

For the eyes of the LORD run to and fro throughout the whole earth, to show Himself strong on behalf of those whose heart is loyal to Him (2 Chronicles 16:9).

God knew Abraham's consistent heart, and Abraham knew the Lord's unchanging faithfulness to His Word. Abraham loved God, and trusted Him with childlike faith, walking in unquestioning obedience. Why did God choose Abraham? Let's let the Lord explain that to us—

> For I have known him, in order that he may command his children and his household after him, that they keep the way of the LORD, to do righteousness and justice, that the LORD may bring to Abraham what He has spoken to him (Genesis 18:19).

The Lord knows us by what's in our hearts (1 Samuel 16:7). He knew Abraham was not perfect. From the time of Adam's fall into sin, not one human has been sinless. However, the Lord knew Abraham exercised his faith to obey Him, demonstrating the reality of his right relationship with God. God trusted Abraham to teach his children to keep His righteous way.

If Abraham's father served pagan idols, who inspired Abraham's incredible faith in the Creator God? The compressed historical account of 2,000 years in Genesis 1–11 doesn't provide many details, but biblical chronology reveals Abraham was born 300 to 350 years after the Flood. His godly ancestor— Noah's righteous son Shem— lived for another 500 years after the flood (Genesis 11:10, 11). Shem was alive for all, or nearly all, of Abraham's 175-year lifespan. They were contemporaries.

A very credible assumption is that Abraham spent family time with his relative Shem, listening to his stories of the frightening Flood and the miraculous account of God's loving provision and protection. With first-hand knowledge of the loving "up -close-and-personal" God, Shem had also witnessed His fierce judgment against wickedness.

What a stunning impact Shem's testimony would have made on Abraham. Certainly, learning of God's interactions with the Flood generation could explain how he developed childlike faith and unquestioning obedience to the Lord. He trusted God to bless those who looked to Him to restore their righteousness, and understood His great displeasure against unrepentant sinners.

Christ warns that the last days of world history will mirror the days of Noah, saying, "For in the days before the flood, people were eating and drinking, marrying and giving in marriage, up to the day Noah entered the ark; and they knew nothing about what would happen until the flood came and took them all away. That is how it will be at the coming of the Son of Man" (Matthew 24:38–39, NIV).

WHY DID ABRAHAM'S FAMILY LEAVE UR OF THE CHALDEANS?

Genesis 11 concludes its historical backdrop with the migration of Terah, Abraham, Sarah, and Lot, going forth "from Ur of the Chaldeans to go to the land of Canaan; and they came to Haran and dwelt there" (Genesis 11:31). Their journey halted halfway between Ur and Canaan.

The narrative doesn't mention their ages at the time of departure or why their journey was put on pause. As we continue, it becomes clear that the pause must have been God-ordained. Abraham followed in the footsteps of his ancestor Noah, obeying the Lord without question or hesitation. Was God allowing time to multiply their resources? Was Abraham's aging father ailing? Either is a plausible explanation—or, perhaps, both.

Abraham's brother Nahor eventually joined them in Haran, and his family took roots there, making it their homeland. Genesis 24 reveals that Nahor's son had a family—including Laban and Rebekah—who still dwelt in Haran. Abraham's father remained there till the end of his life. Genesis 11:32 says, "So the days of Terah were two hundred and five years, and Terah died in Haran."

The short narrative does not explain the compelling reason for their initial migration, or the duration of time Abraham and Sarah lived in Haran before the Lord called them to continue forward to Canaan. The Lord Himself revealed why the family had initially departed from Ur of the Chaldeans, when He reminded Abraham—

> I am the LORD, who brought you out of Ur of the Chaldeans, to give you this land to inherit it (Genesis 15:7).

When the God of glory called, Abraham responded. How great his influence was to have convinced his father to leave his comforts and conveniences in Ur, with nothing more than an expectation of trading all he had for the life of a nomad. It didn't end like this for Terah, who lived out his final years surrounded by family in Haran, but it would be the exchange Abraham and Sarah would make as soon as God called to them again.

GOD REPEATS HIS CALL TO THE PROMISED LAND

Now we begin the historical account of the patriarchs. The Lord repeated His call to Abraham at the opening of Genesis 12:

> Now the LORD had said to Abram: "Get out of your country, from your family and from your father's house, to a land that I will show you. I will make you a great nation; I will bless you and make your name great . . . and in you all the families of the earth shall be blessed" (Genesis 12:1–3).

When the Lord repeated His call—commanding the then 75-year-old patriarch (v. 4) to go forward—He was setting Abraham apart for the divine purpose of His everlasting covenant. Abraham was quick to obey. Having acquired great wealth, the couple gathered their possessions to form a large caravan of flocks, herds, and servants to begin their wilderness wanderings in a new land. Genesis 17:17 explains that Sarah was ten years younger than her husband, so she started the journey of her lifetime at age 65. Accompanied by their nephew Lot, the childless couple departed, never more to return. The rest of their family members remained behind in their homeland of Haran.

The Lord appeared to Abraham and said, "*Unto thy seed* will I give this land" (Genesis 12:7, KJV; emphases added). Modern Bible versions generally supply the synonym *descendants* for the word *seed*. God's call to Abraham echoed the covenant promise of the woman's Seed (Genesis 3:15). God enlarged His revelation by telling Abraham, "In you all the families of the earth will be blessed" (Genesis 12:3). This *repeat* and *enlarge* technique is the way God unfolds His everlasting covenant, building one prophecy upon another. As we follow the story of the seed, it progresses through Abraham's son Isaac and grandson Jacob.

The promise to Abraham that "all families of the earth will be blessed" through him shows that the plan of salvation spans all ethnic and geographic boundaries. God chose Abraham to be the father of all—from that time forward. He was not the father only of the biological Jews who were his *physical* descendants; he is the father of all believers who are his *spiritual* descendants.

On this occasion of the Lord's first appearance to Abraham, the righteous man built an altar and worshiped the Lord (Genesis 12:7). Sojourning further, he continued in devoted worship to God—once again building an altar and calling on the name of the Lord (v. 8). Abraham always recognized that God's presence was with him.

GOD MADE ABRAHAM RIGHTEOUS BY FAITH

Abraham knew the history of God's interactions with humanity. He understood God's grace, and submitted to the Lord's sovereign authority. Demonstrating his friendship with God, he was quick to respond to the Lord's voice and yield to His leading. With trusting faith, the childless Abraham believed God when He told him that all the nations of the Earth would be blessed through his descendants, and was justified by God because of his faith. Announced in the Old Testament, it is confirmed in the New:

Then He [the Lord] brought him outside and said, "Look now toward heaven, and count the stars if you are able to number them." And He said to him, "So shall your descendants be." And he believed in the LORD, and He accounted it to him for righteousness (Genesis 15:5–6; compare Romans 4:3).

And therefore *"it was accounted to him for righteousness."* Now it was not written for his sake alone that it was imputed to him, but also for us. It shall be imputed to us who believe in Him who raised up Jesus our Lord from the dead, who was delivered up because of our offenses, and was raised because of our justification (Romans 4:22–25).

In humble dependence on God's word, Abraham believed. God took of His own divine righteousness, and imputed (credited) it to the faith-filled patriarch's account to establish His covenant with Abraham. God later renewed the covenant with Abraham's descendants, and identified Himself as "the God of Abraham, the God of Isaac, and the God of Jacob" (e.g. Exodus 3:6).

Romans 4:22–25 tells us that God's transaction with Abraham was recorded "not for his sake alone . . . but also for us." What did the Apostle Paul mean? The everlasting covenant God made with Abraham is the foundation of both the *Old* and *New Covenants*. The same gift Abraham received—righteousness by faith—is God's promise to all generations of people who will humbly believe His Word and enter into covenant relationship with Him. Everything recorded in the Old Testament is to benefit our understanding of God's gracious interactions with humanity.

The Old Testament contains the foundational truths of the New, and the New Testament explains the Old. Prophecy is never perfectly clear until God fulfills it. Following the story of the Seed to its divine conclusion, the Apostle Paul explains it many centuries later—

Now to Abraham and his Seed were the promises made. He does not say, *"And to seeds,"* as of many, but as of one, "And to your Seed," who is Christ (Galatians 3:16; emphases added).

If you are Christ's, then you are Abraham's seed, and heirs according to the promise. (Galatians 3:29).

What promise? Paul knew Genesis 15:6 recorded God's act of crediting righteousness by faith to Abraham. Scripture also assured Paul that God had purposed Abraham to be the father of many nations, and had declared that all the families of the earth would be blessed through his Seed—his descendant Jesus Christ. Summarizing it for us, Paul explains Abraham's *spiritual* descendants will have righteousness credited to them also (Romans 4:11), and affirms—

Therefore, the promise comes by faith, so that it may be by grace and may be guaranteed to all Abraham's offspring—not only to those who are of the law but also to those who are of the faith of Abraham. **He is the father of us all.** As it is written: "I have made you a father of many nations." He is our father in the sight of God, in whom he believed—the God who gives life to the dead and calls things that are not as though they were (Romans 4:16-17, NIV; emphasis added).

And the Scripture, foreseeing that God would justify the Gentiles by faith, preached the gospel to Abraham beforehand, saying, "In you all the nations shall be blessed" (Galatians 3:8).

Did you notice? Galatians 3:8 says God proclaimed the "gospel" to Abraham all those years ago. *Gospel* means *good news*. What was the good news God announced to Abraham? It was His plan to "justify" people from all nations (Gentiles) by their belief in His everlasting covenant of righteousness by faith. God's plan to redeem humanity has always been salvation by grace through faith, which is why the Apostle Paul trumpeted the news that grace "was given to us in Christ Jesus before time began" (2 Timothy 1:9).

This good-news *gospel* is referred to as the "everlasting gospel" in Revelation 14:6. Before He created the world, our Creator God affirmed that He would become our Substitute, taking the penalty for our sins. In anticipation of the cross, Revelation 13:8 clearly says that He was considered the "Lamb that was slain from the creation of the world." Hebrews 13:20 identifies Christ's blood as "the blood of the everlasting covenant." The good news of salvation is that God—in the Person of Jesus Christ—would ratify His everlasting covenant by shedding His blood to cover the sin-debt of the human race. In 2 Corinthians 5:21, He declared He would take our sin and—in exchange—give us His righteousness.

Describing Abraham's response to the Lord's call, the New Testament declares the patriarch's ultimate understanding of God's everlasting covenant—

By faith Abraham obeyed when he was called to go out to the place which he would receive as an inheritance. And he went out, not knowing where he was going. By faith he dwelt in the land of promise as in a foreign country, dwelling in tents with Isaac and Jacob, the heirs with him of the same promise; for he waited for the city which has foundations, whose builder and maker is God (Hebrews 11:8–10).

What Promised Land was Abraham really awaiting? The author of Hebrews goes on to explain that it was a "heavenly country"—a city God prepared for His covenant people (v. 16). He describes it as "the city of the living God, the heavenly Jerusalem" and the "one to come" (Hebrews 12:22; 13:14). One of the closing chapters of the New Testament describes this holy city—the "New Jerusalem"—coming down from heaven to be God's permanent headquarters on the recreated Earth (Revelation 21:1–2).

Abraham's obedient faith was the pathway to God's eternal blessings. He gave up his life in Haran to seek the eternal life God was offering him.

THE "REPEAT AND ENLARGE" PRINCIPLE OF PROPHECY

Humans learn through repetition. How do we teach a child with age-related limitations? We begin with basics, and as the child is ready to advance to the next level, we repeat and enlarge till they grasp greater knowledge. For example, we don't hammer children with advanced math in their early years. First, we teach them to add and subtract. Once that knowledge is mastered, we enlarge their understanding by repeating basic math principles to teach them to multiply and divide. In due time, they are prepared to learn greater knowledge. If children never grasp the basic principles in any given area of life, further progress is blocked.

God knows exactly where we are in spiritual maturity, and teaches us in the same manner. If the Bible seems confusing at first, we should keep studying, asking for the Lord's help, and using the objective lens of His infinite love to magnify our understanding. He will patiently give us the knowledge we need to understand the beauty of living in relationship with Him.

The Lord foretells the future in a fluid and continuous manner, using a process of repeating what He expressed in the past and enlarging it with additional details. This is the "repeat and enlarge" principle. By adding additional detail to something He has already foretold, the Lord expands our understanding. We must recognize this to avoid confusion and error as we interpret the Bible. In a nutshell, the repeat and enlarge principle is that each subsequent prophecy builds on the previous prophecy, and must be in agreement with the prophecy before it.

God carefully constructs the written history of His interaction with humans to provide us with the greatest clarity. First, He uses a narrow viewfinder to frame a close-up view for our original focus. Reframing the picture with a wider viewfinder, He enlarges our field of vision to include more detail. This process is repeated until we have a panoramic view in our minds.

Did you notice this when we reviewed the first two Creation accounts? First, He revealed Himself as the eternal and self-existing God—Elohim, who created something out of nothing, and who exists above and *outside* His Creation. Repeating the Creation account, He expanded our vision to see Him as the loving "up-close-and-personal" God—using His covenant name of Yahweh (Jehovah), who exists everywhere *inside* His Creation. If we don't grasp that truth, our understanding of the Old Testament is blocked.

In chapters nine and ten, we will see how the Lord redeemed a group of Hebrews and formed the nation of Israel to live in covenant relationship with Him. Later, conflicts among the people caused split loyalties, and Israel divided into the northern and southern kingdoms. Both kingdoms continued in covenant-breaking apostasy. Through prophets such as Isaiah, Jeremiah, Habakkuk, and Zephaniah, God trumpeted His call for national repentance, warning the people that a refusal to repent would result in their captivity. But they hardened their hearts against the Lord for centuries, and refused to submit to His instructions for righteousness. As His judgment against them, God allowed both kingdoms to eventually be taken captive. His judgments had a redemptive purpose—He wanted His people to recognize they needed Him, and to cause them to repent and turn back to Him.

Swept up in this judgment, the righteous Daniel was taken captive to Babylon. God gave Daniel successive prophecies in the repeat and enlarge fashion, providing additional detail in each disclosure. To His prophet Daniel—in chapters 2, 7, and 8—God predicted domination of the earth through the rise and fall of the kingdoms of Babylon, Medo-Persia, Greece, Rome, and a "little horn" power that would arise from Rome. His prediction included the end-time hope of the Messiah rescuing His people to establish an everlasting kingdom—a kingdom where His love and perfect will of righteousness would reign.

The two Creation accounts, and the world history predicted to Daniel, are just two examples of the repeat and enlarge technique used by God to teach us in a progressive, unfolding fashion. This process is apparent throughout Scripture, including in the last book of the Bible, Revelation, where the rise of the United States is prophesied.

THE UNFOLDING REVELATION OF THE EVERLASTING COVENANT

In less than thirty words, God framed a narrow field of view with the announcement in Genesis 3:15 of a coming Redeemer who would crush Satan's head, and then brought our focus to the central truth of substitutionary sacrifice. From Genesis 3:15 all the way to the last two chapters of the Bible in Revelation, God expands our view until we finally achieve a spectacular panoramic vision of His everlasting covenant.

This opens the way for us to become God's forever friends, just like Abraham—the father of us all.

SUMMARY OF "HIS" STORY
Chapter Five

- God makes two kinds of covenants with humanity: 1) Unilateral; and 2) Bilateral.
- God makes and keeps all the covenant promises.
- God chose Abraham to be the "father of all" believers of every generation.
- Abraham's spiritual descendants who are in covenant with Christ are also Abraham's seed, and heirs according to God's promise of righteousness by faith.
- Abraham believed God, and God accounted it to him as righteousness by faith.
- God's covenant with Abraham is the underpinning of both the Old and New Covenants.
- Abraham came from a long line of God followers all the way back to the Garden.
- Noah had three sons—Shem, Ham, and Japheth.
- After the Flood, Noah became drunk and lay in his tent naked. Ham (and likely his son, Canaan), saw him and disrespected him by sharing the spectacle.
- Shem and Japheth upheld God's moral code of love in showing great respect for their father.
- Noah pronounced a curse on Canaan, but blessed Japheth and Shem.
- Noah spoke *prophetically* to announce the covenant-keeping LORD was Shem's God, and pronounced God's covenant blessing of preeminence on Shem.
- *Preeminence* is a covenant term that describes a superior status.
- Shem lived another 500 years after the Flood, and was the progenitor of the Israelites.
- The descendants of Ham and Japeth worshipped idols.
- Abraham's father Terah was a descendant of Shem, but practiced polytheism.
- Abraham was born 300-350 years after the Flood. His godly relative Shem was alive during all, or nearly all, of his life and was likely the influence on his childlike faith and immediate obedience to God's Word.
- Abraham married his half-sister Sarah, who was 10 years younger than he.

- God called Abraham out of the pagan city of Ur. Abraham, Sarah, Lot, and Terah stopped halfway between Ur and Canaan for a period of time.
- After Terah died, God called Abraham forth to Canaan, and he obeyed, not knowing where he was going. God promised to make the 75-year-old childless man the father of a great nation. This is a promise that builds on the Genesis 3:15 announcement of the Seed.
- The Apostle Paul said that God preached the GOSPEL to Abraham when He promised to bless all nations through him.
- Abraham was loyal to God, and God designated him as a friend.
- God chose Abraham to be the ancestor of all believers because He knew the patriarch would teach his household to keep His moral code of love.
- In the Hall of Faith (found in Hebrews 11), Abraham is said to have waited for the heavenly city built by God, and the Promised Land that is a heavenly country.
- Abraham's obedient faith was the pathway to God's eternal blessings.
- God teaches prophecy to us through the principle of *repeat and enlarge*. In a nutshell, each time He repeats a prophecy, it builds on the previous one, and must be in agreement with the prophecy stated before.
- The Lord progressively unfolds His everlasting covenant from Genesis to Revelation in this repeat and enlarge manner.

RATIFIED IN THE FORM OF A VISION

Chapter Six

M any Christians teach that once someone receives Christ as their Savior, the skies will always be blue and life will be smooth sailing. This contradicts the words of Jesus, who tells us, "In the world you will have tribulation; but be of good cheer, I have overcome the world" (John 16:33). God does not promise His people freedom *from* the storms of life. People who are taught that falsehood often become discouraged when unexpected clouds of confusion and sudden strife come upon them.

The man whom God chose as the spiritual father of us all faced many trials in his life, but consistently walked in loyalty to God's will. Abraham's faith-filled and loving obedience ensured the Lord's fulfillment of the covenant promises to him (Genesis 18:19). As we review his history, we will recognize that a life of faith always requires trusting God for provision and protection *during* the storms of life.

From His pledge in Genesis 12 to make Abraham into a great nation, the Lord delayed the delivery of the promised covenant seed for 25 years. Why did God wait so long to fulfill this promise? So that future generations would be certain it was physically impossible for Sarah to conceive on her own, and that Isaac's birth as the *unique "firstborn" covenant son of promise* was the result of God's miraculous touch on the couple's union. (In reference to Isaac, take note of the lower-case treatment of *son*.)

The Lord was preparing humans for the unfolding of the rest of *His Story*, when a young virgin in Bethlehem conceived a child by a different miracle, and delivered a baby named Jesus—the *unique "firstborn" covenant Son of promise*. (In reference to Christ, take note of the upper-case treatment of Son.)

Using the principle of *repeat and enlarge*, God continues to progressively unfold the revelation of His everlasting covenant of righteousness by faith for the salvation of humanity. With each progression, the Lord makes it clear that His promises and covenant blessings conferred on Abraham and his descendants include his *spiritual* descendants—faithful believers from every nation and every generation who are the spiritual seed of Abraham.

GOD REAFFIRMS THE EVERLASTING COVENANT

Departing Haran, Abraham and his entourage began a migratory life, dwelling in tents. They had scarcely arrived in Canaan when the first of three recorded droughts in that land caused severe famine (Genesis 12:10; 26:1; 41:56). In desperation, Abraham and his household packed up their tents to go down to Egypt, where food was plentiful.

However, when the Egyptian Pharaoh laid eyes on the beautiful Sarah, he seized her for his harem. Within Abraham's heart, that natural law of sin we all battle reared its ugly head. For the sake of self-preservation, he created a half-true fake report for Pharaoh. Abraham asked Sarah to say that she was his sister, not his wife (Genesis 12:13). She was indeed his half-sister, but half a truth is still a whole lie. Graciously intervening, God plagued Pharaoh's household. The king of Egypt reacted to the plagues by restoring Sarah to Abraham, and sending them away. The Lord plucked them out from their self-imposed problem of sin, preserving their lives.

Coming up from Egypt, they settled back in their original stopping place in Canaan. The patriarch once again called on the name of the Lord (Genesis 13:4). Soon after their return, divided loyalties between the herdsmen of Abraham and the herdsmen of Lot caused strife. God had prospered each of their flocks, but the sheer number of sheep were overgrazing crowded pastures. Prosperity now demanded separation. In a gesture of unselfish good will, Abraham humbly waived his rights of seniority, allowing his nephew first choice of the land. Lot chose the well-watered plain of Sodom for his flocks, and a return to city-life for himself (vv. 6–13).

First a drought, and now a division among his family. Was Abraham's faith being tested?

It certainly could have been God's intention. We find parallel support for that idea in the New Testament, which explains that the trials of life produce faith and patience to complete our spiritual training (James 1:2–4). After Lot departed in his chosen direction, the Lord spoke to Abraham to repeat and enlarge His promises—

Lift your eyes now and look from the place where you are—northward, southward, eastward, and westward; for all the land which you see I give to you and your descendants forever. And I will make your descendants as the dust of the earth; so that if a man could number the dust of the earth, then your descendants also could be numbered (Genesis 13:14–16).

With renewed assurance that his physical descendants would become a great nation, and the Promised Land of Canaan would be of great national importance to them, Abraham moved forward to settle in the oak grove of Mamre, and built an altar there to the Lord (v. 18).

Now we fast-forward beyond the history of Genesis 14, where the raiding and conquering kings of Mesopotamia attacked Sodom and Gomorrah, and Lot was taken captive. A survivor of the raid on Sodom came to find Abraham, who is referred to as a "Hebrew" for the first time (Genesis 14:13). Abraham gathered a militia together and in hot pursuit went out to defeat the invaders, rescuing Lot. He met up with Melchizedek, the king of Salem (Jerusalem) and a priest of the Most High God, who blessed him. Abraham gave a tenth (tithe) of all his war booty to this king-priest (v. 20).

A sidebar insert to set the record straight. The mysterious Melchizedek introduced in Genesis 14 was not Christ. He is not mentioned again until the New Testament book of Hebrews, which translates a Greek phrase to render it as saying Melchizedek was "without father, without mother, without genealogy, having neither beginning of days nor end of life" (Hebrews 7:3). The intention of the original Greek is more accurately expressed in the ancient texts of the Peshitta, the Syriac Bible, which renders it, "whose father and mother are not written in genealogies."

Melchizedek had parents—he was a human being. Because his ancestry was irrelevant to his ancient kingship and priesthood, it simply was not recorded. He was the only person to hold both positions of king and priest of the Most High God until the Person of Jesus Christ. As King-Priest, Christ's priesthood is superior to the later order of the Levitical priesthood. Thus Christ was in the "order of Melchizedek" and "in the likeness of Melchizedek" (Hebrews 5:6; 7:15). If Melchizedek had been a heavenly being without beginning or end, he would be God Himself, and there would have been no need for another priest to arise. Christ was not a successor of Melchizedek, but Christ's priesthood was similar to his.

GOD RATIFIES THE EVERLASTING COVENANT IN VISION

The awe-inspiring account of Genesis 15 widens our infinity focus. Scripture doesn't reveal Abraham's age here; we only know that some years had passed, and he was less than 85 years old. This story will ease your mind if you have ever felt guilty that your faith has wobbled. God understands.

Here we see the faithful, covenant-making, covenant-keeping God, who comes in a vision to speak again with Abraham, to reassure His friend whose faith was beginning to waver.

After these things the word of the LORD came to Abram in a vision, saying, "Do not be afraid, Abram. I am your shield, your exceedingly great reward" (Genesis 15:1).

Did the great patriarch fear reprisal from the kings he had routed? Or perhaps battles with the pagan population of Canaan? *God promised to be His shield.* It appears Abraham's greatest fear was that God's promise of descendants had not come to pass. He was still without a child all these years after leaving Haran. In a heartfelt response of confusion, he challenged God, saying, "Lord God, what will You give me, seeing I go childless?"

Longing for God's promises to come true, he had grown confused by the delay, and wondered if he would be obliged to follow the common Mesopotamian custom practiced by childless couples who adopted a servant as their heir. He asked God if the trusted steward of his household, Eliezer, would be his only heir (vv. 2–3). The Lord had already assured him, *"I am. . . your exceedingly great reward."* Now, in vision, He expands Abraham's understanding:

> And behold, the word of the LORD came to him, saying, "This one shall not be your heir, but one who will come from your own body shall be your heir." Then He brought him outside and said, "Look now toward heaven, and count the stars if you are able to number them." And He said to him, "So shall your descendants be." And he believed in the LORD, and He accounted it to him for righteousness (Genesis 15:4–6).

The childless man believed the Lord's promise that he would have countless descendants, and God imputed this acceptance to his account as righteousness. Did you notice? God confirms that He rewards *righteousness by faith* to those who trust in Him, and believe in His Word. Although Abraham's history proved his willingness to walk in faithful loyalty to His Creator, the Patriarch was a sinner who needed God's grace—just like the rest of the human race who have a fallen nature. God accounted *righteousness by faith* to Abraham because he believed in God.

The Lord had previously promised to give the physical land of Canaan to Abraham's descendants, who would be as "the dust of the earth" (Genesis 13:16). That certainly seems to refer to the patriarch's *physical* seed. But now, as God repeats and enlarges His promises to Abraham, He declares his descendants would be as "the stars" of the heavens (Genesis 15:5). Could it be that God was referring to the *spiritual* descendants of Abraham from all the nations of the world? Those who wait "for the city. . . whose builder and maker is God"—just as he did—and recognize their true citizenship is in Heaven (Hebrews 11:10; Philippians 3:20)?

Whatever God meant, He then instructed Abraham to prepare animals—a heifer, female goat, and ram (a male sheep) to be split down the middle, as well as a turtle dove and pigeon that were not to be split. This *typified* an ancient covenant ritual for contracts between men, a practice called "cutting a covenant." Arranging the slain animals opposite each other with a path down the middle, each of the pledging parties walked between them to affirm that the same death should happen to them if they broke the covenant.

God was not cutting a covenant with Abraham. God doesn't make contracts with humanity. (Evidence for this will be provided in chapter eleven.) Rather, in a covenantal form that Abraham would understand, the Lord was confirming His everlasting covenant.

Before the time of the solemn covenant confirmation, the Lord put Abraham into a deep sleep. In vision, God spoke to him—prophesying he would live in peace, and die at a good old age, but declaring that Abraham's descendants would be afflicted for 400 years as strangers in a land that was not theirs, and that the fourth generation would finally return to Canaan. God promised to judge the nation that shamefully abused them, adding that He would bring out his descendants from bondage with abundant possessions. The sun went down. It was dark. Then—

Behold, there appeared a smoking oven and a burning torch that passed between those pieces (Genesis 15:17).

Symbols of God's divine presence—the smoking oven and the burning torch—were the only presence to pass between the covenant sacrifices. God alone made the promises, and He alone would keep them. In the *form of a vision*, the Lord alone obligated Himself to fulfill all the terms of His covenant. In the *substance of reality*, He alone would ultimately ratify His covenant nearly two thousand years later.

Salvation belongs to God, and can never be gained by our works—it is only by His grace (Romans 4:1–8; Ephesians 2:8). Motivated by love, works are merely evidence of living in covenant relationship with God. Paul explains that righteousness is imputed by God—apart from works—and quotes from King David, "Blessed are those whose lawless deeds are forgiven, and whose sins are covered; blessed is the man to whom the LORD shall not impute sin" (Romans 4:6–8; Psalm 32:1–2).

GOD GIVES COVENANT NAMES AND A SEAL OF GRACE

Have you ever grown weary waiting on the Lord's timing? Such was the case with Sarah, ten years after they left Haran. Wondering how God would fulfill His promise of children, impatience brewed in her heart. She persuaded her then 85 year-old husband to take her Egyptian maid Hagar as his concubine to produce an heir. In the common practice of the day, the handmaiden's child would be counted as Sarah's.

Ishmael was born to Hagar when Abraham was 86 (Genesis 16:16). He welcomed his firstborn son into the world, and regarded him as the heir of God's promises—not yet realizing that Ishmael was not to be the *unique "firstborn" covenant son of promise*. Thirteen years later, the Lord appeared to 99-year-old Abraham a second time in a visible form, saying—

I am Almighty God; walk before Me and be blameless. And **I will** make My covenant between Me and you, and **will** multiply you exceedingly . . . you shall be a father of many nations. No longer shall your name be called Abram, but your name shall be Abraham; for I have made you a father of many nations. . . . **I will** make nations of you, and kings shall come from you. And **I will** establish My covenant between Me and you and your descendants after you in their generations, for an everlasting covenant, to be God to you and your descendants after you. Also I give to you and your descendants after you the land in which you are a stranger, all the land of Canaan, as an everlasting possession; and **I will** be their God (Genesis 17:1, 2, 4–8; emphasis added).

"I will" is covenant language. God brings five great promises togeth-er to express His will for the everlasting covenant. "I will be their God" becomes the ringing proclamation of the everlasting covenant through-out the rest of Scripture (e.g. 2 Corinthians 6:16; Hebrews 8:10).

In the New Testament, Christ echoes this idea of "walk before Me and be blameless," saying, "Therefore you shall be perfect, just as your Father in heaven is perfect" (Matthew 5:48). Of course, this is impos-sible by human effort, but it is God's *purpose* of righteousness by faith. Working in the human heart to give us the desire and power to do what pleases Him, He promises that "He who has begun a good work in you will complete it until the day of Jesus Christ" (Philippians 1:6; 2:13). He will sanctify us completely, making us spotless, and preserving us blameless at Christ's Second Coming (1 Thessalonians 5:23–24).

The will of God for His covenant people is that they walk in conscious awareness of His divine presence, observing His moral code of love. Life in the Land of Promise has always been subject to remaining in covenant relationship with the Lord. Jesus tells us—

> Strive to enter through the narrow gate, for many, I say to you, will seek to enter and will not be able. When once the Master of the house has risen up and shut the door, and you begin to stand outside and knock at the door, saying, "Lord, Lord, open for us," and He will answer and say to you . . . . "I tell you I do not know you, where you are from. Depart from Me, all you workers of iniquity" (Luke 13:24–27).

After speaking His five "I will" promises, the Lord granted the couple new names—names encoded with covenant blessings. God changed *Abram (exalted father)* to the name *Abraham (father of many nations)*. God changed *Sarai ("my" princess)* to the name *Sarah (Prin-cess)*. Promising to bless Sarah with a son from her own womb, God proclaimed she would be the mother of nations and kings would could from her lineage (Genesis 17:15–16).

At this second appearance of the Lord, Abraham fell on his face in adoration, but his worship was marred with the laughter of doubt. Considering the life-long infertility of his 89-year-old wife and his own advanced years, it seemed impossible that they could produce a child (v. 17).

Ishmael had been Abraham's one and only child for thirteen years. He loved the boy, and made a plea for the Lord to allow him to stand before Him as the heir of covenant blessings. God promised to bless Ishmael and make him a great nation, but left no room to doubt His will—the *unique "firstborn" son of covenant promise* would come from Sarah's womb, and he should be named Isaac—which mean laughter.

Abraham's faith no longer wavered. He was fully convinced God would deliver the promised son and multiply his descendants exceedingly, making him the father of many nations.

I'm always encouraged by the prophet Jeremiah's thoughts of hope in the midst of hopeless situations. He tells us that God's covenant *hesed*—His loving faithfulness, grace, compassion, mercy—is new every morning (Lamentations 3:22–23). God is the God of new beginnings. He has a plan for each person's life, and "gives life to the dead and calls those things which do not exist as though they did" (Romans 4:17). The Apostle Paul, referring to Abraham, said—

And not being weak in faith, he did not consider his own body, already dead (since he was about a hundred years old), and the deadness of Sarah's womb. He did not waver at the promise of God through unbelief, but was strengthened in faith, giving glory to God, and being fully convinced that what He had promised He was also able to perform. And therefore *it was accounted to him for righteousness* (Romans 4:19–22; emphasis added).

At this point, God introduced the rite of circumcision for Abraham and all his physical descendants (Genesis 17:10–11). God instituted it as a sign of consecration that symbolically represented a cleansing of the heart and a commitment to purity.

In the New Testament, the Apostle Paul summarizes the rite of circumcision by saying—

And he received the sign of circumcision, a seal of the righteousness that he had by faith while he was still uncircumcised. So then, he is the father of all who believe but have not been circumcised, in order that righteousness might be credited to them. And he is also the father of the circumcised who not only are circumcised but who also walk in the footsteps of the faith that our father Abraham had before he was circumcised (Romans 4:11–12, NIV).

Circumcision of the flesh was merely symbolic of the inward circumcision of the Holy Spirit— God's sign of sanctifying grace in the Old Testament and the New (Deuteronomy 30:6; Acts 7:51; Romans 2:28; Colossians 2:11). The covenant-related demand of physical circumcision was abolished by the New Covenant. Paul refused to have Titus circumcised—his point being that uncircumcised Gentiles were welcome in the church, and that Jew and Gentile are all one in Christ (Galatians 2:3–5, 3:16, 27–29; Colossians 2:9–14). Paul did not teach that circumcision was sinful, but that it was totally unnecessary for a Christian's connection with God (1 Corinthians 7:19; Romans 3:30; 8:4).

A THIRD APPEARANCE FOR A GRAND ANNOUNCEMENT

A short time later, God appeared again to Abraham a third time. It was Sarah's turn to laugh. Sitting at the door of their tent to find relief from the heat, her husband suddenly saw three men approaching. One was the Lord Himself in the temporary form of a man (Genesis 18:1–33). The other two were of the *created order of beings* that we most commonly think of as angels, also having assumed human form. Abraham invited them to stay for a meal, and dashed into the tent directing Sarah to bake cakes while he prepared a fatted calf. From inside the tent, Sarah eavesdropped on their after-dinner conversation, and heard the Lord announce that she would have a son. What? How could that be true? Convinced her age and life-long infertility precluded the possibility, a wistful laugh arose in her heart.

Scripture proves the visiting Man who spoke was God, telling us, "And the LORD said to Abraham, 'Why did Sarah laugh, saying, 'Shall I surely bear a child, since I am old?' Is anything too hard for the LORD? At the appointed time I will return to you, according to the time of life, and Sarah shall have a son'" (vv. 13–14). Following the meal, the men arose to head toward Sodom, and hospitable Abraham walked along with them to send them on their way.

> And the LORD said, "Shall I hide from Abraham what I am doing, since Abraham shall surely become a great and mighty nation, and all the nations of the earth shall be blessed in him? For I have known him, in order that he may command his children and his household after him, that they keep the way of the LORD, to do righteousness and justice, that the LORD may bring to Abraham what He has spoken to him" (Genesis 18:17–19).

The Lord didn't keep secrets from His friend Abraham. He explained that He was there "Because the outcry against Sodom and Gomorrah is great, and because their sin is very grave" (v. 20). Before passing a judgment of destruction, the Lord wanted to personally investigate their sins. Aware of God's love and righteousness, Abraham exclaimed, "Far be it from You to do such a thing as this, to slay the righteous with the wicked, so that the righteous should be as the wicked; far be it from You! Shall not the Judge of all the earth do right?" (v. 25).

With compassion and intense humility, Abraham began a process of negotiation with the Lord, finally requesting that He spare the cities if just ten righteous people dwelt there. The Lord readily agreed to reserve His judgment for the sake of just ten righteous ones. But wicked Sodom and Gomorrah were doomed, for ten were not found who walked with God. Just before the Lord rained down fire and brimstone to wipe out their sin, the two angels in human form arranged for Lot and a few of his family members to escape (Genesis 19:15–17, 24). Early the next morning, Abraham looked toward the cities, only to see the smoke of a furnace (v. 28).

THE UNIQUE "FIRSTBORN" COVENANT SON OF PROMISE ARRIVES

The story of the seed now progresses. At age 100, Abraham welcomed his son of promise into the world, and named him Isaac (Genesis 21:3). Hagar's heart was heavy with jealousy, for this new development lowered the favored position of her 14-year-old son Ishmael, while elevating that of Sarah and her son. The already strained relationship between the two competing women worsened.

Years later, Abraham held a great feast when Isaac was weaned (customarily between the ages of three to four). Ishmael ridiculed little Isaac, mocking him during the party. This was the last straw for Sarah, who now insisted that Abraham's first son be sent away, along with his mother. The patriarch was greatly upset, for he loved Ishmael.

> But God said to Abraham, "Do not let it be displeasing in your sight because of the lad or because of your bondwoman. Whatever Sarah has said to you, listen to her voice; for in Isaac your seed shall be called. Yet I will also make a nation of the son of the bondwoman, because he is your seed" (Genesis 21:12–13).

God had a purpose for the line of the covenant seed. Heeding the voice of the Lord, Abraham sent his concubine Hagar and his son Ishmael away, and a time of tranquility seemed to follow.

THE SPIRIT OF THE LORD

Through the writings of Moses, God progressively unfolds His everlasting covenant. Scripture introduces the mission of the Messiah to restore humanity's righteousness, so that humans could live in covenant relationship with the Lord. Christ's mission is more fully developed in the New Testament, coming to a dramatic conclusion in the very last chapter of Revelation.

In like manner, the role of the Holy Spirit is introduced in the Old Testament, and more fully developed in the New, where the attributes of His personality, intelligence, volition, and power are fully proven. God frames a narrow view of the Holy Spirit in the Old Testament, mentioning the title of "Holy Spirit" only three times—

Do not cast me away from Your presence, And do not take Your Holy Spirit from me (Psalm 51:11).

But they rebelled and grieved His Holy Spirit; So He turned Himself against them as an enemy (Isaiah 63:10).

Where is He who put His Holy Spirit within them? (Isaiah 63:11).

The evidence of the Holy Spirit's ministry is abundant in the Old Testament, but in all other references He is simply called "Spirit." The Holy Spirit was active in Creation, and His omnipresence—an attribute of God—is described in David's beautiful writing of Psalm 139 (Genesis 1:2; Job 26:13, Psalm 104:30, 139:7).

The Spirit's operations in the Old Testament are quite similar to how the New Testament identifies His ministry. For example, the Holy Spirit: reproved humanity, convicting them of their sins, while striving to restrain sin (Genesis 6:3); had the sanctifying influence of the washing of regeneration to give people a new heart (Deuteronomy 30:6; Ezekiel 11:19–20, 36:26–29); was given to the people of God to instruct them (Nehemiah 9:20); and was the inspiration of wisdom (Exodus 31:1–6; Isaiah 11:2). To those who called on the name of the Lord in faith, the Spirit restored righteous thinking and acting; empowered people for service to God (Exodus 31:2–5; Numbers 27;18; 1 Samuel 16:12–13; Judges 14:6); and inspired the prophets (Genesis 41:38; 2 Samuel 23:2). His presence could be grieved away (1 Samuel 16:14; Psalm 51:11; Isaiah 63:10). God declared the operation of the Holy Spirit to be the abundant supply of His power—

"Not by might nor by power, but by My Spirit," says the LORD of hosts (Zechariah 4:6).

The Holy Spirit dwelt in many godly saints of the Old Testament who opened their hearts to His leading—particularly priests, prophets, and leaders of God's people. In other cases, His actions in the Old Testament are described as coming upon people with power or dwelling within them for periods of time to help them perform special tasks.

It would seem the primary difference in New Testament times was that the Holy Spirit's indwelling presence was given universally to God's people in the power of the finished work of Christ—the same power that resurrected Jesus from the grave (John 14:17–18; Philippians 3:10). After Christ's ascension, the Holy Spirit was sent as a gift of God's grace to dwell in all of God's covenant people, so that Christ could live in their hearts by faith (Ephesians 3:16–17). The Spirit came to continue the ministry of Christ here on earth, while Jesus serves in Heaven at the throne of God as the Last Adam (the new representative of humanity) and the High Priest of God's people.

A COMING TRIAL OF FAITH

As we have witnessed in this Chapter, each time the Lord repeated and enlarged the revelation of His everlasting covenant, Abraham's faith became stronger. Close to a twenty-year gap of silence exists between Abraham's history in Genesis 21 and 22.

For those who take only a casual approach to Bible reading, what happens next raises questions regarding the character of God. The Lord had a test in store for Abraham, and to us it seems like the test of a lifetime.

Join me in the next leg of our journey to see his amazing response.

SUMMARY OF "HIS" STORY
Chapter Six

- God continued to unfold His covenant with Abraham progressively—clarifying each time that the blessings are for all of Abraham's faithful spiritual descendants.
- From the time God repeated His call to Abraham at age 75, the patriarch had to wait 25 years before the promised covenant seed (Isaac) was delivered.
- God wanted all future generations to know that Isaac's birth as the unique "firstborn" son covenant son of promise was a result of His miraculous power to make the couple fertile.

- God was preparing humanity for the unfolding of the rest of His Story, when a young virgin in Bethlehem conceived a child by another miracle, and delivered a baby named Jesus—the unique "firstborn" covenant Son of promise.
- Soon after arriving in Canaan, a severe drought and famine drove Abraham and his household down to Egypt. When they returned to Canaan, strife broke out that resulted in family division.
- God reaffirmed His covenant with Abraham, saying his descendants would be as the "dust of the earth" and would inherit Canaan.
- Lot was taken captive in a raid on the city of Sodom; after rescuing him, Abraham had a meet-and-greet with a king-priest, and tithed his war booty to him.
- God gave a vision to Abraham, promising to be his shield and exceedingly great reward, and promising him his descendants would be as the "stars" in heaven.
- Abraham believed God, and God accounted it to him as righteousness by faith.
- In the form of a vision God alone ratified the covenant, by passing through the slain animals.
- Centuries later, God ratified the covenant in the substance of the Person of Jesus Christ.
- God did not "cut a covenant" with Abraham. God doesn't make contracts with humans.
- Sarah grew impatient in waiting for an heir, and persuaded her husband to take her handmaiden, Hagar, as a concubine to produce a son.
- Hagar gave birth to Ishmael—Abraham's first son was born to him at age 86.
- Ishmael was not the covenant son of promise, but a flesh-attempt to fulfill God's promise.
- When Abraham was 99, God appeared to him a second time, telling Abraham to walk before Him and be blameless—in the covenant language "I will" God made five covenant promises.
- God gave covenant names to the couple, and instituted a seal of His covenant grace—circumcision—a national ordinance for the distinction of His covenant people in the Old Testament.
- Circumcision was a sign of consecration as a cleansing of the heart, and a commitment to purity of the descendants who would bring forth the holy Seed.

- Circumcision of the flesh was merely symbolic of the inward circumcision of the Holy Spirit.
- God appeared to Abraham a third time, announcing that Sarah would have the covenant son of promise by the end of the year.
- Ishmael was age 14 when Isaac was born. Several years later, he mocked the covenant son Isaac at his weaning party. Ishmael and his mother Hagar were sent away, with God's promise to make Ishmael a great nation.
- The Holy Spirit's role is introduced in the Old Testament, and more fully developed in the New.

COVENANT CONFIRMATION AND RENEWAL

Chapter Seven

D id you realize you're learning God's beautiful covenant language on this journey? It is critical to know, as it proves to be the key that unlocks the identity of the Messiah-Christ. We now understand: 1) the Hebrew word *shalom*—translated into English *as peace*—is layered with concepts of God's covenant blessings that bring completeness to life; 2) the Hebrew word *hesed* is covenant language that describes God's actions of *love, lovingkindness, mercy, grace, steadfastness, faithfulness,* and *loyalty*, all integrated into one word; and 3) *grace* is a covenant word translated from Greek, which means *God's unearned, undeserved favor.*

Continuing our review, now you also recognize: 4) *seed*, which points ultimately to Jesus as the Seed; 5) *Root*, referring to Jesus' human ancestry; 6) *preeminence*, describing superior status; 7) *circumcision*, which refers to the Holy Spirit's influence on human hearts; and 8) *"I will,"* which is covenant language indicating God's promises. Further, we have considered the covenant concepts of: 9) *substitutionary sacrifice*; 10) *righteousness by faith*; and 11) *son of promise*.

It's time to expand our covenant vocabulary with three additional definitions: 12) while the word *firstborn* in Scripture can indicate order of birth, in terms of the covenant *firstborn* refers *to a position of preeminence*; 13) the word *begotten* can refer to a physical parentage, but in covenant language *begotten* means *chosen for a covenant purpose*; and 14) the beautiful covenant term *only begotten* means a *unique, one-of-a-kind, son of promise* who is the rightful heir to the covenant blessings. Armed with those definitions, we are better prepared to understand the stories that follow.

GOD PUTS ABRAHAM'S ABSOLUTE LOYALTY TO A TEST

The Lord God clearly commanded that children should not be sacrificed on the altars of pagan idols. In fact, He regarded the practice as an abomination—He abhorred the disgusting practice (e.g., Leviticus 18:21; Deuteronomy 12:31; 18:10; 2 Kings 17:17–18).

Perhaps knowing this is what makes God's request of Abraham in Genesis 22 so jarring, if we aren't looking through the lens of His infinite love.

> Now it came to pass after these things that God tested Abraham, and said to him, "Abraham!" And he said, "Here I am." Then He said, "Take now your son, your only son Isaac, whom you love, and go to the land of Moriah, and offer him there as a burnt offering on one of the mountains of which I shall tell you" (Genesis 22:1–2).

Why would God request Abraham to sacrifice Isaac, his *only unique one-of-a-kind covenant son of promise?* It's irrational and incongruent to God's holy nature. We will see that the Lord never intended for the sacrifice to be carried out.

In absolute trust, the old man arose early in the morning, split the wood for the burnt offering, saddled his donkey, and took off for Mount Moriah with Isaac and two servants. Nearing the place on the third day of their journey, Abraham told the other two men, "Stay here with the donkey; the lad and I will go yonder and worship, and we will come back to you" (Genesis 22:5).

Laying the wood for the offering on his son's back, Abraham took the fire pot and a knife, and began the journey to the mountain which God had appointed. As the old father and his son made the trek to Mount Moriah, Isaac asked, "Father . . . . Where is the lamb for a burnt offering?" Abraham answered, "My son, God will provide for Himself the lamb for a burnt offering" (v. 8).

What trust Abraham had in the Lord! What astonishing trust Isaac had in the Lord! The strapping young man, now perhaps 20 years old, willingly climbed up on the altar to be bound and slaughtered. Determined to kill his son, Abraham lifted the knife in his hand high into the air—

> But the Angel of the LORD called to him from heaven and said, "Abraham, Abraham!" So he said, "Here I am." And He said, "Do not lay your hand on the lad, or do anything to him; for now I know that you fear God, since you have not withheld your son, your only son, from Me" (Genesis 22:11–12).

> Then the Angel of the LORD called to Abraham a second time out of heaven, and said: "By Myself I have sworn, says the LORD, because you have done this thing, and have not withheld your son, your only son—blessing I will bless you, and multiplying I will multiply your descendants as the stars of the heaven and as the sand which is on the seashore" (Genesis 22:15–17).

Who was this Angel of the Lord? Before His incarnation as the Person of Jesus Christ, Scripture reveals that the Lord made numerous appearances on Earth. Coming in a visible, tangible manner, these events foreshadowed His incarnation. Many Bible scholars agree that Scripture's use of the term "the Angel of the Lord" is rightly interpreted as a pre-incarnate manifestation of the Messiah-Christ. In context *the Angel of the Lord* proves to be God. Following Christ's incarnation, the Angel of the Lord never reappears. (As we studied in

Chapter Four, the word angel simply refers to the *office of messenger*, not to a *created order* of being.)

That very day, the Angel of the Lord—the Lord Himself—*supernaturally provided* a ram caught in a thicket. Nearly 2,000 years later, Roman soldiers laid the wood for the offering on Christ's back. Carrying His cross, they led the *supernaturally provided* Lamb of God outside the gates of Jerusalem to a little knoll, the hill of Calvary—the appointed place near Mount Moriah. Abraham had named that place, "The-LORD-Will-Provide" (Genesis 22:14).

How was the patriarch's trust so firmly established? Jesus told some Jews who accused Him of being demon-possessed, "Your father Abraham rejoiced to see My day, and he saw it and was glad" (John 8:56). I believe this happened when God ratified the covenant in the form of a vision to Abraham in Genesis 15. Abraham knew that God's *only unique one-of-a-kind covenant Son of promise* would be crucified and resurrected, and trusted God would likewise raise his son. Surely, he had taught Isaac this. Consider what the New Testament has to say about this event—

> By faith Abraham, when he was tested, offered up Isaac, and he who had received the promises offered up his only begotten son, of whom it was said, "In Isaac your seed shall be called," concluding that God was able to raise him up, even from the dead (Hebrews 11:17–19).

What grateful worship they must have offered that day before they descended Mount Moriah to rejoin the two men awaiting them. As Abraham promised, they returned together.

Sarah died at 127 years old (Genesis 23:1). Abraham lived 38 years longer, and eventually married another concubine, Keturah, with whom he had six more sons. Nearing his life's end, he gave gifts to his eldest son Ishmael and other six sons, and sent them eastward—away from Isaac (Genesis 25:1–6). Abraham broke custom and gave his entire estate to Isaac as the heir of preeminence (v. 5). Customarily, this birthright went to the oldest son of the clan, who would be recognized as the head of the family after his father's death, and receive a double share of the inheritance (Deuteronomy 21:17).

As God had promised, Abraham died at a good old age, reaching 175-years old (Genesis 15:15; 25:7). His sons Isaac and Ishmael buried him in the same cave as Sarah (Genesis 25:9). Abraham's faithful history made a deep impression on the ancient world, and is still today tightly interwoven in the Jewish, Christian, and Muslim religions.

GOD RENEWS THE COVENANT WITH ISAAC

Thirty-five years before his death, Abraham had sent his trusted steward Eliezer hundreds of miles away to his relatives in Haran to seek a worthy wife for Isaac. He assured Eliezer that God would "send His Angel"—implying the Angel of the Lord—before him (Genesis 24:7). Abraham was convinced of God's divine guidance to protect and perpetuate the covenant promises for future generations. The same Lord who rescued Isaac from the altar of sacrifice would secure the selection of his wife.

At the age of 40, Isaac married Rebekah. She suffered barrenness for nearly 20 years, and Isaac pleaded in prayer for God to open her womb, trusting the Lord's promise and involvement to provide covenant descendants. Rebekah conceived, but had a difficult pregnancy—two children seemed to be fighting in her womb. When she prayed for understanding, the Lord answered with a message that sheds light on her actions years later—

And the LORD said to her: "Two nations are in your womb, two peoples shall be separated from your body; One people shall be stronger than the other, And the older shall serve the younger" (Genesis 25:23).

Isaac was 60 years old when his twin sons were born (v. 26). Esau came out first, and the second-born immediately followed, grabbing hold of Esau's heel. They named him Jacob—meaning *one who supplants* another by replacement. Jacob's early story seems to mirror the meaning of his name, but we must remember that God knew his heart potential, and so told Rebekah that he would enjoy the covenant blessing of preeminence.

Looking nothing alike, the twins acted nothing alike. Isaac preferred Esau—a skillful hunter, and real man's man. Rebekah preferred her mild-mannered son Jacob—a settled man, who dwelt in the tents more than in the fields. The day came when reckless Esau sold his birthright to Jacob for a bowl of lentil stew, and Scripture tells us, "Thus Esau despised his birthright" (v. 34). At the age of 40, Esau took pagan wives, who were "grief of mind to Isaac and Rebekah" (Genesis 26:34–35). The holy covenant seed would not come from his line.

Another severe drought hit the land, and Isaac thought to go down to Egypt, as his father Abraham had done during the first famine. But God showed up visibly to dissuade him, and renewed the everlasting covenant with Isaac—

> Then the LORD appeared to him and said: "Do not go down to Egypt; live in the land of which I shall tell you. Dwell in this land, and **I will** be with you and bless you; for to you and your descendants I give all these lands, and **I will** perform the oath which I swore to Abraham your father. And **I will** make your descendants multiply as the stars of heaven; **I will** give to your descendants all these lands; and in your seed all the nations of the earth shall be blessed; **because Abraham obeyed** My voice and kept My charge, My commandments, My statutes, and My laws" (Genesis 26:2-5; emphasis added).

The Lord renewed His *righteousness-by-faith* covenant on the basis of Abraham's obedience to all His commandments—God's moral code of love—and became the covenant God of Isaac. He prospered Isaac with a hundredfold increase during the drought (Genesis 26:12).

When Isaac was close to 137 years old (age determination segment follows), his eyes were too dim to see. Recognizing his advanced years and his own mortality, he intended to bestow the *clan* firstborn blessings on Esau, although he knew the rash actions of his son had recklessly, but legally, transferred this birthright to Jacob.

Through what seems like unconscionable deceit and sophisticated trickery, Rebekah disguised Jacob as Esau (Genesis 27:15–16) and insisted he appear before his aged father with a ceremonial meal she had prepared, before Esau could return from the field to prepare another. Let's give Rebekah the benefit of doubt for a moment. God told her that Jacob would enjoy preeminence, which could have been her underlying reason to commit fraud on her husband. Nevertheless, Isaac was tricked into passing the *clan* firstborn blessings onto Jacob, and he would become the head of his father's household. Jacob would be master over Esau.

Later, Esau arrived at Isaac's tent and learned his blind father had pronounced the blessing on Jacob—a blessing he could not rescind. Both men were visibly shaken to recognize the deceit. Esau cried out, weeping bitterly. Hatred filled his heart, and he blamed his twin for supplanting him twice. Thinking his father's death would be imminent, he planned to kill Jacob when the days for mourning had passed.

Outside the tent, Rebekah heard Esau's intentions and told Jacob, ". . . arise, flee to my brother Laban in Haran. And stay with him a few days, until your brother's fury turns away" (Genesis 27:43–45). Isaac agreed, recognizing God intended to continue the covenant seed through Jacob's line. Isaac pronounced the Abrahamic *covenant* blessing upon Jacob before he departed, and charged his son not to marry a Canaanite, but rather to choose a wife from his uncle Laban's daughters (Genesis 28:1–4).

The "few days" of life in Haran for Jacob turned out to be 20 years, and Rebekah likely never saw her son again. The twists and turns of Jacob's story occupy half the book of Genesis. His life was a checkered course of conflict, and God guided him through it all.

GOD RENEWS THE COVENANT WITH JACOB

Searching Scripture to determine Jacob's age when he fled his home for Haran, I was surprised to learn he was close to 77 years old—just beyond middle-aged, since he lived another seventy years (Genesis 47:28). Beginning the 500-mile journey, Jacob ran for his life toward a family he had never met. As the sun went down, the weary man stopped for the night. Here he had his first encounter with God. Jacob wasn't looking for God, but God was watching over him. In a divinely-given dream, the Lord renewed His everlasting covenant with Jacob, just as He had with Isaac—

He dreamed, and behold, a ladder was set up on the earth, and its top reached to heaven; and there the angels of God were ascending and descending on it. And behold, the LORD stood above it and said: "I am the LORD God of Abraham your father and the God of Isaac; the land on which you lie **I will** give to you and your descendants. Also your descendants shall be as the dust of the earth . . . and in your seed all the families of the earth shall be blessed. Behold, I am with you and **will** keep you wherever you go, and **will** bring you back to this land; for **I will** not leave you until I have done what I have spoken to you" (Genesis 28:12-15; emphasis added).

Jacob awoke in fear and awe. Pouring oil on the stone he had used as a pillow to consecrate it to the Lord, he named the place Bethel. He vowed faithfulness to the Lord, and—recognizing God as his provider—he promised to return a tenth of all he received to Him (vv. 18–22). So God became known as the *God of Abraham, the God of Isaac, and the God of Jacob.*

Genesis 29 tells the story of Jacob's arrival in Haran. He immediately laid eyes on his cousin Rachel, and it was love at first sight. He desired to marry her, and when he met her father Laban, he offered to work seven years to receive her hand in marriage. At the close of the seven years, Jacob asked for his wife Rachel. Now the deceiver Jacob was deceived by his uncle Laban, who tricked him to first marry his older daughter Leah, by veiling and substituting her in the wedding ceremony.

Laban then agreed Jacob could marry his beloved Rachel at the end of his wedding week with Leah (Genesis 29:27–28). But his tricky uncle—who had now become his father-in-law— compelled him to work an additional seven years for her. Jacob had labored hard the first seven years as a single man. Now he married twice in the space of a week. This double union didn't end so happily-ever-after. His preference for Rachel over Leah caused painful family issues.

Jacob's family grew. "When the Lord saw that Leah was unloved, He opened her womb" (Genesis 29:31). A woman's societal prestige was measured by how many sons she bore. Leah gave Jacob six sons and a daughter named Dinah. Her handmaid Zilpah became his concubine and bore him two more sons. His beloved Rachel was barren for the first six years of their marriage, so she gave him her handmaid Bilhah, who bore two sons (Genesis 30:4–8). God opened Rachel's womb near the close of Jacob's fourteen years of indentured labor to unethical Laban (vv. 22–24). She gave birth to Joseph when Jacob was 91 years old.

Although a poor man, Jacob longed to return home to his family in Canaan. Instead, Laban talked him into staying longer as a partner in his sheep industry (Genesis 30:27–36). Through continued family infighting, Jacob labored another six years in Haran. Laban and his sons were not pleased with the outcome (Genesis 31:1–2). Deceptive Laban changed the terms of their deal ten times, but the Lord was watching and rebuked Laban by beating him at his own game, ensuring the livestock born met the terms of the deal in favor of Jacob (vv. 7–9). Jacob's overwhelming success was gained through God's favor.

Twenty years had now passed. It was time to go home. The Lord commanded Jacob, "Return to the land of your fathers and to your family, and I will be with you" (v. 3). While Laban and his sons were shearing sheep at a far distance, Jacob slipped away with his caravan of two wives, two concubines, eleven sons, one daughter, servants, and his vast flocks (vv. 17–21). He was unaware that Rachel had stolen her father's household idols. We'll consider the outcome of this situation in our next chapter.

Greatly apprehensive about Esau's reception, Jacob hoped to appease him with generous gifts. Jacob prayed that the two could be reconciled, and proceeded cautiously. As the group neared his estranged brother, Jacob purposefully separated himself from his wives, children, and caravan, and spent a lonely night on the other side of the Jabbok River. That night Jacob wrestled with a Man until the breaking of day. The Man turned out to be the Lord, and He asked to be let go. Jacob refused, declaring, "I will not let You go unless You bless me!" (Genesis 32:26). The Man said—

*"Your name shall no longer be called Jacob, but **Israel**; for you have struggled with God and with men, and have prevailed."*

Then Jacob asked, saying, "Tell me Your name, I pray." And He said, "Why is it that you ask about My name?" And He blessed him there. And Jacob called the name of the place Peniel: "For I have seen God face to face, and my life is preserved" (Genesis 32:28–30; emphasis added).

Where did the name "Israel" originate? Just as God had given covenant names to Abraham and Sarah, the Lord gave Jacob a new name encoded with covenant blessings. Jacob had struggled with God and prevailed, and now God would strive on his behalf. Israel became Jacob's covenant name. God became known *as the God of Israel* (e.g. 1 Kings 18:36).

Jacob had struggled with Laban, and prevailed with God's help. Although he had yet to realize it, his struggle with his twin brother was over, for God had strived on his behalf to change Esau's heart. When the two came face-to-face again, Esau "ran to meet him, and embraced him, and fell on his neck and kissed him, and they wept" (Genesis 33:4).

Reunited, at last, without animosity. It had been a long time coming, but nevertheless, their union didn't last long. Perhaps in recognition of their different natures, they parted ways in a friendly manner. Jacob turned west to the Promised Land, and Esau went to Seir to become the father of the Edomite nation. Scripture does not record another reunion between them until their father Isaac died at 180, and his twin sons buried him (Genesis 35:28–29).

GOD'S CHOSEN PRINCE, JOSEPH

Though Jacob remains a central figure, Genesis 37-50 revolve around Joseph. His family had moved from Haran to Canaan with the six-year-old in tow. Scripture is silent about the time it took the caravan with women, children, and flocks of slow-moving sheep to travel those 500 miles, and doesn't explain the time lapse between major events happening after their arrival, and before Rachel gave birth to her second son. Some estimate that five to ten years passed before Rachel's difficult delivery in childbirth caused her death (Genesis 35:16–19). Joseph could have been between 10–16 years old when his brother Benjamin was born and his mother died.

Genesis 37 shares how Jacob loved Joseph above all his sons. He gave him a special tunic of many colors, implying that he was the royal son who would be the future leader of the clan. His brothers envied and hated him, barely tolerating his presence. Joseph was a dreamer, and an interpreter of dreams. One particular dream clearly signaled that his brothers would one day bow to Joseph's dominion over them. The men reacted with fury when he shared the dream. Oblivious to how his dreams irritated others, he later shared another. This one suggested that all his family members would bow to him. Even Jacob rebuked his favorite son—but he mulled the matter over in his mind (Genesis 37:11). What the family had yet to recognize was the divine inspiration of these dreams. Joseph was God's chosen prince—and the Lord would use him to save His people.

One day Joseph's father sent him to check on his half-brothers, who were feeding the flocks over 50 miles away. At the sight of him approaching, their tempers flared and hatred boiled into a conspiracy to murder him. Stripping off his multicolored tunic, they threw him into a pit, and soon sold Joseph as a slave to a passing merchant's caravan. Down to Egypt went the favored son in shackles—at the age of seventeen (Genesis 37:18–27). The brothers dipped his tunic in the blood of a goat and presented it to their father, claiming a wild beast had devoured Joseph. Stunned, Jacob wept and mourned. His grief would endure for 22 years.

In Egypt, Potiphar, an officer of Pharaoh, bought Joseph as a slave. God blessed Joseph, causing his rise in authority to become steward of Potiphar's entire household. Joseph was handsome and well-built. Potiphar's wife lusted after Joseph and threw herself at him. In loyalty to God's moral code of love, Joseph refused her advances. The spurned woman falsely claimed he had violated her. Off to prison went God's chosen prince (Genesis 39:20).

The Lord was still with Joseph, and gave him favor in the sight of the prison master, who promoted him to have authority over all the prisoners (vv. 21–23). During his two years of imprisonment, Joseph gained notoriety as an interpreter of dreams (Genesis 40). A day came that he was called before Pharaoh to interpret his two troubling dreams that court magicians could not. In his dreams, the king of Egypt had seen seven fat cows devoured by seven gaunt cows, and similarly seven plump heads of grain devoured by seven thin heads (Genesis 41:1–7).

Joseph explained that God had shown Pharaoh that seven years of great plenty had arrived, only to be followed by seven years of severe famine. He suggested the king appoint a discerning and wise man under his authority, to collect and store up grain during the seven plentiful years, and thereby prevent starvation in the land during the seven-year famine. In astonishment, Pharaoh said to his servants, "Can we find such a one as this, a man in whom is the Spirit of God?" (v. 38). He appointed Joseph as prince over all his kingdom, second only to Pharaoh himself.

For seven years, Joseph gathered abundant grain and laid up supplies in the cities. Then, as the Lord had predicted, a severe famine struck. People came to Egypt from every direction to buy grain (vv. 25–49, 57). Genesis 42 provides a picture of Joseph's family in Canaan. Two years into the famine, Jacob and his household were in dire straits. Learning of Egypt's great supply of grain, Jacob sent ten of his sons—all but Benjamin—to purchase supplies.

It had been 22 years since the brothers had seen Joseph. As the governor of the land of Egypt, dressed and styled as an Egyptian, and the last person they'd expect to hold such power, Joseph was unrecognizable to them. Just as the Lord had shown Joseph in a dream, his brothers bowed low before him. He quickly determined to see if their hearts had changed before he revealed his identity. Joseph didn't acknowledge that he recognized them. He spoke only through an interpreter, so the brothers assumed the governor didn't understand their Hebrew language.

Although Joseph was very generous with them, he tested their character in various ways. He cleverly manipulated circumstances to make them appear guilty of criminal intent. To motivate them to bring Benjamin before him, he detained one brother as a hostage. The others returned home heavy-hearted, but loaded with generous supplies—they even found the money they had paid for grain had been restored to their sacks (Genesis 42:35). In anguish, they begged their father Jacob to allow Benjamin to return with them to secure the release of their brother Simeon. Earnest pleading and extravagant promises finally convinced the old man to allow his only remaining son by Rachel to make the trip (Genesis 43:13–15).

So Benjamin went with his brothers to Egypt. Overcome with emotion at the sight of Benjamin, Joseph withdrew to his chamber to weep privately. Washing his face, he returned to oversee a banquet for them, and seated them according to their birth order. The men looked in astonishment at one another. Joseph directed his Egyptian attendants to present Benjamin with unusual favor for the youngest member of a clan. He provided a portion of food to him five times greater than the others (Genesis 43:34). His brothers scarcely raised an eyebrow. Now Joseph knew that his brothers' hearts had changed—envy and jealousy had been removed.

Genesis 45 reveals Joseph unable to restrain himself any longer. Desiring to maintain dignity before the Egyptians, he sent the servants attending the banquet away. Twenty two years of pent up emotion gushed forth from his heart. Finally speaking in Hebrew, Joseph made himself known to his brothers, saying—

"Please come near to me." So they came near. Then he said: "I am Joseph your brother, whom you sold into Egypt. But now, do not therefore be grieved or angry with yourselves because you sold me here; **for God sent me** before you to preserve life. For these two years the famine has been in the land, and there are still five years in which there will be neither plowing nor harvesting. And **God sent me** before you to preserve a posterity for you in the earth, and to save your lives by a great deliverance. **So now it was not you who sent me here, but God**; and He has made me a father to Pharaoh, and lord of all his house, and a ruler throughout all the land of Egypt . . ." (Genesis 45:4-8; emphasis added).

"Posterity" is the word translators used here for the Hebrew word meaning *remnant*—a small, remaining portion of a thing. Joseph understood God's providence. With spiritual maturity, he affirmed three times that it was God who had sent him to Egypt. The Lord planned it all, and purposed his life's circumstances to preserve the covenant-keeping remnant. God was protecting the covenant seed who would pass along His covenant blessings to future generations.

Joseph had no ill will toward his brothers, and vowed his care for the next five years of famine and beyond. He requested that they hurry home and bring his father Jacob and the clan down to live near him. Pharaoh heard the report. It pleased him, so he directed Joseph to load their animals with supplies and send carts to retrieve weaker family members. Presenting generous gifts to the brothers, Pharaoh affirmed a land grant for Goshen—a fertile area of Egypt—upon their return. They went home and had to confess their crime to their father as they shared the news that Joseph was alive and governed all Egypt. Jacob's heart stood still in disbelief, until seeing the carts and supplies coming down the dusty road. Eager anticipation of joining his favorite son revived him (Genesis 45:26–28).

God's covenant blessings rested on faithful Joseph. The Lord turned his situation around as he went from a pit to a prison, and then was promoted to the palace of Egypt with a plan to save his own starving relatives—the remnant of God's covenant people on Earth. Seventy members of Jacob's clan immigrated to Goshen, the fertile area where they could graze their flocks and begin a new life (Genesis 46:27, 47:1–12).

Jacob arrived in Egypt at age 130, and lived in peace there for the next seventeen years. At the time of his death at age 147 (Genesis 47:28), Jacob was mourned a full 70 days, according to Egyptian culture for dignitaries. He had asked to be buried in the Promised Land. Out of respect for him and for Joseph, a great number of high-ranking Egyptians joined the funeral procession, providing an escort of horses and chariots all the way back to Canaan.

Now that their father had been buried, guilt from the past arose in the hearts of Joseph's brothers. They feared what he might do. Bowing before him, they offered to become his personal slaves. Joseph acknowledged their previous evil intents, but comforted them—

Joseph said to them, "Do not be afraid, for am I in the place of God? But as for you, you meant evil against me; but God meant it for good, in order to bring it about as it is this day, to save many people alive . . ." (Genesis 50:19–20).

Joseph lived by faith in a covenant-making, covenant-keeping God, and he died in the same faith at the age of 110 (v. 26). His body was embalmed and placed in a coffin. The return of his remains to Canaan awaited a future fulfillment—a day when Moses and the Israelites would carry his body back to the Promised Land.

THE AGE OF JACOB AT JOSEPH'S BIRTH

This segment of age calculations is interesting, but of no great spiritual importance. Some inquiring minds like to know.

Jacob was 130 when he joined Joseph in Egypt (Genesis 47:9). Joseph was 39 at the time. He had entered Pharaoh's service at the age of 30 and had already served Pharaoh for 9 years—seven abundant and two lean (Genesis 41:46, 45:6). The difference in their ages is 91 years (130 minus 39 = 91). Jacob was 91 years old when Joseph was born.

Joseph had been born at the end of Jacob's 14 years of service to Laban (Genesis 30:22–26). If Jacob was 91 at the time, and had already been in Haran for 14 years, he was around 77 at the time he fled to his uncle Laban's home. Jacob's father Isaac was 60 years older than him (Genesis 25:26), so Isaac was about 137 when he was deceived to give Jacob the *clan* firstborn blessing, then knowingly bestowed the covenant blessing to him before he departed for Haran.

ECHOES OF LESSONS FROM THE PAST

The lives of the patriarchs reverberate with lessons for us. From Abraham, we learn the blessing of trusting God, walking in obedient faith, and looking to God's future Promised Land at the end of time.

From Isaac, we learn to pray for God's promises to come to fruition, and to be quick to recognize and reverse emotionally-driven decisions that deny God's will.

Jacob's life clearly demonstrates that success is gained through God's favor, and that we must hold on until God blesses us. We also note the disastrous consequences caused by parental favoritism of one child above another. Jacob's preference for Joseph created insecurities and resentment in the hearts of his ten older sons. Jacob shows us the need to forgive children's shortcomings—he had to forgive those ten sons for lying all those years about the fate of Joseph. His life showcases how God can reverse our situation at His appointed time. God blessed Jacob to be reunited with his beloved son, and to enjoy prosperity again before he died.

From God's chosen prince, Joseph, we learn that if we remain faithful to God, He remains faithful to us. The up-close-and-personal presence of the Lord never left Joseph. Even in Joseph's darkest moments, God continued to bless him. His inspiring example teaches us to forgive others, and to be reconciled as far as possible when those who have harmed us have experienced a heart change.

The greatest lesson Joseph teaches is to recognize God's providence. God is in control. When bad things happen, we need to trust God's ultimate purpose for allowing them, and realize that our loving Lord will work all things together for our *eternal* benefit when we walk in covenant faithfulness with Him (Genesis 50:20; Romans 8:28).

SUMMARY OF "HIS" STORY
Chapter Seven

- Covenant language and concepts include: 1) *shalom*; 2) *hesed*; 3) *grace*; 4) *Seed*; 5) *Root*; 6) *preeminence*; 7) *circumcision*; 8) *"I will"*; 9) *substitutionary sacrifice*; 10) *righteousness by faith*; 11) *son of promise*; 12) *"firstborn"*—describing a position of preeminence; 13) *"begotten"*—meaning chosen for a covenant purpose; and 14) *"only begotten"*—meaning a unique, one-of-a-kind, son of promise.

- God put Abraham to a test when He asked Abraham to sacrifice Isaac. The Lord never intended for the actual sacrifice of Abraham's "only begotten" son of promise.

- "The Angel of the Lord" is rightly interpreted as a preincarnate appearance of Christ.

- "The Angel of the Lord" stopped Abraham, and *supernaturally provided* a lamb for the slaughter. Jesus Christ is the true *supernaturally provided* Lamb of God.

- God renewed His everlasting covenant with Isaac because Abraham had obeyed His commandments, His moral code of love by which He governs the earth.

- Before Jacob was born, God announced his preeminence over his older twin Esau.

- Rebekah schemed to get Isaac to unknowingly give the *clan* birthright blessing to Jacob.
- Recognizing it was Jacob's line that would produce the seed of the covenant, Isaac also pronounced the *covenant* blessing on Jacob before he left for Haran.
- On the trip to Haran, God renewed His everlasting covenant with Jacob.
- Jacob fell in love with his cousin, and worked seven years for Rachel's hand in marriage.
- Laban deceived Jacob, marrying off his older daughter Leah to him first. At the end of their wedding week, Laban allowed him to marry Rachel, but forced him to work seven more years for her. Jacob married two sisters within the space of a week.
- Joseph was born to Jacob and Rachel near the end of his 14 years of indentured labor.
- Jacob worked as a partner to Laban for six more years, and God gave Jacob overwhelming success in developing the flocks that were his earnings.
- God called Jacob to return to Canaan at the end of the 20-year period.
- While Laban and his sons were shearing sheep many miles from their home place, Jacob slipped away with his two wives, two concubines, 11 sons, one daughter, servants, and flocks.
- God gave Jacob the covenant name of *Israel* after he wrestled with God all night.
- Joseph's dreams as a teenager proved he was God's chosen prince.
- At the age of 17, Joseph was thrown into a pit by his brothers, then sold into slavery.
- God's covenant blessings remained on Joseph. The Lord took him from a pit to a prison, before using him to rescue God's remnant people.
- After wisely interpreting Pharaoh's dreams, Joseph was made governor of Egypt, and oversaw a project to store up enough grain during seven years of plenty to prevent starvation for all the land during seven years of severe famine.
- Joseph realized it was God's providence that had brought him to Egypt.
- Joseph's family was restored to him, and moved to Egypt, being given the fertile land of Goshen for their dwelling—with the blessing of the Pharaoh.
- Jacob was reunited with his son Joseph for 17 years before he died. His remains were taken back to Canaan in an amazing funeral procession of honor.

RIGHTEOUSNESS BY FAITH AND RECONCILIATION

Chapter Eight

Trying to work your way into heaven is legalism. Legalism is the classic earmark of all false forms of religion. Obedience is not legalism. Obedience is love, and the highest expression of worship to our righteous Lord. Obedience is the pathway to God's covenant blessings.

In this chapter we will drill down on the definition of *righteousness* to understand God's character, and the two aspects of *righteousness by faith* that He offers humanity by His grace. Will the God of unselfish love and compassion inflict unceasing torture on the wicked in hellfire? Were the Ten Commandments of God's moral code of love known to the ancient people of Genesis? Scripture gives us undeniable answers to these questions.

THE RIGHTEOUSNESS OF GOD

How can a finite human—within the boundaries of limited time and understanding—comprehend an infinite God? He is without beginning or end, has unlimited power and knowledge, and is present everywhere at the same time. God is beyond the capacity of human comprehension.

Though we cannot fully grasp God's invisible qualities, we can contemplate His self-revelation to humanity. The more we behold Him, the better we know Him. Jesus said that to know Him is eternal life (John 17:3). Only as we gain an infinity focus on His self-revelation in Scripture can we begin to glimpse His majesty, glory, and holiness. In an effort to achieve this, let's look at two dimensions of the personality of God—

- "God is love" (1 John 4:8). He is not just loving, His essential *nature* is love. His nature of unselfish love makes Him holy, completely separated from sin. God cannot sin. Love does no harm. His *nature* of love is the wellspring of His *character* of light.

- "God is light" (1 John 1:5). His *character* is righteous—He is morally perfect, which causes His light to be eternally bright. God's light has no variation of rising or setting, and it is never eclipsed by His turning away from righteousness (James 1:17). When God revealed Himself to Moses, we learn that His character of righteousness reflects His glory. Moses asked to see the glory of God. In response, the Lord hid Moses in the cleft of a rock, passing by and proclaiming His character, saying, "The LORD, the LORD God, merciful and gracious, long-suffering, and abounding in goodness and truth, keeping mercy for thousands, forgiving iniquity and transgression and sin, by no means clearing the guilty" (Exodus 34:6–7). That is God's *character*.

Can we separate God's nature of love from His character of light? No. They are inseparably intertwined. His unselfish love is the source of His eternal light. He governs by the power of love and righteousness—doing all things for the eternal benefit of humanity.

Dialing in an infinity focus, and looking through the lens of infinite love, our view of God is cleared of preconceived opinions and distortions of truth. We see that His moral excellence guides everything He does (Psalm 145:17). We find that His interactions with us are right, reasonable, consistent, and correct. God makes no mistakes. His work on our behalf produces an eternity of everlasting peace and harmony.

HEAVEN'S BANKING SYSTEM

How do we understand the process of *imputed* righteousness that is foundational to God's plan of salvation? Some folks have grown up in church and can quote Scripture on this topic, but have little appreciation for it. The following illustration will help us relate. I call on you to use your imagination to lock in a mental image of this process.

Imagine you have amassed a bank debt of $50 billion through deceptive practices. You must cover the debt or suffer the consequences, but you realize that even if you worked the rest of your life, you could never earn enough to make a dent in the debt. Facing legal action, your heart is gripped with fear. Will the judge sentence you to perish in prison?

Suddenly, the CEO of the world banking system steps forward to be your benefactor. International laws prevent him from simply erasing the records of your account, but with mystifying mercy and generosity, he covers your debt by assuming it. He hands you a legal draft to transfer your *debt* to his personal account, and exchange his good *credit* for yours. You take it to the bank, and your debt is covered—your account is reconciled. Can you imagine the feelings of newfound loyalty you would have for your gracious benefactor?

This meager illustration merely hints at the incredible heavenly transaction that occurred when our Creator God stepped forward to become the Person of Jesus Christ. The Messiah-Christ was our Benefactor. God's justice system wouldn't allow our debt to be simply erased, so He assumed the debt for us. He bore our sins, and credited His righteousness to us in the great exchange (2 Corinthians 5:21). God's grace wrote the check—our faith takes it to the bank to reconcile our account. The Bible defines this process as *imputed* righteousness.

It is a legal covenant transaction that we can bank on to put us in right *standing* with God. Christ died for the sins of the whole world, but that does us no good unless we choose to enter into covenant relationship by accepting Him as our Savior. When we do, we must accept Him as our rightful Lord and King, too. Our citizenship is then transferred to His kingdom and we become subjects of His heavenly banking system (Colossians 1:13). He covers our debt of sin and credits His perfect record of obedience to our overdrawn spiritual account. Christ's righteousness becomes ours. God declares us *justified* (not guilty), and our relationship with Him is reconciled. He takes us from foe to friend—restoring our mutual bond that results in peace with God.

> For if by Adam's offense death reigned through him, how much more will those who receive God abundance of grace and the **gift of righteousness** reign in life and triumph over sin and death through the one Man, Jesus Christ (Romans 5:17; *author's paraphrase*).

After sin entered the hearts of humanity in the Garden of Eden, no option was left for human effort to reverse the death penalty. Only preposterous pride entertains the idea that good works could erase a record of guilt, and earn favor with a holy God (Isaiah 64:6).

In the eyes of the Lord, *righteousness by faith* in Him is the only righteousness that exists for humanity.

"RIGHTEOUSNESS BY FAITH" IS A RELATIONAL TERM

"All unrighteousness is sin" (1 John 5:17). Sin is unrighteousness that renounces the holy character of God, and is intolerable to Him. Only as we recognize our sin, turn to Him, and confess our condition with deep remorse can we count on God's intervention to restore us, based on His covenant promise in Christ Jesus, who paid our sin penalty. "If we confess our sins, He is faithful and just to forgive us our sins and to cleanse us from all unrighteousness" (1 John 1:9).

Referring to humanity, *righteousness by faith* is defined in two aspects. The first eliminates sin's penalty and puts us in *right standing* with God. The second emancipates us from sin, and empowers right living in His eyes. Righteousness by faith is a relational term—it is how God relates to His people and how His covenant people relate to Him. It describes covenant relationship.

Justification by faith is an **act** of God's grace—a climactic moment in the lives of believers that is the first aspect of salvation. This happens when we open our hearts to accept God's great gift, receiving Christ as our Savior, and His righteousness is imputed (credited) to us. Our status "in Christ" puts us in right standing, or right being, with God.

This is the foundation of God's everlasting covenant and humanity's hope for eternal life. That's good news, but it gets better.

Sanctification by faith is a **work** of God's grace—an ongoing process that is the second aspect of salvation, and sets us apart from sin as we die to self-will. When we accept Christ as our Lord and walk with Him through life, He empowers us to live according to His will and to reflect His righteousness, "that the life of Jesus also may be *manifested in our mortal flesh*" (2 Corinthians 4:11; emphases added). Paul also proclaimed, "It is God who works in you both to will and to do for His good pleasure," and declared "I can do all things through Christ who strengthens me" (Philippians 2:13; 4:13). As God works to recreate His image within us, He imprints His moral code of love within our hearts (Hebrews 8:10), and causes us to be what He calls us to be. Paul said, "This is the will of God, your sanctification" (1 Thessalonians 4:3).

Let's summarize the *two aspects of righteousness* that God pours out by His grace:

- The ***imputed*** righteousness of Christ occurs when His record of complete conformity to God's commandments is credited to us. This is the first aspect of salvation—justification. God declares us "not guilty" and delivers us from the *penalty* of sin. This puts us in *right standing* with God, and reconciles our relationship with Him. When justified, we can say, "I have been made righteous and saved from the penalty of sin."

- The ***infused*** righteousness of Christ occurs as His perfect moral character is infused in us by the indwelling Holy Spirit. The Spirit empowers us to live according to God's will, separated from sin. This is the second aspect of salvation—**sanctification**. God delivers us from the *power* of sin. As we remain in this lifelong process, we remain in covenant relationship with the Lord, and can correctly say, "I am being made righteous and saved from the power of sin."

The third aspect of salvation is ***glorification***. This will happen at Christ's Second Coming. He will return for His covenant people, and—at the sound of His voice—His faithful ones who "sleep in the dust of the earth" will come forth in the "resurrection of life" (Daniel 12:2; John 5:28–29). The Apostle Paul assures us, "we who are alive and remain until the coming of the Lord will by no means precede those who are asleep . . . the dead in Christ will rise first . . . [and we] shall be caught up together with them in the clouds to meet the Lord in the air" (1 Thessalonians 4:15–18). In the "twinkling of an eye" He will clothe His beloved with immortality, and they will have glorified bodies like His own (1 Corinthians 15:51–55). This is the final victory over death, and results in His glorious rescue from the *presence* of sin.

WILL GOD INFLICT UNCEASING TORTURE ON THE WICKED?

"For God so loved the world that He gave His only begotten Son, that whoever believes in Him should not perish but have everlasting life" (John 3:16). Do you see the juxtaposition here? There is only one of two contrasting choices. Either a person believes and inherits everlasting life, or they don't believe and perish—because they don't inherit everlasting life. The word *perish* means *utter destruction*.

For well over 150 years after Christ's death, the early church fathers believed mortal beings either chose the way of life, or chose the way of death. So how did the concept of an immortal soul enter the realm of Christianity?

A brilliant theologian and Christian apologist—Tertullian of Tunisia—wrote *A Treatise on the Soul* around AD 200, and his words echoed Satan's great lie to Eve, "You will not surely die" (Genesis 3:4). Tertullian had been a pagan philosopher before his conversion to Christianity, following the teachings of Plato. In turn, Plato was a student of Socrates, and both of these Greek philosophers taught the immortality of the soul. Indoctrinated by their unbiblical philosophy, Tertullian never abandoned his preconceived notion. Error insulated his mind against truth in this instance, and he introduced the fatally-flawed concepts of the immortal soul and unceasing torment in hell fire.

Now for our *most crucial* sidebar insert yet. Do you believe the sinister attack on God's character that claims He will burn people in hell through unceasing ages? The distorted teaching of *continual and unimaginable torment in hell* is as popular in our day, as was the false teaching about the coming Messiah that religious leaders promoted in Jesus' day. It is the underlying reason many reject Him and practice atheism.

How can Scripture possibly describe God's *nature* as unselfish love, and His *character* as righteous light, if He would burn people in unceasing torment? He will not! The God of abundant mercy and amazing grace will indeed destroy sinners in the *eternal fire* of hell at His final judgment of the wicked—but He assuredly will **not** torture mortals with an unceasing process of punishing. In the first place, *mortal beings* could not survive such a process. In the second place, such an act would make Him a worse monster than the mass murderers Hitler of Germany, Mussolini of Italy, or Pol-Pot of Cambodia.

Does that sound like double talk? The adjectives *everlasting*, *eternal*, or *forever* from the original Bible languages have no absolute meaning of their own, but are *relative terms* that gain their meaning from the person, object, or process they describe. Their meaning *relates* to the subject they are describing. An example of a *relative term* that will be familiar to your vocabulary is the word "tall." I am six feet tall; my cousin is 4'10" tall. The Statute of Liberty is 305-feet tall; a Chihuahua puppy might be only 5-inches tall. "Tall" is relative to the person or object on it describes.

When the words *everlasting*, *eternal*, or *forever* are used in relationship to God as their subject, these words reflect an *infinite existence* since He is infinite—God alone has immortality at this time (1 Timothy 6:16). At Christ's Second Coming, He will gift the faithful with immortal existence and they will live with Him throughout eternity (1 Corinthians 15:51–55). Because He is eternal, Christ will reign *forever*—throughout endless ages (Revelation 11:15).

Now take close notice of this sharp contrast. When the words *everlasting*, *eternal*, or *forever* are used in relationship to mortal humanity or perishable things as their subject, these words reflect their temporary nature and simply mean *as long as the person or thing exists*.

For example, Samuel was to live in the tabernacle of the Lord "forever" (1 Samuel 1:22). He lived there only for the length of his life. Jonah claimed he was barred in the whale "forever" (Jonah 2:6), but the great fish spewed him forth after just three days and nights. "Eternal judgment" is not an endless process of judging, but it has eternal results; "eternal redemption" is not an endless process of being redeemed, but has eternal results (Hebrews 6:2; 9:12).

Scripture declares the cities of Sodom and Gomorrah were "set forth as an example, suffering the vengeance of eternal fire" (Jude 1:7). Are they still on fire today? Of course not. The results of this fire were eternal, but the *eternal fire* completed its work, destroying Sodom and Gomorrah—those cities perished and no longer burn. When people experience the eternal and *unquenchable* fire of hell, that fire will not be quenched until it finishes its work and they perish—eternally.

From the pulpit of popular preachers, the idea of "gnashing of teeth" is often used as proof of unimaginable torment in hell fire. It sounds horrifying, doesn't it? Do you know what this term *gnashing of teeth* meant to people in the first century? It was an expression of anger and frustration, not of physical anguish. Consider this verse: "When they heard these things they were cut to the heart, and they gnashed at him with their teeth" (Acts 7:54, compare Psalm 35:16). Angry sinners will still be gnashing their teeth at God when their final destruction comes.

"But the wicked shall perish; and the enemies of the LORD, like the splendor of the meadows, shall vanish. Into smoke they shall vanish away" (Psalm 37:20). Both the Old Testament and the New describe how they vanish—

> "For behold, the day is coming, Burning like an oven, And all the proud, yes, all who do wickedly will be stubble. And the day which is coming shall burn them up," Says the LORD of hosts, "That will leave them neither root nor branch . . . You shall trample the wicked, For they shall be ashes under the soles of your feet On the day that I do this," Says the LORD of hosts" (Malachi 4:1, 3).

The Lord is not slack concerning His promise, as some count slackness, but is long suffering toward us, not willing that any should perish but that all should come to repentance. But the day of the Lord will come as a thief in the night, in which the heavens will pass away with a great noise, and the elements will melt with fervent heat; both the earth and the works that are in it will be burned up (2 Peter 3:9–10).

The God of love and mercy takes no pleasure in the death of the wicked (Ezekiel 33:11). That day of disaster will be His unusually "strange act" to end sin forever (Isaiah 28:21). At one time, God cleansed the earth of sin with the great Flood—turning Earth into a lake of water. At the end of time, He will cleanse the earth of sin once again—turning Earth into a lake of fire.

One thousand years after the righteous are resurrected, so shall the unredeemed be raised in a second resurrection (Revelation 20:5). They, too, will hear Christ's voice from their graves, and come forth to what Jesus labeled, "the resurrection of condemnation"—their chosen final destiny (John 5:28, 29). Paul tells us that God will pour out His holy and righteous wrath against sin upon "the sons of disobedience" (Colossians 3:6; compare Ephesians 2:2; 5:6; Revelation 6:16). When God turns the Earth into a lake of fire to destroy all sin, the book of Revelation describes the final punishment of hell fire as the "second death" for the wicked (Revelation 2:11; 20:6, 14; 21:8). They will perish (John 3:16).

Christ bore our sins in His own body, and died as our Substitute. The Bible tells us, "But we see Jesus, who was made a little lower than the angels, for the suffering of death crowned with glory and honor, that He, by the grace of God, **might taste death for everyone**" (Hebrews 2:9; emphases added).

What death did He taste *for us*, and *in place of us*? He could not have served as our Substitute by tasting just the first death. Aside from Enoch and Elijah, all people of every generation who have ever lived on Earth have experienced the first natural death at the end of their lives. Christ was not our Substitute for that experience.

The penalty of sin is the *second death* that Revelation so vividly describes. To pay the full penalty of sin, Jesus had to *taste* the second death experience of total separation from God—but it had no power over Him and He came forward victoriously. Hallelujah! If we are "in Christ," we will not experience that second death.

What follows the flames of hellfire that burn so hot they destroy every trace of sin? The Lord will recreate Earth into the paradise that He originally intended.

> Now I saw a new heaven and a new earth, for the first heaven and the first earth had passed away. Also there was no more sea. Then I, John, saw the holy city, New Jerusalem, coming down out of heaven from God, prepared as a bride adorned for her husband. And I heard a loud voice from heaven saying, "Behold, the tabernacle of God is with men, and He will dwell with them, and they shall be His people. God Himself will be with them and be their God. And God will wipe away every tear from their eyes; there shall be no more death, nor sorrow, nor crying. There shall be no more pain, for the former things have passed away" (Revelation 21:1–4).

TRANSFORMED BY THE SPIRIT

Governing by the power of love and righteousness, God created Adam and Eve in His image, imprinted His moral code of love in their hearts, and gave them *free will* for the sake of love. What was the clear choice He offered them? Either receive His love and accept His counsel to *live*, or reject His love and refuse His counsel to *die*. You know the rest of the story. They conformed to Satan's will, and passed their fallen nature onto the rest of the human race.

But God had a plan, didn't He? And what a plan it was! A plan God made before He created humanity—our Creator would become our Substitute and die to pay our sin penalty for us (Revelation 13:8). A plan to restore moral purity in human hearts when they entered into His everlasting covenant of *righteousness by faith*.

> The counsel of the LORD stands forever, the plans of His heart to all generations (Psalm 33:11).

God's approval of Abel, Enoch, Noah, Seth, Shem, Job, Abraham, Isaac, Jacob, and Joseph wasn't only because they trusted in the substitutionary death of the coming Messiah for imputed righteousness. No.

He worked in them to imprint His moral code of love in their hearts, and to cause them to walk in faithful obedience to Him. The power of the Holy Spirit influenced and renewed their minds, setting them apart from sin. Motivated by love, they followed the Lord's will in loyalty to His covenant, and remained in covenant relationship with Him.

What are the evidences of the Holy Spirit's work within their hearts? He circumcised and purified their hearts, transformed their minds, and influenced their desire to live in submission to God. He provided them the power to follow God's will, and developed their godly characters. The ancients who entered into God's everlasting covenant walked in His will, refusing to conform to the wickedness of the world around them.

Today, all Christians are advised, "Do not conform any longer to the pattern of this world, but be transformed by the renewing of your mind. Then you will be able to test and approve what God's will is—his good, pleasing and perfect will" (Romans 12:2, NIV). Only by the Holy Spirit's power can this be achieved, as God works in us to do His will (Philippians 2:13).

GOD'S MORAL CODE OF LOVE

Do you recall how many years Moses' writing covered in the book of Genesis? He packed a highlight-reel of approximately 2,000 years in just the first eleven chapters, then recorded the dramatic life sketches of all the patriarchs to add close to 300 years more. Genesis covers more than half the history of the entire Bible—more than all other books combined. That's why we have invested so much time in reviewing God's interactions with humanity in Genesis.

Moses couldn't write detailed accounts in this one book, but we've learned a lot from him about God's everlasting covenant. Many people mistakenly believe that God didn't provide commandments to follow during the days of Genesis.

Why did God choose Abraham as the "father of all" believers for the rest of time (Romans 4:11)? He knew Abraham would command his children and his household to "keep the way of the LORD, to do righteousness and justice, *that the LORD may bring to Abraham what He has spoken to him*" (Genesis 18:19; emphasis added). Don't miss the underlined purpose statement the Lord revealed in that text—obedience has always been the pathway to God's covenant blessings. Why did God renew the covenant with Isaac? The Lord said it was "because Abraham obeyed My voice and kept My charge, My commandments, My statutes, and My laws" (Genesis 26:5).

Since our Creator bestowed free will to the human race and governs by love, His righteousness required that He define His expectations of love. In fairness to humanity, a holy God had to define boundaries of acceptable human conduct immediately. He installed His Ten Commandment moral code of love from the beginning to protect His entitled rights as Creator and the rights of humankind that love demands.

God did not find it necessary to explain His existence at the beginning of Genesis. His existence is assumed. He simply had Moses write, "In the beginning God created." What the Lord inspired Moses to record in the book of Genesis assumes God's commandments as a way of life during the first 2,300 years of history. The record of the patriarchs' walk of obedient faith to God demonstrates His moral code of love was imprinted on their hearts and minds. If God had no commandments in place, could there have been any sin? Scripture defines sin as ignoring and breaking God's law (1 John 3:4).

God's moral code of love is reiterated by both the spoken and written Word of God in the events Moses recorded in Exodus, when God verbally reminds His people of His will, and later writes His Ten Commandments on tablets of stone, directing Moses to place them inside His ark of the covenant (His throne in the tabernacle), *under* the mercy seat. This placement indicated two things: His Ten Commandments are the foundation of His government, and His redeeming mercy always supersedes His righteous judgment to destroy sin.

Let's see how the record of Genesis shows us that these same Ten Commandments were in place from Creation as God's moral code of love.

God clearly commanded loyalty to Him as the one true God. His covenant people were to demonstrate loyalty by not turning to pagan gods. We have reviewed many stories of His people in Genesis showing reverence for God alone, building Him altars to sacrifice spotless lambs which symbolically represented the coming Messiah—the Lamb of God who was slain from the foundation of the world (Revelation 13:8). Jacob knew this code of loyalty: "Jacob said to his household and to all who were with him, 'Put away the foreign gods that are among you, purify yourselves, and change your garments'" (Genesis 35:2). He wanted his household cleansed of defilement and consecrated to the Lord alone. This evidences that the patriarchs knew the *first of God's Ten Commandments:* "You shall have no other gods before Me" (Exodus 20:3).

Did God prohibit the worship of images? Pagans bowed down before their household gods—carved images thought to bring fertility or other blessings—and carried small figurines of mini-gods as protective charms. But God's people knew better. In an effort to erase all idolatry, Jacob commanded both men and women who had departed from Haran with him to surrender the strange gods they had carried with them, as well as the earrings they wore as charms against evil, and he buried these idolatrous items under an oak tree near Shechem (Genesis 35:4). The patriarchs knew the *second of God's Ten Commandments*: "You shall not make for yourself a carved image . . . . you shall not bow down to them nor serve them" (Exodus 20:4–5).

God expected His people to treat His name with respect and reverence. The ancient covenant people reverently called on the name of the Lord from the time of godly Seth forward (Genesis 4:26). Knowing His loving provision for His own people, but His fierce anger against sin, the patriarchs had great respect for the name of the Lord—the God of Abraham, Isaac, and Jacob—demonstrating they understood the *third of God's Ten Commandments*: "You shall not take the name of the Lord your God in vain" (Exodus 20:7).

God initiated the seventh-day rest at Creation as a special time of *sanctification* and *relationship*. It is the only day of the week that God blessed and set apart from the other six days (Genesis 2:1–3). Don't you think God expected continued observance of this special day? Moses' distilled account of 2,300 years in Genesis does not mention it again, but it is implied. In the story of the Exodus that we will consider in our next chapter, Moses clearly records the truth of God's expectation of continued observance of His Sabbath day.

Well before the Hebrews reached Mount Sinai, where God reminded them of His Ten Commandments and delivered them written by

His own finger in stone, the Lord ordered preparation for the Sabbath day (Exodus 16:22–26). We have every reason to believe His covenant-keeping patriarchs kept the seventh day in a special manner, and understood the *fourth of God's Ten Commandments*: "Remember the Sabbath day, to keep it holy. Six days you shall labor and do all your work, but the seventh day is the Sabbath of the Lord you God. In it you shall do no work" (Exodus 20:8–10).

God's moral code of love included showing respect for parental authority, which is seen throughout the history of Genesis. Covenant-keeping sons of the patriarchs recognized the authority of their fathers over the clan, and respected both their fathers' and mothers' instructions. As Jacob mourned the false news of Joseph's death, "all his sons and all his daughters arose to comfort him" (Genesis 37:35). Shem and Japheth honored Noah, whereas Noah pronounced a curse on Ham's son Canaan for dishonoring him (Genesis 9:22–27). The patriarchs understood the *fifth of God's Ten Commandments*: "Honor your father and mother" (Exodus 20:12).

You know that God expected His people to respect human life. He punished Cain for murdering Abel (Genesis 4:8–13). He soon intensified His instructions on the matter, revealing that blood symbolically represented life. He prohibited human consumption of animal blood, and established the death penalty for any animal or man who unlawfully took human life, because humans were made in His image (Genesis 9:4–6). The patriarchs definitely knew the *sixth of God's Ten Commandments*: "You shall not murder" (Exodus 20:13).

Do you believe God cared about the purity of sexual relationships? He judged wicked Sodom and Gomorrah, destroying those cities since they had "given themselves over to sexual immorality" (Jude 1:7; compare Genesis 18:20; 19:4–5, 24; Ezekiel 16:49–50). When Potiphar's wife tried to seduce Joseph into an adulterous affair, the handsome young steward revealed his moral character. Joseph said, "You are his wife. How then can I do this great wickedness, and sin against God?" (Genesis 39:9). There's no question the patriarchs understood the *seventh of God's Ten Commandments*: "You shall not commit adultery" (Exodus 20:14).

God placed protective boundaries on personal property, and taught His covenant people it was wrong to steal. Jacob did not realize his wife

Rachel had stolen her father's carved pagan gods as they left Haran. When Laban caught up to them and confronted Jacob about this theft, Jacob innocently reacted, saying, "With whomever you find your gods, do not let him live. In the presence of our brethren, identify what I have of yours and take it with you" (Genesis 31:32).

When Joseph was governor of Egypt and his brothers bowed before him, he sought to create a valid reason to keep his brother Benjamin with him. Secretly hiding his special cup in Benjamin's sack as all the brothers prepared to return to Canaan, Joseph sent his steward to catch up with them and accuse them of theft. Their horrified response reveals they associated stealing with a sin deserving of death (Genesis 44:4, 6–10). No question about it, the patriarchs understood the *eighth of the Lord's Ten Commandments*: "You shall not steal" (Exodus 20:15).

We can be certain the Lord's moral code of love included truthfulness. God, who cannot lie, hates lying. As Jesus said, Satan is the "father of lies" (John 8:44). The first lie recorded on planet Earth happened in the Garden of Eden when Satan told Eve, "You will not surely die" (Genesis 3:4). That lie sent the human race into a tailspin. The story of Jacob's deceit to gain the clan firstborn blessings demonstrates lying and deceit were known to be evil (Genesis 27). The patriarchs were aware of the *ninth of the Lord's Ten Commandments*: "You shall not bear false witness" (Exodus 20:16).

God knew how important contentment is to the human psyche, and recognized that the act of coveting would entrap people in greater sin. The most striking example is poor Eve, who coveted the forbidden fruit and false wisdom it offered (Genesis 3:6). Seduced by Satan, she fell into the greater sin that contributed to the first couple's expulsion from the Garden of Eden. Her son Cain copied her sin of covetousness. Cain coveted the favor his brother received and murdered his own flesh and blood (Genesis 4:3–5). Knowing this history, surely the patriarchs understood the *tenth of God's Ten Commandments*: "You shall not covet" (Exodus 20:17).

God's Ten Commandments are the reflection of His righteous character, and have always been His Sovereign will for His everlasting covenant people and His government of love. They serve as His foundational Charter of Rights—boundaries of love, specifying His rights as the Sovereign Creator and the rights of humanity. He imprinted His Ten Commandment law of love in the hearts of His people during the age of Genesis, and He still imprints them on the hearts of His people today (Hebrews 8:10–12).

RIGHTEOUSNESS WILL REIGN FOREVER

The original Hebrew language describes the Ten Commandments as ten *words* or ten *instructions*. These words are a transcript of God's righteous character, and are actually ten promises of what the Lord will achieve in our hearts as we submit to Him.

God has a plan to make His people righteous by their faith in Him. This isn't a mystical event—it affects real change in the hearts of believers as the Holy Spirit works to conform them to the image of Christ. It produces the mind of Christ, who opens our understanding to God's revealed will; and the humble attitude of the Person of Jesus, who submitted to God's will (1 Corinthians 2:16; Philippians 2:5).

It was the Lord's pleasure for His righteousness' sake [in accordance with a steadfast and consistent purpose] to magnify instruction and revelation and glorify them (Isaiah 42:21, AMP).

Jesus came to magnify the Lord's instruction, and so He did. In His Sermon on the Mount, He magnified the Ten Commandments, equating anger and hate with the spirit of murder, and lust with the spirit of adultery (Matthew 5:21–22, 27–28). He did not abolish the Ten Commandments written by God's own finger. In fact, He died to pay the penalty for our breaking of that moral law of love. Reflect on this thought for a moment—if God had planned from the beginning to abolish the Ten Commandments, Jesus died in vain to pay our penalty for breaking them.

Our Creator God came, as Paul explained, "in the likeness of sinful flesh, on account of sin: He condemned sin in the flesh, that the righteous requirement of the law might be fulfilled in us who do not walk according to the flesh but according to the Spirit" (Romans 8:3–4). Coming as a sin offering to condemn sin—not sinners—Jesus' purpose was to "destroy the works of the devil" (1 John 3:8), and abolish the power of sin over His covenant people, so that the righteous requirement of His law of love might be fulfilled in us as we are empowered by the Holy Spirit.

God expects His people to live a life of righteousness by faith, "that the life of Jesus also may be manifested in our mortal flesh" (2 Corinthians 4:11). His perfect moral life proved God's Ten Commandment Law is just. Our destiny is to become like Jesus (Romans 8:29).

Our hearts should overflow with love for our wonderful Benefactor, and surge with loyalty for the One who loves us and gave Himself for us. Love should motivate us to obey Him as our Lord, and walk in harmony with His requirement of righteousness, by which He will reign forever.

When we enter into the experience of His everlasting covenant and walk according to the Spirit, there is no condemnation for those who are "in Christ Jesus" (Romans 8:1). He frees us from the *penalty* and *power* of sin, making us *righteous by faith*, and reconciling our relationship with Him.

SUMMARY OF "HIS" STORY
Chapter Eight

- Trying to earn salvation is legalism. Legalism is the classic earmark of all false religions.
- Obedience expresses love for God, and is the highest form of worship.
- God's *nature* is unselfish love; God's *character* is righteous—He is morally perfect.
- God governs by the power of love and righteousness. Moral excellence guides all of His interactions with humanity for our eternal benefit.
- All sin is unrighteousness that renounces the holy character of God, and is intolerable to Him.
- *Righteousness by faith* is the only righteousness that exists for humanity.
- *Righteousness by faith* is a relational covenant term—describing how God relates to His people and how His covenant people relate to Him.

- *Righteousness by faith* is defined as two aspects—justification (an *act* of God that delivers us from the *penalty* of sin) and sanctification (a *work* of God that delivers us from the *power* of sin).

- Glorification will be the final aspect of salvation, at Christ's Second Coming, when He calls His people forth from the grave and clothes them with immortality.

- The Bible tells us only God is immortal at this time.

- Mortal humans have one of two choices: believe in Him and inherit everlasting life, or don't believe and perish (because they don't inherit everlasting life).

- The pagan philosophy of immortal souls, promoted by Socrates and Plato, was adopted by Tertullian of Tunisia, who later converted to Christianity.

- Tertullian introduced to Christianity the fatally-flawed concept of the immortal soul and unceasing torment in hellfire.

- Everlasting, eternal, and forever, are relative terms. Their meaning is derived from the nature of the subject they describe.

- God's nature is immortal. When *everlasting*, *eternal*, and *forever* are related to God as their subject, these words reflect His infinite existence.

- When *everlasting*, *eternal*, and *forever* are related to *mortal beings* or *perishable things* as their subject, these words reflect their temporary nature and simply mean *as long as the person or thing exists.*

- Sodom and Gomorrah were set forth as an example of "suffering the vengeance of eternal fire." The fire completed its work. They no longer burn.

- When mortal beings experience the *eternal* and *unquenchable fire* of hell, that fire will not be quenched until it finishes its work and they perish—eternally.

- "Gnashing of teeth" is an expression of anger and frustration, not physical anguish.

- The final judgment of hellfire will burn up mortal souls—they will perish and vanish.

- God takes no pleasure in the death of the wicked. His day of disaster will be His unusual, "strange act" to quench sin forever.

- Revelation describes the final punishment as the "second death."

- Jesus tasted the second death for us, but victoriously arose.

- The Holy Spirit worked in the hearts of God's ancient covenant people in Genesis.

- The record of Genesis demonstrates that God's people knew—and lived by—His Ten Commandments, which are the foundational principles of His government of love.
- Christ died to pay humanity's penalty for breaking God's moral law of love—the Ten Commandments. He did not abolish them.
- God's plan is to make His covenant people righteous—empowering their loving obedience.
- His righteousness will reign throughout eternity.

THE LORD HEARS—THE LORD REMEMBERS

Chapter Nine

He was a special baby, and she knew it. Could he be the one? Jochebed had heard the stories of God ratifying the covenant with Abraham and warning him that the Hebrews would be enslaved 400 years—a timeframe that was almost fulfilled (Genesis 15:13–14). All of Israel expected a soon-coming deliverer to rescue them from their descent into slavery. Could this child be that deliverer?

Stories of the covenant-keeping God had been handed down by oral tradition for over 2,500 years. From childhood Jochebed had known that generations earlier a Pharaoh had appointed Joseph as Egypt's governor, and served as a welcoming and gracious host to Israel's immigrating clan, granting them the land of Goshen. Their settlement started peacefully. Jacob and Joseph lived good lives in Egypt, though not all welcomed the presence of their family. Foreigners and shepherds were an abomination to Egyptians (Genesis 43:32, 46:34). Israel's clan was both, and felt the sting of social isolation from the general population. Did Jochebed realize this barrier of discrimination served God's purpose of preventing intermarriage with native pagans to protect the Hebrews' identity as His people?

"Israel" was the covenant name the Lord gave Jacob after their all-night wrestling match (Genesis 32:28). Years later, God appeared to Israel in vision, directing him to take his household down to Egypt, promising He would go with them and make them a great nation there (Genesis 46:2–5). Arriving in Goshen, the clan totaled 75 persons (Genesis 46:27; Acts 7:1–14).

One thing is for certain—God keeps covenant with those who keep covenant with Him, and walk before Him in loving obedience to His commandments (Nehemiah 1:5; Deuteronomy 7:9, 8:18; 1 Kings 8:23; Daniel 9:4). He promised the patriarchs their seed would multiply greatly (Genesis 15:5; 26:4; 28:14). Seventy Hebrews went down to Egypt, and they flourished there.

At the time of their departure, Moses records the rounded number of 600,000 men, and later in the wilderness tallies the census of men twenty years or older at 603,550 (Exodus 12:37; Numbers 1:44–46). If we consider women and children, the staggering implication is that the Israelite population had reached over two million people. Although this is a matter of debate, historical records indicate Egypt's total population at the time to have been four million, and the Pharaoh is quoted in Scripture as saying, "Look, the people of the children of Israel are more and mightier than we" (Exodus 1:9).

Pharaoh was alarmed that the Israelites outnumbered the Egyptians. This new king hadn't known Joseph, and he became paranoid at the thought that these Hebrews might join forces with invading nations in an effort to overthrow his government. To thwart that possibility, Pharaoh enslaved them. Under the whips of slave-drivers, by day they groaned as they built the Pharaohs' supply cities with brick and mortar. Expecting God to perform another miracle for His people, by night they moaned in prayer for the deliverer to arrive. Yet the more the Pharaohs afflicted them, the more they multiplied. Nothing humans do can thwart the plans of Almighty God.

As we follow the story of the seed with an infinity focus, we expect Satan to do all within his power to try to annihilate the coming Seed—the Messiah-Christ whom God had prophesied would crush his head under his feet (Genesis 3:15; Romans 16:20). Now, "that serpent of old, called the Devil and Satan, who deceives the whole world" (Revelation 12:9) surely wondered if this was the time that God would send His Deliverer. Satan inflamed the heart of the reigning Pharaoh to order that all male Hebrew babies be thrown into the Nile River and drowned (Exodus 1:22). The king was desperate to control their burgeoning population.

Jochebed prayed. Prompted by faith, she concealed her baby boy for three months (Exodus 2:2; Hebrews 11:23), endangering the lives of her family—including a three-year old son named Aaron, and his older sister Miriam. When the peril could no longer be risked, she constructed a small waterproof ark, wrapped her baby in a blanket, set him adrift in the Nile, and instructed Miriam to follow along the river bank with a watchful eye to see the outcome of his rescue (Exodus 2:4). This was not the first time God used an ark to save His covenant seed.

Bathing in the Nile that day, Pharaoh's daughter was led by God to the location where the ark had lodged among the reeds. Seeing the basket, the princess sent her handmaiden to bring it to her. She opened the lid and recognized that it was a Hebrew baby that her father had ordered to be destroyed, but her heart welled with pity and maternal desire when he cried. She wanted him for her son, and suddenly faced a dilemma. How would she feed this baby?

Quick-thinking Miriam ran to her, saying she knew of a wet nurse, but not revealing the woman was the baby's mother. Pharaoh's daughter agreed to pay wages to the woman, establishing proof the princess had rightful claim over the boy as her adopted son (Exodus 2:9). In His providential working, the Lord ensured Jochebed would raise her own son for many years. The child grew, and his Levite parents obviously instructed him in the way he should go.

Eventually the young lad was delivered to the princess, and she named him Moses— meaning "drawn" [from the water]. Living as a prince, Moses was educated in all the wisdom of the Egyptians—math, sciences, and the recently formalized language art of reading and writing. The New Testament tells us that Moses was "mighty in words and deed" (Acts 7:22), but the trappings of wealth and pomp left him discontented. Our Creator has put eternity in each human heart, and nothing but a restored relationship with Him can fill the void and make sense of our lives (Ecclesiastes 3:11). Nothing can bring true satisfaction except the hope of eternal life which God promised before time began (Titus 1:2). The New Testament Hall of Faith says of Moses—

> By faith Moses, when he became of age, refused to be called the son of Pharaoh's daughter, choosing rather to suffer affliction with the people of God than to enjoy the passing pleasures of sin, esteeming the reproach of Christ greater riches than the treasures in Egypt; for he looked to the reward. By faith he forsook Egypt, not fearing the wrath of the king; for he endured as seeing Him who is invisible (Hebrews 11:24–27).

One day Moses went to observe the Israelites and saw an Egyptian beating one of his people without mercy. Looking around and not seeing any witnesses, Moses killed the Egyptian and buried him in the sand. The next day, he returned for a visit and saw two fellow Hebrews fighting. Dismayed, he intervened. The man who had started the fight sneered, "Who made you a prince and a judge over us? Do you intend to kill me as you killed the Egyptian?" Shocked, Moses realized that people knew what he'd done (Exodus 2:14). The story reached Pharaoh, who sought to kill him, but Moses fled to the desert in the land of Midian, at the age of 40 (v. 15; Acts 7:23), where he married the daughter of a local priest, and had two sons.

Moses did not write the Book of Exodus as a biography, but as an historical account of the covenant-making, covenant-keeping God of Abraham, Isaac, and Jacob. So we will pick up our journey with God's actions to fulfill His everlasting covenant.

GOD REMEMBERS HIS COVENANT WITH ABRAHAM, ISAAC, AND JACOB

> Now it happened in the process of time that the king of Egypt died. Then the children of Israel groaned because of the bondage, and they cried out; and their cry came up to God because of the bondage. So God heard their groaning,

and God remembered His covenant with Abraham, with Isaac, and with Jacob. And God looked upon the children of Israel, and God acknowledged them (Exodus 2:23–25).

The up-close-and-personal God *heard*. God *remembered*. Do you think an all-knowing God forgets things and needs to be reminded? No. When Scripture says God *forgets* a matter, it means He takes no action on it. Conversely, when Scripture says God *remembers* a matter, it means He is ready to act. God *looked upon* them. God *acknowledged* their situation. The rest of the book of Exodus records God's continued actions to fulfill the same everlasting covenant of *righteousness by faith* He made with Abraham, Isaac, and Jacob.

Moses had been on the back side of the desert tending sheep for 40 years when something spectacular suddenly happened—"the Angel of the LORD appeared to him in a flame of fire from the midst of a bush" at Horeb, the mountain of God. Seeing that the bush was not being consumed, Moses approached to examine the strange phenomenon. The Angel of the Lord—the Lord Himself serving as the Messenger—suddenly spoke to him.

And the Angel of the LORD appeared to him in a flame of fire from the midst of a bush . . . So when the LORD saw that he turned aside to look, God called to him from the midst of the bush and said, "Moses, Moses!" And he said, "Here I am." Then He said, "Do not draw near this place. Take your sandals off your feet, for the place where you stand is holy ground." Moreover He said, "I am the God of your father—the God of Abraham, the God of Isaac, and the God of Jacob." And Moses hid his face, for he was afraid to look upon God (Exodus 3:2, 4–6).

The Lord explained that He had seen the oppression of the Egyptian taskmasters, and knew the sorrow of His people. He planned to rescue them and bring them to "a land flowing with milk and honey," telling Moses to go as His representative before the people and Pharaoh. Moses balked and used the empty argument of "Who am I?" to accomplish such a task (Exodus 3:11). Though the One who was sending him promised to be with him, Moses persisted to resist, claiming he wouldn't know what to say if people asked God's name.

> And God said to Moses, "I AM WHO I AM." And He said, "Thus you shall say to the children of Israel, 'I AM has sent me to you.'" Moreover God said to Moses, "Thus you shall say to the children of Israel: 'The LORD God of your fathers, the God of Abraham, the God of Isaac, and the God of Jacob, has sent me to you. This is My name forever, and this is My memorial to all generations'" (Exodus 3:14–15).

I AM—the self-existent, eternal God who *is* and *will be*—promised that the people would heed Moses' voice, declared He would stretch out His hand with mighty wonders, and assured him that Pharaoh would release the Israelites from bondage. God further confirmed His promise, made centuries earlier to Abraham, that the people would not leave the country empty-handed, but would come out with great possessions (Exodus 3:18–22; Genesis 15:14). Through continued reassurances, the Lord tried to persuade a reluctant Moses that He would be with him, but Moses feared for his life and had no desire to return to Egypt.

So Moses said, "O my Lord, I am not eloquent, neither before nor since You have spoken to Your servant; but I am slow of speech and slow of tongue" (Exodus 4:10). This claim was a flimsy excuse of false modesty, to which Moses added a request that the Lord send someone else. This angered God. God agreed to send Aaron with him, saying in a seemingly sarcastic response, "I know that he can speak well." Further assuring Moses that all the men who sought his life forty years earlier were now dead, the Lord sent him on his way to Egypt (Exodus 4:10–14, 19). "Then Moses took his wife and his sons and set them on a donkey, and he returned to the land of Egypt. And Moses took the rod of God in his hand" (Exodus 4:20).

God told Moses to make this formal declaration to Pharaoh, and it is an amazing covenant declaration—

Then you shall say to Pharaoh, 'Thus says the LORD: "Israel is My son, My firstborn. So I say to you, let My son go that he may serve Me . . ."' (Exodus 4:22–23).

Do you recognize the covenant language here? The Lord called Israel His *firstborn*. *Firstborn* in covenant language refers to a *position of preeminence*. Israel was not the first nation, but the Lord designated the whole nation as *His firstborn* son of the everlasting covenant, ranking them first in covenant relationship as the preeminent son of God.

Look at Moses' words to the nation of Israel 40 years later: "Of the Rock who begot you, you are unmindful, and have forgotten the God who fathered you" (Deuteronomy 32:18). *Begotten means chosen for a covenant purpose*, just as Isaac was called Abraham's "only begotten son" (Hebrews 11:17)—meaning *a unique, one-of-a-kind son of promise* who is the rightful heir to the covenant blessings. Moses declared that the Lord was the Father of Israel, and had chosen them for His covenant purposes.

"God remembered His covenant with Abraham, with Isaac, and with Jacob" (Exodus 2:24). In His perfect timing, the Lord was ready to bring His people out of the darkness of their bondage and into His marvelous light.

"Therefore say to the children of Israel: 'I am the LORD; **I will** bring you out from under the burdens of the Egyptians, **I will** rescue you from their bondage, and **I will** redeem you with an outstretched arm and with great judgments. **I will take** you as My people, and **I will** be your God. Then you shall know that I am the LORD your God who brings you out from under the burdens of the Egyptians. And **I will** bring you into the land which I swore to give to Abraham, Isaac, and Jacob; and **I will** give it to you as a heritage: I am the LORD'" (Exodus 6:6–8; emphasis added).

God's seven "I will" statements—His covenant language of promise—signified that God was about to reveal Himself more fully than ever before. The Israelites would know Him intimately by His covenant name, the LORD Jehovah ("Yahweh" in Hebrew).

PLAGUES, PASSOVER, AND PASSING THROUGH THE WATER

Moses was 80 years old, and his brother Aaron was 83, when they stood before the new Pharaoh (Exodus 7:7). From that point forward, they delivered the Lord's repeated demand of Pharaoh: "Let My people go" (vv. 16; 8:1, 20; 9:1, 13; 10:3).

From Exodus 7:14 through 11:10, the Lord performed great signs and wonders, and delivered three groups of three plagues each—the first three falling on Egypt and Israel alike, the next six falling on Egypt alone—foretelling the timing and severity through Aaron and Moses. During these nine plagues, Pharaoh vacillated from time to time, but continued to harden his heart against the Lord. God's two Levite representatives warned the prideful king that the tenth plague would kill all the firstborn (oldest) of the land—animals and children, including the Pharaoh's own son. Though he had seen clear evidences of the Lord's power, Pharaoh scoffed at the idea and rejected the warning, clinging to his notion of the power of pagan gods.

The tenth plague was to be a direct and devastating visitation from God. To protect the Israelites, the Lord instituted a Passover ceremony. For seven days prior to the Passover meal, no leaven was to found in their homes. God required each household to select a spotless male lamb as a sacrifice, and to personally apply the blood of the Passover lamb—smearing it on the doorposts of their homes—to be spared according to His promise, "And when I see the blood, I will pass over you; and the plague shall not be on you to destroy you when I strike the land of Egypt" (Exodus 12:13). To eat the Passover meal of the roasted sacrifice, unleavened bread, and bitter herbs, they were to be fully dressed and ready to go, eating in haste.

The rich symbolism of the Passover pointed to Christ's ministry of atonement for humanity's sins. Since leaven represented sin, the unleavened bread symbolized Jesus' sinless life. Bitter herbs symbolized His suffering. The Apostle Paul identifies Christ as our one true *Passover Lamb*, saying, "For indeed Christ, our Passover, was sacrificed for us" (1 Corinthians 5:7). His sacrifice—typified in the Passover lamb—is of no value to us unless we personally accept Him as Savior and Lord, having His blood applied to our account.

Following the tenth plague, the Egyptians feared for their lives, and begged Israel to leave. Moses directed the children of Israel to ask for silver, gold, and clothing, and the fearful Egyptians were all too eager to comply. The Lord gave Israel favor to plunder the Egyptians, but having no time to make provisions for their hasty departure, they merely took their unleavened dough, bound in their kneading bowls with cloth.

The Lord intended to prove to the Egyptians that He alone was God, and purposed to accomplish the destruction of Pharaoh, his army, and his weapons of war. Maneuvering the Hebrews' exodus in a clever manner, the Lord led Moses to change directions after their departure. Israel became seemingly trapped—closed in by the Red Sea—setting the stage for a final confrontation with Pharaoh.

The ever-vacillating king lamented freeing his talented workforce and losing the riches of Egypt. He heard the report of their wandering, and—thinking Israel was bewildered and lost—he disregarded God's manifested power, deciding to pursue Israel (Exodus 14:1–9). When the Israelites saw the menacing threat of his approaching chariots, they cried out in fear, bemoaning their decision to follow Moses—

> And Moses said to the people, "Do not be afraid. Stand still, and see the salvation of the LORD, which He will accomplish for you today. For the Egyptians whom you see today, you shall see again no more forever. The LORD will fight for you, and you shall hold your peace" (Exodus 14:13–14).

Instructing Moses to stretch forth his shepherd's staff over the sea, the Lord sent a strong east wind all that night to divide the water, and dry the sea bed (v. 21). Israel passed through the midst of the sea on dry ground, with walls of water to their right and left (Psalm 78:13). The Angel of God—the Lord Himself in a pillar of cloud, and a pillar of fire—went before them as their advance guard, and stood behind them as their rear guard (Exodus 14:19, 24).

The Lord looked down upon the pursuing army, and clogged their chariot wheels, slowing their advance. Disheartened and ready to turn back, Pharaoh's army recognized the Lord was fighting for Israel (v. 25), yet at the king's command they marched onto the dry sea bed. Moses watched their procession, then stretched out his staff again at God's direction. The Lord caused the walls of water to collapse, and the churning sea returned to its full depth and "covered the chariots, the horsemen, and all the army of Pharaoh that came into the sea after them. Not so much as one of them remained" (Exodus 14:28). That day the Lord fulfilled His "I will" covenant promises to save Israel from bondage.

As the Israelites looked upon the dead Egyptians scattered along the seashore, they marveled at the Lord's demonstration of power, and feared Him and His servant Moses (vv. 30–31). In praise to the Lord, the people sang, "The LORD is my strength and song, and He has become my salvation; He is my God, and I will praise Him; my father's God, and I will exalt Him" (Exodus 15:2). Yet their burst of praise was soon forgotten. The miracle God performed at the Red Sea made no lasting impact on their attitude toward Him.

THE LORD SAVED THEM—THEN HE SOUGHT OBEDIENCE

It took three months for the multitude of people with all their plunder to reach Mount Sinai. Scripture records four stops—four encampments—along the way. A distinct pattern of their unbelief and total disregard for God's saving grace emerges.

Three days into their journey they arrived at Marah. The people complained against Moses because the water they found there was bitter. Moses cried to the Lord, and God graciously healed the water (Exodus 15:22–25). The Lord established a statute and an ordinance to test their character—

If you diligently heed the voice of the LORD your God and do what is right in His sight, give ear to His commandments and keep all His statutes, I will put none of the diseases on you which I have brought on the Egyptians. For I am the LORD who heals you (Exodus 15:26).

Continuing onward, they camped at Elim, before advancing on the thirtieth day of their journey to a desert area named the Wilderness of Sin (Exodus 16:1), camping somewhere between Elim and Mount Sinai. Showing no respect for God's gracious redemption, the people whined about their lack of provisions and sarcastically claimed it would had been better if God had killed them in Egypt, where they at least had plenty to eat.

Once again, God graciously responded to their grumbling, directing quail to them and raining down a honey-like wafer bread from heaven. Looking at the bread, the people asked, "What is it?"—which is the meaning of the word *manna*, as it came to be known. God instructed a daily quota of manna be gathered according to their actual individual need, advising that any excess would simply spoil by the next day. However, on Friday—the day before the Lord's Day—they were to gather twice their quota, which God promised would not spoil. This allowed for His prescribed Sabbath rest—

Then the LORD said to Moses, "Behold, I will rain bread from heaven for you. And the people shall go out and gather a certain quota every day, that I may test them, whether they will walk in My law or not" (Exodus 16:4).

The oppressive Pharaohs had not allowed the people days off to rest and worship, so they were not in the habit of observing the Sabbath. The Lord intended to test them to see if—now that they had opportunity—they would obey His commandment. This indicates He had expected continued Sabbath observance since Creation. Moses reinforced God's instruction, saying—

"This is what the LORD has said: 'Tomorrow is a Sabbath rest, a holy Sabbath to the LORD. Bake what you will bake today, and boil what you will boil; and lay up for yourselves all that remains, to be kept until morning'" (Exodus 16:23).

When some of the people went out on the Sabbath to collect manna, their disobedience displeased the Lord, causing His rebuke—

How long do you refuse to keep My commandments and My laws? See! For the LORD has given you the Sabbath; therefore He gives you on the sixth day bread for two days. Let every man remain in his place; let no man go out of his place on the seventh day. So the people rested on the seventh day (Exodus 16:28–30).

Moses led the people onward to Rephidim (Moses later named the location "Massah" and "Meribah")—where they found no water. Becoming hostile, the people rose up against him, saying he had brought them out of Egypt to kill them by thirst. The Lord's patient and loving concern, demonstrated through miracle after miracle, had achieved little effect on their hard-hearted disobedience. Moses feared they would stone him (Exodus 17:1–4).

Moses cried out again to God. The once reluctant prophet, who had claimed with false modesty that he wasn't an eloquent speaker, had developed the true humility of depending totally on the Lord. The Lord responded, promising Moses that He would stand before him "on the rock in Horeb" (Exodus 17:6)—he was back where he had seen the burning bush! Now the Lord instructed him to take his staff and strike the rock. In full confidence of faith, Moses struck the rock in the view of all the people, and the Lord brought gushing water forth to prove His covenant presence and provision was among them (vv. 5–7).

Moses later referred to the Lord as "the Rock" (Deuteronomy 32:4, 15, 18, 30). Paul echoes the declaration that the rock symbolized the Messiah-Christ: "For they drank of that spiritual Rock that followed them, and that Rock was Christ" (1 Corinthians 10:4).

The Amelekites—a brutal tribe of nomadic raiders—came out to attack Israel's encampment at Rephidim (Exodus 17:8). As the battle raged, Moses stood at the top of a hill with his staff lifted before God. As long as Moses held the rod high, the Israelite army, led by Joshua, prevailed in battle, but soon he could not help but lower his weary arms. Each time he did, the Amelekites began winning. Moses' brother Aaron and Hur, the son of Caleb, finally steadied his arms, one man holding up his left hand and the other his right. Joshua and the Israelites won the battle by Moses' effort combined with the Lord's power (vv. 8–13).

The location of Rephidim is unknown, but Scripture places this campsite on Mount Horeb, where the Lord appeared in the burning bush. It was not more than a day's march from Mount Sinai, where God planned to appear to the whole nation of Israel.

Midian was nearby. Moses had sent his wife Zipporah and two sons there to his father-in-law Jethro. Now Jethro came out to the wilderness camp to return the family to Moses (Exodus 18:1–5). The next day he watched his overwhelmed son-in-law listen as the Israelites brought him their various problems to solve, from morning to night.

Moses judged the people's cases, making known "the statutes of God and His laws" (v. 16). What laws of God were in place at this time? These were the same commandments, statutes, and laws of the Lord followed by Abraham and the patriarchs (Genesis 26:5).

Jethro recommended that Moses choose God-fearing men of good character to hold various positions of authority to hear these cases. Moses heeded Jethro's counsel, appointing able men who judged the people at all times, bringing only the difficult cases to him (Exodus 18:17–27).

In the third month, they departed Rephidim and arrived to camp at Mount Sinai, where God would become their King (Exodus 19:1–2).

GOD SPEAKS THE CHARTER OF RIGHTS FOR HIS GOVERNMENT OF LOVE

Moses went up Mount Sinai, and the Lord directed him to deliver these words to Israel—

"'You have seen what I did to the Egyptians, and how I bore you on eagles' wings and brought you to Myself. Now therefore, if you will indeed obey My voice and keep My covenant, then you shall be a special treasure to Me above all people; for all the earth is Mine. And you shall be to Me a kingdom of priests and a holy nation.' These are the words which you shall speak to the children of Israel" (Exodus 19:4–6).

What covenant was in place when God spoke these words? Only one—the everlasting covenant of *righteousness by faith*—by which

Moses and the elders judged the people's cases according to His commandments. God wanted Israel to rely on His Holy Spirit and obey, like His people had done from the beginning. Calling all the people to serve as priests—as He does today (1 Peter 2:9–10)—He desired that they live separated from sin to rightly represent Him on earth.

"I bore you on eagle's wings and brought you to Myself" is covenant love language. The Lord—their Father God—had protected them, and was attempting to teach them to fly. Many years later, when the second generation of Israel reached the edge of the Promised Land, Moses repeated this metaphor: "As an eagle stirs up its nest, hovers over its young, spreading out its wings, taking them up, carrying them on its wings, so the LORD alone led him"—*him* being His covenant son, the nation of Israel (Deuteronomy 32:11–12).

Calling all the people together, Moses relayed God's words, and they collectively responded, "All that the LORD has spoken we will do" (Exodus 19:7–8). The Lord told Moses that He would come in a cloud to speak with him audibly, and the whole nation would hear and believe forever that Moses was His true representative (Exodus 19:9).

Because centuries of slavery under Egypt's pagan influence had shrouded their appreciation of the Lord's holiness and requirements of righteousness, God required strict preparation. God directed that all first consecrate themselves for inward cleansing, and wash their clothes for outward cleansing. The Lord announced that He would summon the people by the sound of a ram's horn in three days, and told Moses to warn that anyone who approached and touched the mountain would die (vv. 9–13).

On the morning of the third day, the Lord came down in His majestic glory. A thick cloud of smoke covered the mountain, accompanied by a powerful fireworks display of thunder and lightning. The ram's horn blasted loud and long. The earth quaked and the people trembled, afraid they would die if God spoke to them. Moses assured them, "Do not fear; for God has come to test you, and that His fear may be before you, so that you may not sin" (Exodus 20:20). The Lord desired to impress awe and respect for Him upon their hearts to deter them from transgressing His divine moral code of love. They had yet to learn how to recognize and follow His gentle leading.

Moses spoke, and the Lord responded in His majestic audible voice (Exodus 19:16–19). The trembling people stood afar off. Moses pressed into God's presence in the cloud. God spoke audibly to the people His Ten Commandments to remind them of His expectations of reciprocal love to Him, and morality and love toward humanity.

In the original Hebrew, God's instructions are literally called *Ten Sayings*. Likewise, the Greek translates them as the *Decalogue*, meaning *Ten Words*. Because the Lord spoke in the imperative—implying He expected a ready response of action—English translators called them the *Ten Commandments*. In our last chapter, we clearly saw these obligations of love for God and fellow human beings were imprinted on the hearts of the patriarchs of Genesis. They were not new to God's people.

Now, the Lord simply repeated His known Charter of Rights for His government of love within the context of His everlasting covenant. God began to speak these words of instruction—the *Ten Commandments*—by identifying Himself as the people's Savior, saying, "I am the LORD your God, who brought you out of the land of Egypt, out of the house of bondage" (Exodus 20:1–2). In other words, *I redeemed you by grace, now listen to Me.*

God's words found in Exodus 20:3–17—the Ten Commandments— don't apply an "if . . . then" construction, where an offense is followed by a penalty. They are merely His expressed boundaries that unite duty and morality.

God's instructions spoken in the negative can be interpreted as, "Living in covenant relationship with Me, you will never have another God above me, bow down to carved images, take My name in vain, murder, commit adultery, steal, lie, or covet." His instructions spoken in the positive can be interpreted as, "Living in covenant relationship with me you will celebrate the Sabbath, enjoying and extending its blessings to others, and you will respectfully honor your parents." That is what living in an everlasting covenant relationship with Him is all about. And that is what He will work in the human heart by His Spirit (Zechariah 4:6; Philippians 2:13).

A point of interest is the fourth commandment regarding the Sabbath. It is the only commandment that begins with the word

"Remember." God's boundaries around His special day of rest included no work for the individual, for servants, for strangers within their gates, or for animals. The Lord explains the day to be a memorial of Him as Creator, reminding the people that He blessed the Sabbath day and made it holy at Creation (Exodus 20:8–11). Soon afterward, He revealed the Sabbath day was the sign that He is the one who sanctifies His people—setting them apart from sin (Exodus 31:13). Years later, Moses repeated God's Ten Commandments to the next generation, noting that the Sabbath also served to remind the Lord's people that He is their Deliverer-Redeemer (Deuteronomy 5:12–15). The Sabbath memorialized Creation, redemption, and sanctification.

God's Ten Commandment law of love clearly reveals the purposes of His everlasting covenant of *righteousness by faith*—He intends to rescue His people from sin and death, renew a right spirit within them, and restore them to moral purity as they live by the power of His love.

In our next chapter, we will see how Scripture defines a body of civil, social, and ceremonial laws that served as the constitution for the new nation of Israel. They were written in a document called the *Book of the Covenant*, a temporary covenant of law that is historically referred to as the *Old Covenant*. For the want of a better word, God "layered" this covenant on top of His everlasting covenant to govern a people who refused to follow the leading of the Holy Spirit. Certainly, the Ten Commandments continued to represent the *Charter of Rights* of God's government, and were at the heart of the historical Old Covenant.

For now, consider that God's *Charter of Rights*—His Ten-Commandment Law of Love—is also the heart of the *New Covenant*—

> For this is the covenant that I will make with the house of Israel after those days, says the LORD: I will put My laws in their mind and write them on their hearts; and I will be their God, and they shall be My people (Hebrews 8:10).

Jesus said, "If you love Me, keep My commandments," adding, to show how love motivates us to obey, "And I will pray the Father, and He will give you another Helper, that He may abide with you forever" (John 14:15–17). Paul assures us that God pours out His divine love into our hearts by the power of the Holy Spirit (Romans 5:5), and "love is the fulfillment of the law" (Romans 13:10).

Paul tells us, "For by grace you have been saved through faith, and that not of yourselves; it is the gift of God, not of works, lest anyone should boast" (Ephesians 2:8–9). *Righteousness by faith* is the only way unholy humanity can acquire right standing before a holy God. God's amazing grace motivates us to walk in obedience by His power. Obedience is not legalism; obedience is love. God gives the Holy Spirit to those who desire to obey Him (Acts 5:32), so that "it is God who works in you both to will and to do for His good pleasure" (Philippians 2:13). God gets all the glory for making us *righteous by faith*.

Cry out to Him now—He hears . . . He remembers!

SUMMARY OF "HIS" STORY
Chapter Nine

- *Israel* was the covenant name God gave to the Patriarch Jacob. His descendants became known as the Israelites. They were Hebrews.
- The household of Jacob/Israel went down to Egypt during a famine, where they were given the land of Goshen. God went with them, and promised to make them a great nation there.
- Seventy clan members arrived in Egypt—the remnant of God's people on Earth.
- God multiplied them over 400 years in Egypt to an implied number of 2,000,000 people.
- Moses spent his early years being trained by his Levite parents, then grew up as the prince of Egypt, but later identified with his fellow Hebrews.
- At 40, Moses fled Egypt to save his life, and spent 40 years on the backside of the desert.
- God heard the groaning of Israel, remembered His covenant with Abraham, Isaac, and Jacob, and planned His action to deliver them.
- Appearing to Moses in a burning bush, the Lord called him to lead His covenant people.

- The Lord called the nation of Israel His firstborn son—and demanded Pharaoh release them. *Firstborn* is covenant language for a *position of preeminence*.

- God was a Father to Israel, and Moses said He had *begotten* them. *Begotten* is covenant language meaning *chosen for a covenant purpose*.

- Before God released His final plague on Egypt, He instituted the Passover, to point to Christ's atoning ministry. After their exodus, the Lord purposely hemmed His people in at the Red Sea to set up a final confrontation with Pharaoh.

- Pharaoh pursued the people, who murmured against God's plan as the king's army approached.

- God parted the Red Sea, and Israel crossed over on dry ground. When Pharaoh tried the same, God closed in the waters, drowning Pharaoh's army.

- Israel praised God as their Savior, but feared Him and Moses. Three days later, Israel arrived at Marah, where they murmured against God—and God healed the bitter water.

- A month into their journey, camped in the Desert of Sin, the Israelites sarcastically mocked God for lack of provision—He sent quail and manna.

- God tested the Israelites to see if they would obey His Sabbath commandment now that they had opportunity. When some didn't, He rebuked them—demonstrating that He had expected continued observance of the Sabbath from Creation.

- Moses led the people onward to Rephidim at Mount Horeb. There was no water, and the nation of Israel reacted faithlessly and with such hostility that Moses feared for his life.

- At Rephidim, the people tempted God again, and He brought water from a rock.

- Jethro visited Moses at Rephidim. Moses listened to his advice, and instituted positions of varying authority for men to judge in Israel, following the commandments and laws of God's everlasting covenant—known and followed by the patriarchal fathers of the Book of Genesis.

- In the third month, the Israelites arrived at Mount Sinai.

- God gave Moses words of covenant love and assurance to deliver to the people.

- When God showed up in His majestic glory, the people were afraid to have Him speak to them.

- God sought to put awe and respect for Him into their hearts.

- God spoke Ten Words of instruction to all the people, explaining His Charter of Rights in His government of love, reminding them of His everlasting covenant.
- These Ten Commandments were not the historical *Old Covenant* of civil, social, and ceremonial laws written in the *Book of the Covenant*, but were at the heart of the covenant and prove to be the foundation of both the Old and New Covenants.
- God expects loving obedience from all of His covenant people.

THE OLD
COVENANT

Chapter Ten

W hat did Jesus say about the writings of Moses? "For if you believed Moses, you would believe Me; for he wrote about Me.
But if you do not believe his writings, how will you believe My words?"
(John 5:46–47). Moses' inspired words in the Book of Exodus reveal a
beautiful picture of the everlasting covenant of *righteousness by faith* in
Christ Jesus that many people have overlooked. Confusion abounds
within Christianity about what transpired at Mount Sinai.

As we journey through the rest of *His Story* in Exodus, we'll see
that God's actions at Mount Sinai did nothing to change His plan of
salvation. First, let's map out the twists and turns that casual Bible
readers often miss.

Expect the Bible's order of Mount Sinai events to be as follows:

1) The Lord *speaks* His Ten Commandments to the whole nation
   of Israel;
2) God speaks *civil, social, and ceremonial laws* to Moses alone as
   the proposed constitution for the new nation of Israel;
3) Moses repeats God's words to the people, and they accept this
   body of law;

4) Moses writes on animal skin or parchment—in his own hand-writing—the document called the *Book of the Covenant*, including in this constitution the Lord's spoken words of the Ten Commandments;

5) Moses reads the *Book of the Covenant* to the people, and the Hebrews once again agree to His form of government;

6) Moses *ratifies* this constitution, and the terms of the *Book of the Covenant* become what is historically referred to as the Old Covenant (the *Book of the Covenant* and the *Old Covenant* are synonymous);

7) The Lord writes His Ten Commandment moral code of love on two stone tablets—with His own finger—on two separate occasions.

8) The people build the tabernacle of God.

In our last chapter we saw that "God remembered His covenant with Abraham, with Isaac, and with Jacob" (Exodus 2:24), and took action to save their descendants from the cruelty of their captors in Egypt. As their loving Redeemer, He patiently endured their doubt and mocking, leading them to Mount Sinai in a pillar of cloud and a pillar of fire. God demonstrated His power and provision through numerous miracles along the way.

The Lord knew that their memory of His holiness and His government of love had been eclipsed by centuries of bondage in a pagan nation. At Mount Sinai He spoke directly to the people to remind them of His Ten Commandments—known to the patriarchs of Genesis—that represented His standard of righteousness and boundaries of love. When Moses recounted this experience in Deuteronomy 5:4, he said that the Lord appeared on the mountain in the midst of a fiery cloud of glory and spoke to the entire nation of His redeemed people "face to face"—an expression that simply means "without a mediator."

Trembling from the sound of His majestic voice and the display of His glory, the fearful people chose not to hear directly from the Lord again, asking instead that Moses serve as their mediator. The people distanced themselves, standing afar off (Exodus 20:19).

MOSES WRITES THE BOOK OF THE COVENANT—
CIVIL/SOCIAL/RELIGIOUS LAWS FROM GOD

Moses pressed in to the Presence of the Lord on the mountain. There the Lord delivered legislation to serve as Israel's constitution under His authority as their Sovereign King. Moses chronicled these terms in Exodus 20:22 to Exodus 23:33, which lists civil, social, and religious ceremonial laws concerning: altars; treatment of servants; violence; animal control; responsibility for property; moral and ceremonial principles; justice for all; a seventh-year rest for the land to lay fallow (with repetition of the law for the weekly seventh-day Sabbath rest for the people); the institution of three annual feasts; and conditions for the Lord's presence to accompany the nation to the Promised Land.

Coming down from the mountain, Moses delivered to the people all that the Lord had spoken regarding the legislation He had put forth, including the severe judgments for breaking these laws. With the emotionally-stirred enthusiasm of crowd mentality, the people said in a collective voice, "All the words which the LORD has said we will do" (Exodus 24:3).

Once they agreed to this body of law, Moses set all the words down in writing, recording them in the *Book of the Covenant*, and rose early to build an altar with twelve pillars—representing the twelve tribes of Israel. He sent young men up to present burnt offerings to the Lord. Catching the sacrificial blood in basins, he sprinkled half of it on the altar (vv. 4–6), then read the *Book of the Covenant*, repeating the Lord's inaugural address as King to all the people.

> Then he took the **Book of the Covenant** and read in the hearing of the people. And they said, "All that the LORD has said we will do, and be obedient." And Moses took the blood, sprinkled it on the people, and said, "This is the blood of the covenant which the LORD has made with you according to all these words" (Exodus 24:7–8; emphasis added).

The New Testament sheds additional light on this scene: "Therefore not even the first [meaning former] covenant was dedicated without blood. For when Moses had spoken every precept to all the people according to the law, he took the blood of calves and goats, with water, scarlet wool, and hyssop, and sprinkled both the book itself and all the people, saying, 'This is the blood of the covenant which God has commanded you'" (Hebrews 9:18–20).

This ceremony at Mount Sinai ratified a special temporary covenant between God and Israel, referred to as the *Mosaic Covenant*, and commonly called the *Old Covenant*. What was its purpose? The terms written in the *Book of the Covenant* were a systematic code of laws that served as a constitution for Israel's nation.

The Ten Commandments were at the heart of the covenant as God's *Charter of Rights* for His government of love (Deuteronomy 4:13). The various civil and social laws were intended to achieve and enforce the Lord's standard of righteousness, and the penalties were intended to impress upon a rebellious people the seriousness of sin. This *Old Covenant* dictated by God and written by Moses' hand didn't replace God's everlasting covenant. In fact, the ceremonial laws pointed to the ministry of the coming Messiah, and the continuation of God's plan of salvation He had announced in the Garden of Eden, and ratified in the form of a vision to Abraham.

The Apostle Paul makes clear that God never intended the *Old Mosaic Covenant of Law* to be a means of salvation for the people. He had already redeemed His people from bondage through their faith in following the cloud and crossing through the waters of the Red Sea—they were "baptized into Moses" (1 Corinthians 10:2). The covenant God made with Israel at Mount Sinai was never in conflict with His everlasting covenant of *righteousness by faith*—

> Now to Abraham and his Seed were the promises made. He does not say, "And to seeds," as of many, but as of one, "And to your Seed," who is Christ. And this I say, that the law, which was four hundred and thirty years later, cannot annul the covenant that was confirmed before by God in Christ, that it should make the promise of no effect. For if the inheritance is of the law, it is no longer of promise; but God gave it to Abraham by promise. . . . Therefore the law was our tutor to bring us to Christ, that we might be justified by faith (Galatians 3:16–18, 24).

This book of the *Old Covenant* law written out by Moses was simply a *tutor* to convict people of sin and lead them to Christ. *Tutor* in the original Greek was used to describe a slave who was not so much a teacher, but a strict supervisor of moral behavior and a guardian for youth till they matured. Ratified at Mount Sinai, the *Old Covenant Law* did not annul God's plan of salvation by grace, but was a temporary covenant of laws that optimized understanding of the everlasting covenant of *righteousness by faith*. It could not bring salvation to anyone through obedience. In fact, to obey required the Holy Spirit's grace working on the heart.

When Christ renewed the everlasting covenant on the basis of His more perfect sacrifice, He delivered an inaugural address as the Sovereign King in the Sermon on the Mount (Matthew 5:1–7:27). This constitution of the New Covenant makes demands equally impossible to achieve by human effort, requiring dependence on the Holy Spirit and God's divine grace to meet His righteous standards. Christ magnified the spiritual interpretation of His moral Law of Love, then commanded, "Therefore you shall be perfect, just as your Father in heaven is perfect" (Matthew 5:48). Peter echoed Christ's command, saying, "as He who called you is holy, you also be holy in all your conduct, because it is written, 'Be holy, for I am holy'" (1 Peter 1:15–16).

THE LORD WRITES HIS TEN COMMANDMENTS ON STONE

Back now to Mount Sinai. After ratifying the covenant, Moses took Aaron and his sons, along with seventy of the elders of Israel, up the Mount to participate in a covenant meal with the Lord (Exodus 24:9–10). Then the Lord said to Moses—

"Come up to Me on the mountain and be there; and I will give you tablets of stone, and the law and commandments which I have written, that you may teach them" (Exodus 24:12).

Leaving the others behind, Moses and his assistant Joshua went up into the Lord's cloud of glory for six days. On the seventh day, the Lord called Moses alone to come farther up the mountain into His presence (Exodus 24:12–18).

The Lord's desire was to dwell among His people. As the Father who begot Israel, God called the nation His *firstborn* covenant *son* (Exodus 4:22). To express the intimacy of covenant relationship, He later referred to national Israel as His wife, while identifying Himself as their loving Husband who provided all their needs and expected covenant fidelity in return. The Lord considered idolatry as *adultery* (Jeremiah 3:8)—unfaithfulness to their exclusive relationship with Him.

Knowing Israel's passion for pagan gods, He wanted to deter them from running off to play the harlot with those inanimate foreign lovers that offered only empty promises. So now the Lord told Moses to collect an offering from those who had willing hearts and would contribute toward building Him a portable sanctuary where His presence could be visibly manifested in their midst as they traveled—

And let them make Me a sanctuary, that I may dwell among them. According to all that I show you, that is, the pattern of the tabernacle and the pattern of all its furnishings, just so you shall make it (Exodus 25:8–9).

From Exodus 25:10 to Exodus 31:11, Moses records the Lord's detailed instructions of the way to build His sanctuary, prepare the articles of furnishings, appoint the priesthood, and even to prepare the holy anointing oil and incense for use in the sanctuary.

Then the Lord said, "Speak also to the children of Israel, saying: 'Surely My Sabbaths you shall keep, for it is a sign between Me and you throughout your generations, that you may know that I am the LORD who sanctifies you.'" (Exodus 31:13). What does God promise here? He promises that it will be by His power—the power of His Spirit—that people will be sanctified—set apart from sin!

And when He had made an end of speaking with him on Mount Sinai, He gave Moses two tablets of the Testimony, tablets of stone, written with the finger of God (Exodus 31:18).

The stone-hard evidence of God's moral code of love was written by God's own finger—on both sides of two tablets of stone (Exodus 32:15).

Moses had been up the mountain with God for 40 days and nights (Exodus 24:18), and was unaware that the same people who had entered into covenant with the Lord just before he ascended had wearied of waiting for his return, and had forsaken the Lord who had redeemed them from bondage. In fact—at that very moment—in complete disregard of the divine commandments, they were offering sacrifices to an image of a golden calf and worshiping this pagan idol as their god (Exodus 32:1–6).

The man of faith was unaware, but the all-seeing God realized the people's reckless disregard of Him. How it must have shocked Moses when the Lord erupted with righteous anger against sin and those covenant-rejecting sinners. Explaining the sordid details, the Lord called the nation of Israel a "stiff-necked people," and offered to start a new line of His holy seed through Moses, promising to make him the head of a great nation (Exodus 32:7–10).

Alarmed, Moses argued such action would ruin God's reputation, and pleaded for Him to turn from His fierce wrath, reminding the Lord of His covenant promises to Abraham, Isaac, and Jacob. The humble man was unconcerned about his own position in the Lord's plan. His passion was to protect the Lord's good name. Moses' earnest and unselfish intercession for the people softened the heart of the righteous Judge, who decided to compassionately extend mercy instead of destroying them for their sin (Exodus 32:11–14).

Moses rejoined Joshua and the two descended the mountain, with Moses carrying the two tablets that "were the work of God, and the writing was the writing of God engraved on the tablets" (Exodus 32:16). As they approached the encampment of Israel they heard singing. Arriving at the site, Moses witnessed the unrestrained humans dancing around a golden calf. Enraged, he cast down the two tablets and broke them, burned the idol in the fire, ground it into powder, and scattered it over water that he made the people drink so that what remained of the idol would be no more than human dung (vv. 16–20).

Moses knew God's anger had burned against his brother Aaron for contributing to Israel's great sin by fashioning the golden calf. He was painfully aware that God would have destroyed him had Moses not pleaded on his behalf (Deuteronomy 9:20). When he confronted his brother, Aaron offered a lame rationalization to justify his behavior, claiming he had received the gold from the people and "cast it into the fire and this calf came out" (Exodus 32:24).

Drawing a line in the sand, so to speak, Moses called those who were on the Lord's side to gather together with him. All the sons of Levi went to Moses, and that day he ordered around 3,000 unrepentant pagan men who totally rejected the Lord to be executed to protect the others from their deadly influence of idolatry and immorality (v. 28).

MOSES OFFERS TO ATONE FOR ISRAEL'S SIN

Going up the mountain again, Moses hoped to make atonement for the people's great sin of idolatry, and sought forgiveness for them by making an astonishing offer. If Israel's death penalty for sin could not be forgiven in the Lord's righteous judgment, Moses was willing to stand in as their substitute to make atonement, suggesting, "blot me out of Your book which You have written" (Exodus 32:32). His reference to the *book* is to the Lord's *book of life*, the record of mortal people who will inherit eternal life (compare Psalm 69:28; Daniel 12:1; Revelation 3:5; 13:8). Isn't that amazing? Reflecting Christ-like compassion and humility, Moses asked the Lord to allow him to die the second, eternal death to atone for the people's sins (Revelation 20:14).

And the LORD said to Moses, "Whoever has sinned against Me, I will blot him out of My book" (Exodus 32:33).

To convince the people that sin had consequences, the Lord vowed to "visit punishment upon them for their sin," and sent a plague to the camp, but in His mercy He did not destroy them (vv. 34, 35). In faithfulness to His covenant promises, God told Moses that the people would still go up to the Promised Land, but on account of their sin, He would not go in their midst because His holy presence might consume the stiff-necked people if they violated His covenant again (Exodus 33:3).

"For our God is a consuming fire" (Hebrews 12:29; compare Exodus 24:17; 33:5). His glory and His righteousness consume sin. That is why unholy humans cannot see Him face to face without perishing, at least not until the day His glorified saints will finally see His face (Revelation 22:4). In His mercy, God suggested He would only send an angel (not *the* Angel Himself) to accompany them (Exodus 33:1–3).

This implied no need of constructing the tabernacle for the Lord's dwelling among the people—the tabernacle He had described in detail to Moses and directed be stationed in the very center of the camp. Moses reported this disturbing news to Israel. The people mourned. God called them to repentance, telling them to remove all their jewelry to show their sorrow of heart. In a gesture of immediate obedience, the people stripped themselves of their ornaments, but genuine heart repentance was yet to come (vv. 4–6).

Moses pitched his tent a far distance outside the camp, designating it as "the tabernacle of meeting," and individuals who sought the Lord went there (Exodus 33:7). When Moses walked outside the camp to the make-shift tabernacle, the people watched attentively from their tent doors, desiring for the Lord to renew the covenant with them that they might receive His favor. Throughout the camp a deep longing for the Lord's presence spread, and it came to pass that the Lord appeared in the pillar of cloud to speak with Moses. Each time the Israelites saw this evidence of His presence, they rose in respect and worshiped in their tent doors (vv. 8–10). Genuine repentance had begun.

From the pillar of cloud, the Lord "spoke to Moses face to face, as a man speaks to his friend" (v. 11). *Face to face* is merely a figurative expression to describe the Lord's direct method of communication with Moses. In other words, the Lord spoke to Moses in plain communication, without visions or dreams, and without an intermediary. Within this same passage of Scripture, the Lord clearly warned Moses, "You cannot see My face; for no man shall see Me, and live" (Exodus 33:20). Moses walked in divine awareness of the Lord's presence, but he never saw His face.

At the *tabernacle of meeting*, Moses pleaded for God's favor on the undeserving people, repeatedly requesting that the Lord's presence go with Israel to identify them as His people in the sight of other nations. The earnest prayers of a righteous man are effective (James 5:16), and the Lord agreed to do all he asked, saying—

"My Presence will go with you, and I will give you rest . . . I will also do this thing that you have spoken; for you have found grace in My sight, and I know you by name" (Exodus 33:14, 17).

Moses and the Lord were friends—they knew each other by name. The heart of the man God chose to lead Israel was not centered so much on the covenant blessing of the Promised Land as much as on getting to know his Divine Friend. Enjoying an intimate and close-knit relationship with the Lord gave Moses the holy boldness to say, "Please, show me Your glory" (v. 18). Vowing that no man could see His face and live, the Lord agreed that when Moses next came up the mountain, He would hide Moses in the cleft of the rock and cover him with the palm of His hand to protect him from seeing His face as He passed by—Moses would see only His back, not His face (vv. 20–23).

COVENANT RENEWAL—THE LORD WRITES THE TEN COMMANDMENTS A SECOND TIME

Moses had asked for the Lord to renew the covenant with Israel and restore His favor, which required that the Lord restore the record of His moral code of love by personally rewriting the Ten Commandments with His own finger. Since Moses had broken the first set, it was now his responsibility to provide the two replacement stones, and the Lord commanded that he cut them out and return to the mountain the next morning (Exodus 34:1–2). Moses trekked to the top of the mountain with stones in hand, and the Lord descended in the cloud and stood with him there. According to His promise to reveal His glory to Moses, the Lord passed by him, exalting His grace, and testifying of His invisible qualities of perfect moral righteousness—

"The LORD, the LORD God, merciful and gracious, longsuffering, and abounding in goodness and truth, keeping mercy for thousands, forgiving iniquity and transgression and sin, by no means clearing the guilty, visiting the iniquity of the fathers upon the children and the children's children to the third and the fourth generation" (Exodus 34:6–7).

A sidebar insert—God does not place generational curses on families, but the consequences of sin often do. Beholding sin within the family, children frequently practice the same, and wickedness can take generations to reverse. God's punishment is directed at offenders, not their children. In later years, Israel used a proverb about fathers eating sour grapes and setting the children's teeth on edge (Jeremiah 31:29–31). God didn't like it, and said, "You shall no longer use this proverb in Israel. Behold, all souls are Mine; the soul of the father as well as the soul of the son is Mine; the soul who sins shall die" (Ezekiel 18:3–4; compare Deuteronomy 24:16; Ezekiel 18:20).

Seeing the eternal light of the Lord's righteous character on the mountain, an awestruck Moses quickly dropped to the dirt, bowed his head, and worshiped. Exhilarated and encouraged, Moses called on the Lord asking for His forgiveness, favor, and faithfulness toward the feeble and stiff-necked people, despite their behavior (Exodus 34:8–9).

Because of Moses' pleading prayers, and the Lord's promises to the Patriarchs, God said, "Behold, I make a covenant" (Exodus 34:10). He proceeded to renew the covenant, providing additional warning about the dangers of being ensnared by idol worship. God commanded the people to destroy the altars and ritual sites they found in Canaan, and instructed that they avoid treaties with the Canaanite nations by feasts or through marriage. He declared that He was a jealous God—a God who vigorously protects the integrity of His relationship with His people—and would not tolerate the sin of serving pagan idols (vv. 11–17). Then the Lord repeated commands from the *Book of the Covenant*—emphasizing His moral code, and some of the civil and ceremonial laws (vv. 18–27).

Moses spent a second interval of 40 days and nights with the Lord on Mount Sinai, and God wrote the Ten Commandments on the new set of stones (Exodus 34:28). "And He wrote on the tablets according to the first writing, the Ten Commandments, which the LORD had spoken to you in the mountain from the midst of the fire in the day of the assembly; and the LORD gave them to me" (Deuteronomy 10:4).

After his first 40-day encounter, Moses descended the mountain with a heavy spirit and furrowed brow. This time he left with his face radiant, reflecting the Lord's glory, returning to a subdued and compliant nation.

Moses and the people fulfilled the Lord's instruction for building a sanctuary. The Holy Spirit came upon artisans to enable them to precisely follow each aspect of the divine pattern. God had initially called the entire nation to be a holy priesthood, but the people had refused, asking Moses to act as an intermediator between them and a holy God. In place of a *nation* of priests, the Lord raised up the temporary Levitical priesthood (so-called since all priests had to be of the tribe of Levi).

To understand God's revelation in the Old Testament, we must expect that everything the Lord portrays is the progressive unfolding of His everlasting covenant, and look at His actions through the lens of His infinite love. God did not leave Israel in the dark, but showed them the way of salvation in His sanctuary. "Your way, O God, is in the sanctuary" (Psalm 77:13).

THE GOSPEL MESSAGE OF THE SANCTUARY

The sanctuary was theology expressed in physical type (symbolic form), much more beautiful on the inside than the exterior. It illustrated the everlasting covenant for the benefit of the illiterate. While Moses was trained in the art of reading and writing, the Hebrew nation had been enslaved for centuries. The Lord visually portrayed His covenant of *righteousness by faith* in the sanctuary to help them understand that His plan would both *justify* and *sanctify* them through belief in the coming Messiah. He loved them too much to only save them from the *penalty* of sin—He would release them from the *power* of sin as well.

The three areas of the sanctuary represented God's three aspects of salvation.

THE SANCTUARY OF THE WILDERNESS

INSIDE THE TABERNACLE

1. Holy of Holies
2. Ark of the Covenant
3. Veil of the Holy of Holies
4. Altar of Incense
5. Lampstand
6. Holy Place
7. Table of Showbread
8. Veil of the Holy Place

COVERINGS

9. Outer covering of badger skins
10. Covering of ram's skin
11. Curtain of goat's hair
12. Curtain of fine linen

OUTSIDE THE TABERNACLE

13. Bronze Basin
14. Altar of Sacrifice
15. Gate

THE OUTER COURT REPRESENTED *JUSTIFICATION BY FAITH*

Only one door existed to the 75-by-150 foot courtyard, enclosed by *white linen hangings* (Exodus 27:8–18). The linen border symbolized the practical benefits of righteousness by faith, "to be arrayed in fine linen, clean and bright, for the fine linen is the righteous acts of the saints" (Revelation 19:8). The symbolic significance of a single door is that the Messiah-Christ is the only way to enter into covenant relationship with God. Jesus said, "I am the door. If anyone enters by Me, he will be saved" (John 10:9).

The *altar of burnt offering* was centered midway between this entrance and the actual tabernacle (Exodus 40:29). The guilty brought an innocent creature here, laid their hands on its head, confessed their sin to transfer it to the spotless substitute, and were required to personally put the animal to death, before the priests offered the sacrifices on the altar. Imagine how this practice impressed on the sinner's conscience that the penalty of their sin was death. Priests also sacrificed two spotless male lambs—one at dawn and one at evening, as part of their daily service—to confirm the nation's consecration to God and constant dependence upon Him for atonement from sin.

The blood-stained exterior of the *altar of burnt offering* witnessed against the guilt and horror of sin, and pointed to Calvary's blood-stained Cross. The substitutes sacrificed on the altar symbolically represented Christ—the spotless Lamb of God who takes away the sins of the world (Revelation 13:8; John 1:29). Smoke ascending from the continuously-burning fire represented God's mercy and forgiveness.

The *shining bronze laver* was positioned midway between the altar and the door of the tabernacle. It consisted of a cistern of flowing water and a basin (Exodus 30:18). The basin was a reflection pool where priests searched for polluted spots on their person or garments, and washed away all impurities. Even their hands and feet had to be washed each time they prepared to enter the *Holy Place* of God's Presence, under penalty of death for failure to do so (Exodus 30:21). The Lord was teaching the people to revere His righteous standards and search their consciences for sin, confessing sin to be made spotless through their belief in the Messiah. "If we confess our sins, He is faithful and just to forgive us our sins and to cleanse us from all unrighteousness" (1 John 1:9).

Here the people saw God's first aspect of salvation—*justification by faith*—to release them from the penalty of sin.

THE HOLY PLACE SIGNIFIED *SANCTIFICATION BY FAITH*

The spotless member of the priesthood was prepared to enter the first compartment of the sanctuary, the *Holy Place*, which measured 15-feet wide and 30-feet deep. Covering the interior walls of the tabernacle were magnificent curtains of blue, purple, and scarlet-colored yarn (Exodus 26:1–6; 35:25), resplendent with artistic designs of cherubim embroidered in gold and silver threads. As the priest entered the Holy Place, he would see three articles of furnishing.

The *golden candlestick* stood on the left side (Exodus 25:31–40). No natural light shone in the sanctuary, a covered tent without windows. The *golden candlestick* burned continually to provide the light necessary for the priests to perform their duties (Exodus 27:20; Leviticus 24:2). Representing the light of Christ's glory, it taught the necessity to rely on the eternal light of the Messiah's righteous character for guidance. Jesus said, "I am the light of the world. He who follows Me shall not walk in darkness, but have the light of life" (John 8:12).

This seven-branched *golden candlestick* had a main branch and six branch-like arms with multiple almond-shaped bowls that held the purest hand-pressed olive oil as the fuel source (Exodus 27:20). In biblical symbolism, the number seven expresses completion or perfection, and oil symbolizes the Holy Spirit, who is described as the sevenfold Spirit of God before His throne (Revelation 1:4; compare Isaiah 11:2). Each morning, the priests dressed these seven lamps, snuffing out the flames only one at a time so they could still see to remove the ashes and replenish the oil. The golden candlestick also taught the people to seek the Spirit as their power source daily. Sanctification would be "Not by might, nor by power, but by My Spirit" (Zechariah 4:6).

The *table of showbread* stood on the right side of the *Holy Place* (Exodus 25:23–30). The priest arranged twelve loaves of bread—prepared fresh for each Sabbath (Leviticus 24:5–9) and set out as a show of thanksgiving—in two stacks, representing the twelve tribes of Israel. This memorialized God's constant provision for nourishment. The loaves were flat-bread baked without leaven (a yeast-like ingredient symbolizing corruption). Also known as the "bread of His Presence," the loaves represented Christ as the Word of life. Jesus said, "I am the bread of life" (John 6:35), and also said, "Man shall not live by bread alone, but by every word that proceeds from the mouth of God" (Matthew 4:4). The Lord showed the people that His Word was provided for spiritual nourishment, and *sanctification* came by the faith of Jesus in loving obedience to His Word (Revelation 14:12).

The *golden altar of incense* was located at the far end of the chamber, in front of the veil that guarded the entrance to the innermost compartment. A common priest prayed here daily and listened to the Lord's voice through the veil. On this altar of prayer, a special incense burned continually, morning and night, with fire taken from the courtyard *altar of burnt offering* of sacrifice. The unique formula for the incense compounded fragrant spices and gums. God prohibited its use for any other purpose (Exodus 30:34–38). The *golden altar of incense* represented human prayers mingled with Christ's intercessory prayers, which provide the special sweet-smelling aroma to God (Hebrews 7:25; Revelation 5:8, 8:3–4). As the fragrance of the sweet spices permeated the Holy Place, and the perfumed smoke rose in front of the veil, God demonstrated the need of prayer, and that only through Christ can prayer have efficacy. Christ is our only Mediator and Advocate with the Father (1 Timothy 2:5; 1 John 2:1).

The *Holy Place* signified God's ongoing second aspect of salvation—*sanctification by faith*—to release them from the power of sin.

THE MOST HOLY PLACE REPRESENTED *GLORIFICATION BY FAITH*

The *Most Holy Place* was the innermost sanctuary compartment, also known as the Holy of Holies. It was consecrated by the Shekinah Presence of God that provided the only light there. Its entrance was guarded by a thick hanging veil.

The *ark of the covenant* was the only piece of furniture in the *Most Holy Place*. God also called this piece the *ark of Testimony* (e.g. Exodus 25:22). The most sacred of all sanctuary objects, the ark represented God's earthly throne. Exquisitely designed and fashioned of pure gold, the lid of the ark was called the *mercy seat* and was fashioned as a single piece with a covering cherub on either side of it (Exodus 25:17–22). As God's Presence descended to His earthly throne, He sat between the two cherubim on His mercy seat, heard the priests' prayers, and communed with them.

Inside the sacred *ark of the covenant* under the *mercy seat* were the two tablets of stone upon which God had written His Ten Commandments (Exodus 31:18; Deuteronomy 10:1–5). Those tablets represented the *Charter of Rights* upon which God's government of love is founded, and that His mercy always supersedes His judgments.

By sharp contrast, Israel's constitution of civil/social/ceremonial laws, dictated by God and written by Moses' hand—known as both the *Book of the Covenant*, and later as the *Book of the Law* (explained in our next chapter)—was placed in a pocket on the *outside* of the ark, which indicated the temporary terms of the Old Covenant law.

Only once a year, on the Day of Atonement, was the high priest allowed to enter the *Most Holy Place*. When Christ died on Calvary, the veil in the earthly temple was torn in two—from top to bottom (Matthew 27:51). As High Priest of the covenant, Christ opened a "new and living way" for believers to gain direct and bold access to the Lord's throne of grace (Hebrews 4:16; 10:19–22). Jesus said, "I am the way, the truth, and the life. No one comes to the Father except through Me" (John 14:6). God's covenant people today enter into a Most Holy Place experience through faith in Christ.

The *Most Holy Place* represented entrance into the Lord's eternal Presence, the stage of *glorification by faith* that follows final judgment made in favor of His saints, and provides the grand entry of His covenant people into His literal eternal kingdom.

The sanctuary represented the gospel of the everlasting covenant of righteousness by faith, through its ceremonial types, services, and sacrifices which represented Christ. In fact, the New Testament tells us that the same gospel preached to Christians today was preached to the nation of Israel (Hebrews 4:2).

WAS GOD'S FORMULA OF LAW A COPY OF THE SUZERAINS?

Some modern Bible scholars point out striking parallels between the features of the *Old Mosaic Covenant* and those of Hittite treaties— where the more powerful Hittites were considered the *Suzerains*, and the nations they subjected were called *vassals*. The *Suzerains* provided land grants and military protection to *vassal* nations, with expectations of their allegiance and financial tribute, but their treaties did not present laws from a deity, or duties to a deity. The Lord's *Old Covenant* system of laws was unique from theirs because the laws came from God, and lawbreaking was an offense against His righteousness, yet some scholars suggest the Lord copied this *Suzerain-vassal* formula so that His people would be familiar with the terms.

An infinity focus on Scripture suggests the Creator originated this formula of law from the beginning of time, and that Noah's son Shem and his descendants followed the same government of love that Abraham followed. We must always recall the first eleven chapters of Genesis were merely a highlight reel of 2,000 years of history, and do not provide the details of God's government of love. When the Lord renewed the everlasting covenant with Isaac, He said it was "because Abraham obeyed My voice and kept My charge, My commandments, My statutes, and My laws" (Genesis 26:5).

God says, "For I am the LORD, I do not change" (Malachi 3:6). The New Testament says of our Creator God, "Jesus Christ is the same yesterday, today, and forever" (Hebrews 13:8).

Isn't it more likely that the Hittites copied the Creator's formula, while purposely omitting any mention of obligation to the one true God?

OLD TESTAMENT BELIEVERS WERE SAVED BY GRACE

By their knowledge of God's faithfulness, and understanding that His coming Messiah would pay their death penalty for sin, Old Testament believers trusted that they were justified by faith. Yet, they recognized there was more to God's everlasting covenant—He would restore their righteousness by empowering them to live according to His commandments.

King David said, "He restores my soul; He leads me in the paths of righteousness for His name's sake" (Psalm 23:3). Calling on His name, all Old Testament believers were led and empowered by the Spirit to walk in faithful obedience to the Lord.

The *Old Mosaic Covenant* did not change God's everlasting covenant of *righteousness by faith*.

SUMMARY OF "HIS" STORY
Chapter Ten

- The Lord first *spoke* His Ten Commandments to the whole nation of Israel.
- Then God spoke *civil, social, and ceremonial laws* to Moses alone as the *constitution* for the new nation of Israel.
- Moses wrote the document called the *Book of the Covenant*, and included in this constitution the Lord's spoken words of the Ten Commandments, which serve as His *Charter of Rights*.
- Moses *ratified* this constitution, and the terms of the *Book of the Covenant* became the Old Covenant (the *Book of the Covenant* and the *Old Covenant* are synonymous).
- After the people entered into the Old Covenant, God called Moses up to Mount Sinai to receive the written Ten Commandments.
- God then expressed His desire to dwell among His people, and gave Moses a pattern to build Him a sanctuary and install a priesthood.
- Finally, the Lord wrote His Ten Commandment moral code of love on two stone tablets—with His own finger.
- Returning to camp with the Ten Commandments, Moses burned with anger when he witnessed the people worshiping a golden calf, and he broke the two tablets.
- Moses returned to see God, and sought to make atonement for the people, asking God to allow him to be their substitute by blotting his name out of His book of life.
- God renewed the covenant, and rewrote the Ten Commandments with His own finger.
- The Apostle Paul affirms this Old Covenant law was not meant for salvation, but merely served as a tutor to lead people to Christ.

- The sanctuary was theology expressed in physical format. It illustrated the gospel message of the everlasting covenant and the Messiah's ministry.
- The Outer Court represented *justification by faith*.
- The Holy Place signified *sanctification by faith*.
- The Most Holy Place represented *glorification by faith*.
- The Ten Commandments were *inside* the *ark* of *the covenant*, representing the *Charter of Rights* of God's government.
- The Book of the Law (the Old Covenant) was in a pocket *outside* the *ark of the covenant*, and stood as God's witness against covenant-breakers. This placement represented the temporary nature of the Old Covenant.
- The New Testament tells us that the same gospel (the good news of God's everlasting covenant of *righteousness by faith*) preached to Christians today was preached to the nation of Israel.
- Old Testament believers knew they were *justified by faith*, and that God was working in them to restore righteousness, and leading them in His path of righteous living.

JESUS CHRIST IS THE COVENANT

Chapter Eleven

All three members of the Godhead—the Father, Son, and Spirit— are actively involved in the plan of salvation. By their collective determination, they planned and participate in the everlasting covenant of *righteousness by faith*—the only means of salvation for humanity.

The contents of this chapter require a slow and thoughtful read. It will greatly enhance your understanding of the word "covenant" as used in the Bible, and will show that the life, death, and mission of Jesus Christ was prophesied with vivid detail in the Book of Isaiah. Finally, it will make clear what Jesus nailed to the cross.

"COVENANT"—THE TRUE MEANING REVEALED BY JEWISH SCHOLARS BEFORE JESUS

Words are important. Words reveal our cultural and individual identity as we express our thoughts, purposes, expectations, and emotions. Think about the Lord's self-revelation in the Bible—can the importance of His words be overstated? What if His Word had not been translated into a language we understood? How could we interpret God's will?

The Old Testament was recorded by Hebrews mostly in their Hebrew language, with some Aramaic texts. With the passing of time and the fulfillment of God's prophecies of the Jews being taken captive by other nations, as well as the rise and fall of world-dominating kingdoms that introduced new languages, many Jews living just before Christ's time had lost their ability to read and write Hebrew. They spoke primarily the Greek language, which created a great need to have the Old Testament—the only Scripture of the time—translated into Greek.

Beginning about 250 BC, 72 Jewish scholars made the first translation of the Hebrew texts—beginning with the five books of Moses. Since no language can precisely capture the meaning of another word for word, they translated ideas as well as words to reveal the meaning of the original texts. Their end product bears a striking resemblance to the Dead Sea Scrolls discovered in 1946–1947 in the caves of Qumran, which are the most ancient manuscripts of the original Hebrew texts yet discovered.

This Hebrew-to-Greek translation of the Old Testament is called by the name *Septuagint* ("Translation of the Seventy"), or LXX (Roman numerals for 70). The Septuagint made God's Word available to the Jews who no longer spoke their ancestral Hebrew language, and to the entire Greek-speaking world. Becoming the Bible of the early Christian church, the Septuagint profoundly influenced the writers of the New Testament.

For the purpose of understanding God's covenants, we need to consider how the Jewish scholars translated the one and only Hebrew word for *covenant*, which is *berit* and means to *obligate* or *bind*. The majority of its over 280 usages in the Old Testament relates to God's covenant promises, but *berit* is also used to describe a covenant between humans.

In contrast to the Hebrew language, the Greek language has two words for covenant:

1. *Syntheke* conveys the idea of a *contract*, a *partnership*, or a *treaty*—generally implying equality between the parties negotiating the agreement; and

2. *Diatheke* conveys the idea of a will, or a testament, or a testimony expressing the desired will of an individual—implying

that only one person makes all the promises, holds absolute power over the terms of the covenant, and invites others to enter into covenant by agreeing to abide by the set terms.

When referring to God's arrangements with humanity, those Jewish scholars—working independently from one another—each translated the Hebrew word for covenant into the Greek by employing the term *diatheke*.

In other words, each and every one of these ancient scholars saw all of God's covenants as His *expressed will for humanity*, in which He alone made the promises, and He alone keeps the promises! This explains why Moses thought even the Old Covenant—the *Book of the Law*—was a glorious law (Deuteronomy 4:6–8). He knew that God would keep His promises to enable the people to obey if they yielded to Him.

Likewise, the New Testament authors always employed the Greek word *diatheke* to define each and every covenant God ever made with humanity. Some 33 times, the New Testament writers describe that God alone makes and keeps the covenant promises, and invites us to enter into a covenant relationship of wholehearted love, promising His benevolence and protection in exchange for our loyalty to Him.

In Hebrews 8:10, the Lord said about the New Covenant, "For this is the covenant that I will make with the house of Israel after those days, says the LORD: I will put My laws in their mind and write them on their hearts; and I will be their God, and they shall be My people." This eternal desire of God's heart is expressed throughout the Old Testament.

THE GOSPEL MESSAGE OF ISAIAH

Many scholars call Isaiah "the gospel Prophet." If you have never read past the harsh judgments of his first 39 chapters, it might sound strange to hear Isaiah identified this way. His ministry arose after the nation of Israel had divided into two kingdoms—the kingdom of the north continued under the name Israel, and was guilty of extreme wickedness and rebellion against the Lord; the kingdom of the south became known as Judah, and was following in her sister nation's footsteps. God commissioned Isaiah to both warn and then comfort His people.

A note of interest—the two divisions of the Bible are reflected in the book of Isaiah. The Old Testament has 39 books which focus on humanity's great need of salvation, and warns of God's judgments on those who refuse to live by His righteous standards. The first 39 chapters of Isaiah do likewise, as God's forewarning of condemnation against Judah and other nations for their moral sins and political entanglements. Isaiah's primary message was to the southern kingdom of Judah—he prophesied of their upcoming Babylonian captivity, which transpired 840 years after Mount Sinai. How patient God proved to be with His people.

The first division of Isaiah is sprinkled with grace, emphasizing a need to repent to receive God's forgiveness, and announcing the birth of the Messiah—

"Come now, and let us reason together," Says the LORD, "Though your sins are like scarlet, they shall be as white as snow; Though they are red like crimson, They shall be as wool" (Isaiah 1:18).

For unto us a Child is born, Unto us a Son is given; and the government will be upon His shoulder. And His name will be called Wonderful, Counselor, Mighty God, Everlasting Father, Prince of Peace. Of the increase of His government and peace there will be no end, upon the throne of David and over His kingdom, to order it and establish it with judgment and justice from that time forward, even forever. The zeal of the LORD of hosts will perform this (Isaiah 9:6–7).

The last 27 chapters of Isaiah reflect the same message of hope provided in the 27 books in the New Testament. The Lord had Isaiah declare future hope through prophecies of comfort and the proclamation of the Messiah's ministry. Jesus fulfilled most of Isaiah's prophecies in a literal fashion, while some merely typified Him. Let's examine the relationship between the writings of Isaiah and the Person of Jesus Christ revealed in the New Testament.

Jesus said of Himself, "the Son of Man did not come to be served, but to serve, and to give His life as a ransom for many", and "I am among you as the One who serves" (Mark 10:45, NIV; Luke 22:27). The Apostle Peter identifies Jesus as God's servant, saying, "The God of Abraham, Isaac, and Jacob, the God of our fathers, glorified His Servant Jesus" (Acts 3:13). The term *Servant* is covenant language describing the Messiah-Christ, who served as a *chosen and confidential representative*—a special *Messenger* on a mission to represent God.

Jesus was born to do the will of God, and always sought to please and glorify His Father (John 4:34; 5:30; 6:38; 13:31). As the Divine Servant, He completed the work He was to accomplish on Earth, then the Father honored Him with the glory He had before the world began. He ascended to Heaven to continue His ministry as High Priest of God's covenant people (John 17:4–5; Hebrews 4:14–15).

The Prophet Isaiah recorded four "Servant Songs" about the coming Servant-Messiah. They are called *songs* because of the poetic literary style in which they are written. The key to understanding these Messianic prophesies is to recognize that they depict the *incarnated Christ*. In two of these songs, the One who is speaking is the Second Person of the Godhead *before* His incarnation. He is prophesying about His future when He takes on flesh to become the Servant-Messiah.

Armed with that key to unlock the meaning of Isaiah's recorded Servant Songs, let's see how the beautiful and detailed description of the *Person of Jesus Christ*, His mission, death, resurrection, and exaltation was provided about 700 years before God became incarnated in human flesh.

These prophecies are important to see on our journey, as God progressively unfolds the revelation of His everlasting covenant. When the risen Christ pointed His disciples to the texts of the Old Testament to prove His mission from Scripture, He surely included these.

FIRST SERVANT SONG—GOD IDENTIFIES CHRIST AS THE EVERLASTING COVENANT

Isaiah 42:1–9 is the first Servant Song. Some mistakenly read and interpret the singular *Servant* to represent the collective nation of Israel. Although Isaiah did refer to *national* Israel as the Lord's servant that was called to be His witness to all nations (Isaiah 44:1, 2; 43:10), the nation had closed their ears and eyes to God's leading, and were spiritually deaf and blind (Isaiah 42:19). Repeatedly failing to be God's faithful and true witness, these idolatrous people were on the brink of being taken captive to Babylon (which God allowed for the purpose of bringing them to repentance). They had completely missed the mark of God's high standards of righteous living, and were in great need of His forgiveness (Isaiah 44:21–22). *National* Israel could not fulfill God's mission purpose, for He would not share His glory with the pagan idols they served (Isaiah 42:8; 48:11).

God's identification of His Servant could only be fulfilled in Christ—

Behold! My Servant whom I uphold, My Elect One in whom My soul delights! I have put My Spirit upon Him; He will bring forth justice to the Gentiles. He will not cry out, nor raise His voice, nor cause His voice to be heard in the street. A bruised reed He will not break, and smoking flax He will not quench; He will bring forth justice for truth. He will not fail nor be discouraged, Till He has established justice in the earth; and the coastlands shall wait for His law (Isaiah 42:1–4).

God delights in this Servant-Messiah. Scripture says, "since He Whom God has sent speaks the words of God [proclaims God's own message], God does not give Him His Spirit sparingly or by measure, but boundless is the gift God makes of His Spirit!" (John 3:34, AMP). The *Person of Jesus Christ* would be the Ideal Servant who was gentle and offered compassionate mercy to people who had been bruised and battered by life, and whose spiritual light was flickering and about to be snuffed out. The New Testament provides ample evidence that Jesus fulfilled this prophecy (e.g. Matthew 12:18–21), ministering with divine humility.

The most remarkable revelation of this first Servant Song is now made—

"I, the LORD, have called You in righteousness, and will hold Your hand; **I will keep You and give You as a covenant to the people**, as a light to the Gentiles, to open blind eyes, to bring out prisoners from the prison, those who sit in darkness from the prison house" (Isaiah 42:6–7; emphasis added).

Do you see it? While all three members of the Godhead actively participate in the plan of salvation, it was by their collective *divine will* that they determined the everlasting covenant of *righteousness by faith* would be made available through the human *Person of Jesus Christ*.

Sometime in eternity past, the Three-in-One Godhead decided among themselves that One of them would come to Earth, live a perfectly righteous life incarnated in human flesh, and die as the Substitute for humanity to satisfy their righteous judgment against sin. Before creating our world, they agreed among themselves that the Second Person of the Godhead would become this human instrument. He would open the way for salvation by their collective grace through a believer's faith. God gave the *Person of Jesus Christ* as a covenant to all the people on earth.

Jesus is the everlasting covenant of *righteousness by faith*. In anticipation of His substitutionary death, He was considered the "Lamb slain from the foundation of the world" (Revelation 13:8). By His blood—called "the blood of the everlasting covenant" (Hebrews 13:20)—He would make atonement for all the past, present, and future sins of the world. Hallelujah!

Close to the end of his book, Isaiah recorded the Messiah's words—

"The Spirit of the Lord GOD is upon Me, because the LORD has anointed Me to preach good tidings to the poor; He has sent Me to heal the brokenhearted, to proclaim liberty to the captives, and the opening of the prison to those who are bound; to proclaim the acceptable year of the LORD, and the day of vengeance of our God; to comfort all who mourn, to console those who mourn in Zion, to give them beauty for ashes, the oil of joy for mourning, the garment of praise for the spirit of heaviness;

that they may be called trees of righteousness, the planting of the LORD, that He may be glorified" (Isaiah 61:1–3).

The gospel writer Luke records an event in Jesus' life. He went into a synagogue on the Sabbath, stood up to read, opened a scroll of Isaiah, read those very words, closed the book, and sat down. As all the eyes of the people were fixed upon Him, He said, "Today this Scripture is fulfilled in your hearing" (Luke 4:21).

SECOND SERVANT SONG—CHRIST WILL BRING SALVATION TO ALL NATIONS

In the second Song, Isaiah 49:1–13 records the Second Person of the Godhead speaking of Himself as Messiah after He would be incarnated in the *Person of Jesus Christ*.

He speaks of His mission and spiritual success, beginning with details that identify His human nature, saying, "The LORD has called Me from the womb" and "He has made mention of My name" (Isaiah 49:1). This is an obvious parallel prophecy to Isaiah 7:14, "Therefore the Lord Himself will give you a sign: Behold, the virgin shall conceive and bear a Son, and shall call His name Immanuel." He says in Isaiah 49:2, "He has made My mouth like a sharp sword," a description of Christ's mouth that is echoed in Revelation 19:15, "Now out of His mouth goes a sharp sword, that with it He should strike the nations" (compare Revelation 1:16; 2:16).

Then He adds in Isaiah 49:3, "And He said to me, 'You are My servant, O Israel, in whom I will be glorified.'" We must always interpret by context, and the context of this second Song clearly refers to an individual, distinct from *national* Israel. How is it that the Messiah applies the title *Israel* to Himself?

You will recall that *Israel* is a covenant name first given to Jacob by the Lord (Genesis 32:28). The nation of Israel—the firstborn covenant son of God—was merely a symbolic type of Jesus, who is also referred to as the firstborn covenant Son of God (Exodus 4:22; Colossians 1:15). Remember, God is progressively unfolding the story of the Seed, and through His continued revelation in Scripture the covenant name and concept of *Israel* develops a spiritual application.

It is Christ who is the true *spiritual Israel* who "struggled with God and with men" and prevailed. Just as the seed of Jacob was considered the *sons of Israel* (e.g. Genesis 42:5), those who belong to Christ—the Ideal Servant *Israel*—are His spiritual seed and heirs according to the promises of the everlasting covenant (Isaiah 53:10; Galatians 3:29; Romans 4:13; 9:6–8; 11:17–20; 1 John 3:9). That is not *replacement theology*, but rather *biblical-revelation theology*.

Isaiah 49:4 records the Servant saying, "I have labored in vain, I have spent my strength for nothing and in vain; yet surely my just reward is with the LORD, and my work with my God." Although He would be rejected by *national* Israel, the One who would become *the Person of Jesus Christ*—knitting Divine nature together with human nature—would fulfill the covenant promises to Abraham and bless all the nations on earth.

It was too small a thing for God—in the *Person of Jesus Christ*—to merely come as the Savior of the Jews. In Isaiah 49:5–6, He explained that His first assignment was to minister to the believing remnant of Israel, and next to be a light to the Gentiles. He began His work on Earth, then ascended to Heaven with the promise to send the Holy Spirit, who would empower a missionary movement by His disciples that would spread the good news of the everlasting covenant to the ends of the earth (Acts 1:4–8).

Isaiah 49:7 describes the humiliating treatment of Christ at His first Advent, but a reversal will take place at His second coming, when nobles of all nations, and His former oppressors as well, will bow down to Him (Romans 14:11; Philippians 2:10).

This prophecy repeats the promise to give the Servant as a covenant to the people for the *day of salvation*, when God would come as the Person of Jesus Christ to renew and ratify the everlasting covenant of *righteousness by faith* in the New Covenant, for the benefit of all who have lived on Earth (Isaiah 49:8). He would release sin-sick souls from spiritual darkness, hunger, and thirst (vv. 9–10). No wonder Isaiah's second Servant Song concludes with the heavens and the earth breaking forth into singing for the joy of the Lord's mercy (v. 13).

THIRD SERVANT SONG— MESSIAH'S DEATH AND RESURRECTION

Isaiah 50:4–11 records the third Song, where again the Second Person of the Godhead is speaking of Himself in the future when He would become the Servant-Messiah. Almost certainly, the risen Christ shared this prophecy about His death and resurrection with His followers.

Beginning in Isaiah 50:4–5, He prophesies about His incarnation, saying, "The Lord GOD has given Me the tongue of the learned, that I should know how to speak a word in season to him who is weary. He awakens Me morning by morning, He awakens My ear to hear as the learned. The Lord GOD has opened My ear; and I was not rebellious, nor did I turn away." When Christ walked the Earth, it was through the Holy Spirit that God gave Him words of wisdom for hardened hearts and words of comfort for His lost sheep of Israel. Listening to Jesus, the multitudes were "astonished at His teaching" (Matthew 7:28; 22:33).

These opening lines of Isaiah's third Song contrast Christ's perfect obedience with the disobedience of *national* Israel. Jesus Christ always obeyed the Father, no matter what it cost Him personally. He humbled Himself and was obedient to the point of death upon the cross (Philippians 2:8). His willingness to suffer humiliation, scourging, and to endure the cross for the joy of paying humanity's sin-debt (Hebrews 12:2) is clearly prophesied—

I gave My back to those who struck Me, And My cheeks to those who plucked out the beard; I did not hide My face from shame and spitting. "For the Lord GOD will help Me; Therefore I will not be disgraced; Therefore I have set My face like a flint, And I know that I will not be ashamed" (Isaiah 50:6–7).

Jesus was not ashamed to die in submission to fulfill God's everlasting covenant of salvation by grace, through faith. Knowing torture awaited Him, He resolutely determined to go to Jerusalem to be crucified (Luke 9:51), because He knew generations of people would be saved by His act of love. On the Thursday night before His crucifixion, the high priest accused Jesus of blasphemy for claiming to be the Son of God, and people mocked, spat on, and beat Him. They led Him to the Roman Governor Pilate, who had Jesus scourged with a braided-leather whip that had metal or bone attached to each strand, which lacerated His skin and muscles. Adding insult to injury, Roman soldiers spit in His face and held a mock coronation of a king, dressing Him in a royal purple robe and jamming a twisted crown of thorns deep into His head (Matthew 26:67–68; 27:24–26, 30; Mark 15:17).

Christ willingly offered his back to his tormenters, and did not retaliate against His abusers. The gentle Lamb of God being led to the slaughter knew His victory would come. In Isaiah 50:8–9, He claimed His vindication, foretelling His resurrection and the pronouncement by God that He indeed was the spotless Lamb whose worthy blood paid the penalty of sin. The prophecy ends with His call and warning—

"Who among you fears the LORD? Who obeys the voice of His Servant? Who walks in darkness and has no light? Let him trust in the name of the LORD and rely upon his God. Look, all you who kindle a fire, who encircle yourselves with sparks: Walk in the light of your fire and in the sparks you have kindled—this you shall have from My hand: You shall lie down in torment" (Isaiah 50:10–11).

Jesus prophetically cries out to the unconverted—believe, obey, and be saved. He offers a warning to those who might try to escape moral and spiritual darkness by lighting their own fire of man-made religion, or works to earn salvation. If they did not accept His *righteousness by faith*, they would go to their graves without hope.

This third Servant Song presents us with two questions: 1) Will we fear the Lord, listen to Christ, and walk humbly in His light by faith? If so, we will be saved; or 2) will we reject Christ, light our own torch for guidance, and seek to live according to our own wisdom? If so, we will lie down in torment.

The New Testament says of Jesus, "though He was a Son, yet He learned obedience by the things which He suffered. And having been perfected, He became the author of eternal salvation to all who obey Him" (Hebrews 5:8–9).

FOURTH SERVANT'S SONG—DETAILS OF MESSIAH'S SUFFERING AND DEATH

Isaiah 52:13–53:12 records the fourth and most memorable of the Servant Songs. Undoubtedly, this gospel chapter is the climax of all the prophecies in Isaiah, describing Christ's suffering, death, and resurrection in such specific detail that it proves only God—who knows the end from the beginning—could be the Author of Scripture. The exact fulfillment of this prophecy by the *Person of Jesus Christ* proves beyond a shadow of a doubt that He was no imposter.

Beginning with a promise of victory following the violence Christ would suffer at the hands of men, Isaiah 52:13 says, "He shall be exalted and extolled and be very high." In a startling turn, the very next verse brings the brutality of His beatings to light: "His visage was marred more than any man, and His form more than the sons of men" (v. 14). Jesus would be so disfigured by the flogging of the Roman whip that He would be hardly recognizable. Afterwards, nobles and commoners who began to comprehend the truth of His identity would be speechless, and stand in awe of His self-sacrificing love (v. 15).

Isaiah 53:1 goes on to say that the Messiah's glory was hidden in humiliation. Few believed Jesus was the Christ, as it says, "For He shall grow up before Him as a tender plant, and as a root out of dry ground. He has no form or comeliness; and when we see Him, there is no beauty that we should desire Him" (v. 2). The Lord of glory stepped out of Heaven and arrived in obscurity as a common human baby. Christ was the "Root of Jesse," King David's father (Isaiah 11:10). Coming from the decayed and apparently dead stump of the Davidic line, He appeared without human pomp and circumstance that would draw humanity's desire toward Him. Who would believe this humble child would ascend the throne of David forever, to fulfill God's covenant with the king? (2 Samuel 7:11–13; Matthew 21:9).

Isaiah 53:3 says, "He is despised and rejected by men, a Man of sorrows and acquainted with grief. And we hid, as it were, our faces from Him; He was despised, and we did not esteem Him." The Messiah-Christ Jesus did not appear in the manner people expected, so most despised and rejected Him (Luke 13:34; John 1:10–11). People turned away in disbelief when He was tortured and crucified. The vivid details the gospels offer of His agony still make some close their eyes to that portrait of the Sin-bearing Servant.

Next we see the snapshot of salvation, and we are in the picture—

> Surely He has borne our griefs and carried our sorrows; yet we esteemed Him stricken, smitten by God, and afflicted. But He was wounded for our transgressions, He was bruised for our iniquities; the chastisement for our peace was upon Him, and by His stripes we are healed. All we like sheep have gone astray; we have turned, every one, to his own way; and the LORD has laid on Him the iniquity of us all (Isaiah 53:4–6).

Prone to wander far from the loving Shepherd, like sheep we could not find our way back to Him. To rescue His lost sheep, God had to lay our iniquity on Jesus Christ, and execute His fierce wrath against sin on Calvary's cross (compare John 10:1–18; Matthew 9:36; 18:11–14). The cross of Christ testifies that the penalty for breaking God's law is death. We caused the atrocities of His suffering and death to bear the penalty for our violations of God's government. Christ died the death God's justice demands of us.

The spotless Lamb of God became our Substitute to atone for our sins. Stricken by God, crucified and pierced for our transgressions, the weight of our sins caused Him spiritual anguish, crushing His holy heart. By His stripes of physical agony our spiritual infirmities were healed (1 Peter 2:24). When we accept Christ as Savior and Lord of our lives, we are made whole through *righteousness by faith* and find peace with God.

Isaiah 53:7 predicted His silence in front of His accusers: "He was oppressed and He was afflicted, He was led as a lamb to the slaughter, and as a sheep before its shearers is silent, so He opened not His mouth" (compare Matthew 27:12, 14; 1 Peter 2:23).

The prophecy continues in Isaiah 53:8, 9. "He was taken from prison and from judgment, and who will declare His generation?

For He was cut off from the land of the living; for the transgressions of My people He was stricken. And they made His grave with the wicked—but with the rich at His death, because He had done no violence, nor was any deceit in His mouth." Jesus was escorted from a mock trial during the night by the Jewish leaders directly to Pilate, and no one considered the potential of His life. He was "cut off" in a violent death, crucified between two thieves, yet buried in a rich man's tomb (Matthew 27:38, 57–60).

> Yet it pleased the LORD to bruise Him; He has put Him to grief. When You make His soul an offering for sin, He shall see His seed, He shall prolong His days, And the pleasure of the LORD shall prosper in His hand (Isaiah 53:10).

Isaiah 53:10 explains why Jesus had to die. In anticipation of the cross, He was identified as the spotless Lamb of God slain before the foundation of the world (Revelation 13:8). The death of Jesus Christ accomplished the will of God concerning our salvation. As our Substitute, He had to give His life and shed His blood—"the blood of the everlasting covenant" (Hebrews 13:20)—to atone for our sins. It pleased the Lord that He should fulfill the everlasting covenant to make salvation available to all, and to reconcile the relationship between God and humanity (Ephesians 2:16; Colossians 1:20).

Paul explains the goal of the everlasting covenant of *righteousness by faith*. "For He made Him who knew no sin to be sin for us, that we might become the righteousness of God in Him" (2 Corinthians 5:21). Peter tells us that Christ died that we might live for righteousness—

> For to this you were called, because Christ also suffered for us, leaving us an example, that you should follow His steps: "Who committed no sin, nor was deceit found in His mouth"; who, when He was reviled, did not revile in return; when He suffered, He did not threaten, but committed Himself to Him who judges righteously; who Himself bore our sins in His own body on the tree, that we, having died to sins, might live for righteousness— by whose stripes you were healed. For you were like sheep going

astray, but have now returned to the Shepherd and Overseer of your souls (1 Peter 2:21–25).

Isaiah 53:11–12 declares that Christ will rise above all these circumstances. "He shall see the labor of His soul, and be satisfied. By His knowledge My righteous Servant shall justify many, For He shall bear their iniquities. Therefore I will divide Him a portion with the great, and He shall divide the spoil with the strong, because He poured out His soul unto death, and He was numbered with the transgressors, and He bore the sin of many, and made intercession for the transgressors." In this fourth Servant Song, Isaiah foretells that death is not the end of this Servant, Jesus Christ. He will be resurrected triumphant over death, and exalted in spiritual glory (Philippians 2:9–11). He will rise to become the King of kings and Lord of lords (Revelation 19:16).

Many will learn of the loving Savior, and by knowledge of Him receive His *righteousness by faith* because He bore their iniquities and poured out His life to *justify* them, declaring them *not guilty*. By virtue of His fulfillment of the everlasting covenant of *righteousness by faith*, He crushed Satan's head and now shares the spoils of His spiritual victory over evil and death (Genesis 3:15). As the Last Adam— the new representative of the human race—Christ sits at the right hand of the Father serving as our High Priest today, interceding for us always. "He is also able to save to the uttermost those who come to God through Him, since He always lives to make intercession for them" (Hebrews 7:25).

The Person of Jesus Christ is the everlasting covenant, and we will see in our next chapter exactly how He fulfills God's covenant promises.

WHAT WAS NAILED TO THE CROSS?

Let's return to Moses and the people he led through 40 years of wilderness wanderings. Their story will help us better understand that God's temporary covenant was annulled once the Messiah-Christ ratified the New Covenant.

Although the new nation of Israel had the gospel of the everlasting covenant preached to them, faithless Israel did not enter God's rest. The New Testament tells us, "they could not enter in because of unbelief" and "indeed the gospel was preached . . . to them; but the word which they heard did not profit them, not being mixed with faith in those who heard it" (Hebrews 3:19; 4:2). Only the second generation of Israel would inherit the Promised Land.

Moses wrote the Book of Deuteronomy during the final month of his 120 years of life. It records his farewell addresses to that second generation, standing at the edge of the Promised Land.

Deuteronomy means *the second giving of the Law*. The book documents how the Lord greatly increased the constitutional laws of the *Book of the Covenant* first recorded by Moses' hand in Exodus. It was the renewal of what is historically known as the *Old Covenant* with the second generation of Israelites. Moses referred to this updated covenant document as the *Book of the Law*. Throughout the rest of Scripture, it is referred to either as the *Book of the Law* or the *Book of the Covenant*. The two terms both represent what is commonly referred to as the *Old Covenant*.

Moses identified the Ten Commandments as the heart of the covenant (Deuteronomy 4:13), and later confirmed that God had instructed him to place those two tablets of stone inside the *ark of the covenant* as the foundation of His government of love (Deuteronomy 10:2). They are the Charter of Rights of God's government of love.

The rest of Deuteronomy clearly reveals the principle of repeat and enlarge, as the Lord revisits the terms of the *Book of the Covenant* and adds to the constitutional requirements of civil, social, and ceremonial laws for the nation—including new ordinances for Festivals, annual sabbath days, food and drink offerings, and symbolic sacrificial remedies to pardon sin. All the ceremonial laws symbolically pointed to the ministry of Christ, and were intended to make the people recognize their need for their Messiah. The regulations of ministry of this covenant were accomplished by a temporary priesthood in an earthly sanctuary through substitutionary sacrifices that represented Christ.

Deuteronomy delivers the good news of God's blessings for obedience, but—in His foreknowledge—the Lord told Moses that the Israelites "will forsake Me and break My covenant which I have made with them" (Deuteronomy 31:16). Thus, He had Moses include a long list of curses, found in Deuteronomy 27:11–26 and 28:15–68, to warn the nation of consequences for disobedience and to stand as His witness against them when they sinned.

To renew and reaffirm the covenant with the second generation, Moses delivered this constitution in an address to the nation. Moses wrote all these words of the Lord in the covenant document he called the *Book of the Law*, also referred to as the *Book of the Covenant*. Then he instructed that the *Book of the Law* be placed in a side pocket of the ark, implying its temporary function—

So it was, when Moses had <u>completed writing the words of this law in a book</u>, when they were finished, that Moses commanded the Levites, who bore the ark of the covenant of the LORD, saying: "Take this **Book of the Law**, and put it **beside the ark** of the covenant of the LORD your God, that it may be there as a witness against you" (Deuteronomy 31:24–26; emphasis added).

Let's take a moment to recap the differences between the Ten-Commandment Law of God, and the *Book of the Law*—

The Ten Commandments of God

1) Written by the Lord's own finger;
2) Written on two stone tablets, also known as the *Testimony*;
3) Reflected His righteous character and represented the *Charter of Rights of God's* government of love;
4) God ordered them to be placed *inside* His ark of the covenant (His throne);
5) Have always been the heart of God's everlasting covenant of *righteousness by faith*.

The *Book of the Law* in Deuteronomy (also called the Book of the Covenant)

1) Dictated by God to Moses, who recorded it in human handwriting;
2) Written on animal skins or parchment;

> 3) Contained civil, social, and ceremonial religious laws that were Israel's *constitution*, with the Ten Commandments at the heart of their laws;
>
> 4) God directed it be placed in an **outside** pocket of the *ark of the covenant*, as a witness of God's judgments against unfaithfulness;
>
> 5) Was only relative to the Old Covenant, and annulled in the New

Now, let's consider what the Apostle Paul had to say about the *Book of the Law*. Paul's first published writing of the New Testament was his letter to the Galatians. Judaizers were troubling the church in Galatia, trying to make them keep the works of the old Mosaic Covenant *Book of the Law*. Paul wanted to assure the church members that those civil and ceremonial laws did not apply to New Covenant Christians. To make his point he quotes from Deuteronomy. Let's compare Moses' words about the *Book of the law* to Paul's —

Cursed is the one who does not confirm all the words of this law by observing them (Deuteronomy 27:26).

For as many as are of the works of the law are under the curse; for it is written, "Cursed is everyone who does not continue in all things which are written in the *book of the law*, to do them" (Galatians 3:10; emphasis added).

Remember, Paul liberally used the term law, and it is critical to examine his context to understand to which law he referred. In Galatians 3:10, Paul establishes the context for his entire letter of Galatians. Each time he uses the term *the law* he is—in context—referring to the *Book of the Law*, which represented the Old Covenant. This secondary law was added because of their transgressions against God's Ten Commandment Law of Love (Galatians 3:19).

The Old Covenant document was the tutor to bring Christ's people to Christ. All the ceremonial laws symbolically pointed to Christ's ministry (v. 24). Paul warned Christians that they should not practice these *Old Covenant* ordinances, saying "You, have become estranged from Christ, you who attempt to be justified by law; you have fallen from grace" (Galatians 5:4), and goes on to state in a positive manner, "if you are led by the Spirit, you are not under the law" (v. 18). Even God's covenant people from the Old Testament times who were led by the Spirit were not under the law's condemnation.

From Paul's context in Galatians, we know that all his references to *law* are related to the *Book of the Law*. How does Paul explain that this temporary *Old Covenant* document was done away with? Paul says this in his letter to the Colossians—

"And you, being dead in your trespasses and the uncircumcision of your flesh, He has made alive together with Him, having forgiven you all trespasses, having wiped out the handwriting of requirements that was against us, which was contrary to us. And He has taken it out of the way, having nailed it to the cross. Having disarmed principalities and powers, He made a public spectacle of them, triumphing over them in it. So *[his purpose statement, i.e. 'for this reason']* let no one judge you in food or in drink, or regarding a festival or a new moon or sabbaths, which are a shadow of things to come, but the substance is of Christ (Colossians 2:13–17).

What was nailed to the cross? Certainly, Christ bore our sins in His body and paid our sin debt at the cross (1 Peter 2:24). His precious blood blotted out the certificate of our indebtedness. And, Paul declared, "our old man was crucified with Him, that the body of sin might be done away with, that we should no longer be slaves of sin" (Romans 6:6).

What else was nailed to the cross? In the context of Colossians 2:14–17, we see Paul's reference to food and drink offerings, festivals, and annual sabbaths that symbolically shadowed the ministry of Christ. All of these were recorded in the Old Covenant *Book of the Law*, which also included the listing of God's curses for disobedience, and was placed in the side pocket of God's throne to stand as a witness against unfaithfulness. With the blood of the everlasting covenant being shed on Calvary's cross, the commandments contained in ordinances were abolished.

But now in Christ Jesus you who once were far off have been brought near by the blood of Christ. For He Himself is our peace, who has made both one, and has broken down the middle wall of separation, having **abolished in His flesh** the enmity, that is, **the law of commandments contained in ordinances**, so as to create in Himself one new man from the two, thus making peace, and that He might reconcile them both to God in one body through the cross, thereby putting to death the enmity (Ephesians 2:13–16; emphases added).

When Christ ratified the New Covenant through His blood, He abolished in His body the Old Covenant *Book of the Law*. Those ceremonial laws contained in ordinances which were unique to the Jewish nation—and separated them from the Gentiles—were no longer a dividing factor between the people.

Moreover, the civil laws of the *Mosaic Covenant*—like stoning for sexual sins, idolatry, and blasphemy—were made obsolete, in favor of civil authorities that God ordained to rule the nations. New Covenant believers are subject to the authorities of the land in which they live, with the exception they are not to follow any civil regulation that would require disobedience to God (Romans 13:1, 2; Acts 4:19; 5:29).

What was *not* nailed to the cross? Scripture is clear that God's moral law of love—which reflects His holy character and is summarized in the Ten Commandments—is included in the New Covenant when God writes His laws in our heart (Hebrews 8:10). Further, although most scholars refer to the entire book of Deuteronomy as the *Book of the Law*, we can be certain God didn't discard all of the principles included in that law that He had previously emphasized elsewhere in Scripture. For example, the description of covenant love and loyalty, "You shall love the LORD your God with all your heart, with all your soul, and with all your strength" (Deuteronomy 6:5), which Christ repeated in Mark 12:30, or even the health laws contained in the document that He mentioned earlier in Genesis 7:2–8 and Leviticus 11.

In Romans 8 Paul writes about the Ten Commandment law of God, saying that if we are walking in covenant relationship with Christ—

There is therefore now no condemnation to those who are in Christ Jesus, who do not walk according to the flesh, but according to the Spirit. For the law of the Spirit of life in Christ Jesus has made me free from the law of sin and death. For what the law could not do in that it was weak through the flesh, God did by sending His own Son in the likeness of sinful flesh, on account of sin: He condemned sin in the flesh, *that the righteous requirement of the law might be fulfilled in us* who do not walk according to the flesh but according to the Spirit (Romans 8:1–4; emphasis added).

The *Person of Jesus Christ* is the everlasting covenant of *righteousness by faith* determined by the Godhead before creating our world. Through this covenant, each member of the Godhead—the Father, Son, and Spirit—participates in the work of salvation, ensuring that the righteous requirement of their Divine moral code of love is fulfilled within those who enter into covenant relationship.

SUMMARY OF "HIS" STORY
Chapter Eleven

- The Hebrew language has only one word for covenant—*berit.*
- The Greek language has two words for covenant—*syntheke* and *diatheke.*
- *Syntheke* implies a contract between equal partners. This term is never used to describe God's covenants (God doesn't make contracts with humanity).
- *Diatheke* implies a will/testament/testimony that expresses the desired will of an individual. Only one person makes all the promises, holds absolute power over the terms of the covenant, and invites others to enter into covenant with them by agreeing to abide by the set terms.
- The Septuagint (LXX) was the first Hebrew-to-Greek translation of the Old Testament. Even though 72 Jewish scholars worked independently of one another, they all chose the word *diatheke* to describe all of God's covenants.
- The New Testament writers always used the word *diatheke* when referring to God's covenants.

- Jesus is identified in both the Old Testament and the New as the Servant of God.

- Isaiah's Servant Songs depict the *incarnated* Christ. In two of these songs, the Second Person of the Godhead speaks of the future when He will take on flesh.

- The first Servant Song is the recorded words of God, identifying Christ as the Everlasting Covenant. *National* Israel could not fulfill this prophecy in their apostate condition.

- The second Servant Song is a soliloquy of the Second Person of the Godhead, speaking of Himself *after* He would be incarnated in the Person of Jesus Christ. He prophesies about His human nature, and identifies Himself as *Israel*.

- Israel is a covenant name that develops a spiritual application.

- The Third Servant Song records another soliloquy that prophesies about the Messiah's willingness to suffer and die to pay the penalty of sin, and His victory in resurrection.

- The Fourth Servant Song describes Christ's suffering, death, and resurrection in such detail it proves only God could foretell these details. Their exact fulfillment in the New Testament proves that Christ was no imposter.

- The fourth Song also pictures why He had to die—we are in the picture.

- Jesus *is* the everlasting covenant of *righteousness by faith*.

- Deuteronomy is a covenant document called the *Book of the Law by Moses*, and named either by that term or the *Book of the Covenant* by Bible writers.

- When God renewed the covenant with the second generation of Israel, He added ordinances and commands to Israel's constitution, as recorded in Deuteronomy.

- Additional terms of the covenant included sacrificial remedies to pardon sin, food and drink offerings, festivals, and annual sabbaths that all pointed to the ministry of Christ.

- God included a list of curses for disobedience.

- Moses placed the *Book of the Law* in a side pocket of the Ark as God's witness against sin; this placement indicated the temporary nature of the Old Covenant.

- The *Book of the Law* was annulled when Christ ushered in the New Covenant.

- The Ten Commandments were inside the *Ark* as the foundation of God's government.

- The Ten Commandments were not abolished; they are part of the New Covenant.

THE BIG REVEAL

Chapter Twelve

The Messiah is the central figure of the Old Testament as well as the New. Through 4,000 years of His interactions with humanity recorded in the Old Testament, the Lord led His people by the light of His eternal humility. Is it difficult to think of God in that light? Only humility can govern by love that seeks reciprocal love. Only resolute humility could fulfill the promise that one of the Godhead would step out of Heaven to become the human *Suffering Servant* portrayed in Isaiah, who would pay humanity's sin-debt by His death, then be resurrected to glory and reign on the throne with God the Father.

His Story can be understood only through a knowledge of God's progressive revelation of His everlasting covenant of *righteousness by faith*. We have reviewed relevant Old Testament stories that have increased our infinity focus and taught us God's covenant language. This has prepared us for the big reveal of the Messiah's identity.

The member of the Godhead who humbled Himself to take on the flesh of humanity became forever identified by these covenant titles: 1) the *Anointed One*—the *Messiah-Christ*, who would be the *Servant*; 2) the *Seed of the woman*—who became the *Son of Man*; 3) the unique *only begotten covenant Son of God*—considered *firstborn*; 4) the eternally pledged *Lamb of God* who paid humanity's sin-debt; 5) the *Savior* who ratified the everlasting covenant with His own blood; 6) the *last Adam*—who represents humanity as the new *High Priest*; and, most significantly, 7) the *Surety* or *Guarantor* of the covenant. These covenant titles prove to be the key that unlocks the understanding of His true identity.

This is our "Aha!" moment when we see how the Person of Jesus Christ fulfilled all the roles of the promised coming Messiah who would renew the everlasting covenant with *spiritual* Israel.

THE ETERNAL GOD IS THE MESSIAH

In Hebrew the covenant title *Messiah* means *the Anointed One*, and the Greek word *Christ* is an equivalent title. The Old Testament contains over 125 prophesies of the coming Messiah, and the historical account of Jesus' life proves He fulfilled them all.

Dr. Peter Stoner—a former chairman of the departments of mathematics, astronomy, and engineering at Pasadena College in California—chose just eight of those prophesies to which he applied the "principle of probability." The results? The odds were a *trillion X trillion X billion to one* (that's 1 followed by 33 zeros) that anyone could fulfill even eight of the 125 prophesies. Just think what the odds would be for all 125. It couldn't just happen!

When the Lord of glory came down to take on the flesh of humanity in the Person of Jesus Christ, this was not His first personal appearance on Earth. We have seen that before His incarnation as Jesus, He appeared as a Man both to Abraham (when He personally investigated the sins of Sodom and Gomorrah—Genesis 18) and to Jacob (in an all-night wrestling match, when the Lord bestowed the covenant name *Israel* to him—Genesis 32:24–31).

He frequently appeared as *the Angel of the Lord* (meaning the *Messenger* of the Lord) who was distinct from the Father, and never appeared again after His incarnation. One such instance of His appearing as *the Angel of the Lord* was to Moses from a burning bush. When Moses asked His name, God said, "I AM WHO I AM . . . Thus you shall say to the children of Israel, 'I AM has sent me to you'" (Exodus 3:13–14).

In the New Testament, Jesus declared Himself to be the eternally pre-existent God. "Most assuredly, I say to you, before Abraham was, I AM" (John 8:58). The "I AM" God—the God of *history*, and the *present*, and the *future*—stood physically before the people, and the people picked up stones to kill Him for blasphemy because He claimed to be God. Sadly, in today's world *His Story* is often taught in the wrong manner, just as it was in Jesus' time. If He came to stand before our generation today, many would likely react by casting rocks of doubt at Him.

In seven "I AM" statements, Jesus repeatedly presented Himself as the great "I AM" of the Old Testament.

"I am the bread of life. He who comes to Me shall never hunger, and he who believes in Me shall never thirst" (John 6:35).

"I am the light of the world. Whoever follows me will never walk in darkness, but will have the light of life" (John 8:12, NIV).

"I am the door. If anyone enters by Me, he will be saved" (John 10:9).

"I am the good shepherd. The good shepherd lays down his life for the sheep" (John 10:11, NIV).

"I am the resurrection and the life. He who believes in Me, though he may die, he shall live. And whoever lives and believes in Me shall never die" (John 11:25–26).

"I am the way and the truth and the life. No one comes to the Father except through Me" (John 14:6).

And the seventh statement is very telling, "I am the vine, you are the branches. He who abides in Me, and I in him, bears much fruit; for without Me you can do nothing. If anyone does not abide in Me, he is cast out as a branch and is withered; and they gather them and throw them into the fire, and they are burned" (John 15:5–6).

Salvation is absolutely secure for those who remain "in Christ"—living in covenant relationship with Him. However, if we allow something to destroy that union with Him, we die spiritually and become barren branches that produce no fruits of righteousness. The final fate of dead branches is to face divine judgment at the end of time, and be cast into hell-fire to suffer the second death and perish (Revelation 21:8).

Moses told the Israelites, "The eternal God is your refuge, and underneath are the everlasting arms" (Deuteronomy 33:27, NIV). Isaiah refers to Him as the *Angel of God's Presence*, saying, "So He became their Savior. In all their affliction, He was afflicted, and the

Angel of His Presence saved them; in His love and in His pity He redeemed them; and He bore them and carried them all the days of old. But they rebelled and grieved His Holy Spirit; so He turned Himself against them as an enemy, and He fought against them" (Isaiah 63:8–10).

In the last book of the Old Testament, the Lord prophesies of sending John the Baptist to announce His coming, "Behold, I send My messenger, and he will prepare the way before Me." Then He immediately identifies Himself as the *Messenger of the covenant*: "*And the Lord, whom you seek, will suddenly come to His temple, even the Messenger of the covenant, in whom you delight. Behold, He is coming*" (Malachi 3:1; emphasis added). The Old Testament ends on this note.

Now we move to the Big Reveal of the New.

THE SEED OF THE WOMAN BECOMES THE SON OF MAN

As soon as sin shattered the Lord's sphere of righteousness in the Garden of Eden, God announced His everlasting covenant by saying to Satan, "I will put enmity between you and the woman, and between your seed and her Seed; He shall bruise your head, and you shall bruise His heel" (Genesis 3:15).

As we considered in chapter four, in less than 30 words God outlined an ongoing battle between Satan and his followers with the human descendants of Adam and Eve, and established the doctrine of the Incarnation, the promised covenant Seed. He would be wounded by that old serpent, before He crushed the head of Satan.

To bring His Seed into the world God selected a young virgin named Mary, who was betrothed in marriage to a carpenter named Joseph. A betrothal was a legally-binding marriage covenant, only dissolvable by divorce. It was a time of preparation for the union of two lives, during which the husband and wife lived separately and restrained from physical intimacy.

A quick sidebar-insert. To best understand any story about Jesus' life and ministry, all Gospel accounts should be considered, as they build on each other. John's Gospel uniquely puts greater emphasis on signs and conversations, rather than making Christ's preaching the main focus. The *synoptic gospels* (Matthew, Mark, Luke) describe similar events of Christ's life written to different target audiences. Each author shared the details they perceived as relevant to their readers. Luke—the only Gentile writer of the New Testament (Colossians 4:11, 14)—was an excellent historian whose research and interviews provide an explanation of the assumed Jewish perspective that the story of Jesus is part of God's progressive unfolding of the everlasting covenant.

In other words, the New Testament narrative simply picks up where the Old Testament left off.

Luke details the account of the angel Gabriel's visit to young Mary. Announcing that she was chosen by God to bear and nurture His young covenant Son, Gabriel explained that the Holy Spirit would do a miraculous work to plant the covenant Seed in her womb. After puzzling through this idea, Mary responded, "Behold the maidservant of the Lord! Let it be to me according to your word" (Luke 1:38).

The angel departed, the Holy Spirit wrought the miracle, and the virgin conceived the existing *Second Person of the Godhead*. His Divine nature was knitted together in the womb with her human nature, fulfilling God's promise made in the Garden (Genesis 3:15). Jesus had no human father!

Mary immediately departed to the hill country to visit with her relative Elizabeth, who was married to the priest Zacharias. God had granted this righteous couple their heart's longing. Elizabeth had been barren in her younger years, and was finally pregnant with their son who would become John the Baptist. Upon Mary's arrival, the baby in Elizabeth's womb leaped for joy, and she addressed Mary as the mother of her Lord (Luke 1:40–44). In Luke's account, first Mary and then Zacharias broke into song—

And Mary said: "My soul magnifies the Lord, and my spirit has rejoiced in God my Savior. For He has regarded the lowly state of His maidservant; for behold, henceforth all generations will call me blessed. . . . He has helped His servant Israel, **in**

remembrance of His mercy, as He spoke to our fathers, to Abraham and to his seed forever" (Luke 1:46–48, 54, 55; emphasis added).

Zacharias was filled with the Holy Spirit, and prophesied, saying: "Blessed is the Lord God of Israel, for He has visited and redeemed His people, and has raised up a horn of salvation for us In the house of His servant David, as He spoke by the mouth of His holy prophets, who have been since the world began, that we should be saved from our enemies and from the hand of all who hate us, **to perform the mercy promised to our fathers and to remember His holy covenant, the oath which He swore to our father Abraham**" (Luke 1:67–73; emphasis added).

All present knew these events meant God had remembered His everlasting covenant and was taking progressive action to fulfill His covenant promises to Abraham.

Mary remained with them for three months, then returned to Nazareth. As she shared the story of her conception with her betrothed husband, he struggled to believe it. Joseph was faithful to the Mosaic Law (Matthew 1:19), but his compassionate heart thought to quietly divorce her rather than have her stoned for adultery. God intervened by sending an angel to Joseph, declaring, "She will bring forth a Son, and you shall call His name JESUS, for He will save His people from their sins" (v. 21). Joseph received Mary as his wife, but did not know her intimately "till she had brought forth her first-born Son" (vv. 24–25).

Luke's regard for historical detail had him record the date that the Roman Emperor Caesar Augustus issued a decree requiring that all people be registered. Joseph and his very pregnant betrothed wife Mary "went up from Galilee, out of the city of Nazareth, into Judea, to the city of David, which is called Bethlehem" (Luke 2:4). Mary delivered her baby and wrapped Him in swaddling cloths (v. 7).

In self-sacrificing love, the Lord of glory stepped out of Heaven, lowering Himself to be incarnated in human flesh and presented on Earth, not in a plush palace, but a cold hard-stone feeding trough for cattle and sheep.

"But you, Bethlehem Ephrathah, though you are little among the thousands of Judah, yet out of you shall come forth to Me the One to be Ruler in Israel. Whose goings forth are from of old, from everlasting" (Micah 5:2).

No earthly fanfare accompanied His arrival. However, the hosts of Heaven's angels adored Him for His humility, and showed up as sky-witnesses, appearing to shepherds in the field to announce the arrival of the Messiah, bringing "good tidings of great joy which will be to all people, for there is born to you this day in the city of David a Savior, who is Christ the Lord. And this will be the sign to you: you will find a Babe wrapped in swaddling cloths, lying in a manger" (Luke 2:10–12). The shepherds rushed to Bethlehem to see the Lord, afterwards making it widely known that this Child had arrived. Mary pondered these things in her heart (vv. 16–19).

Gentiles described as *magi* or *wise men* from the East had been studying the story of a coming Redeemer and searching the skies for a sign. When they saw His star, they traveled far to reach Jerusalem. On arrival, they met with Herod the Great—the king of Israel—and explained that they were seeking the one born King of the Jews so they might worship Him. Herod summoned scribes who were experts in Old Testament prophecies to learn where it was prophesied the Messiah would be born, and they advised him it was Bethlehem (Micah 5:2). Then Herod secretly met with the wise men to determine when the star had risen, and instructed them to return to him when they found the Child, cunningly pretending that he also wanted to worship Him.

Drawn to His light, these Gentile wise men followed the star that moved and settled above the Bethlehem home where Joseph, Mary, and Jesus lived for a short time following His birth. They presented gifts of gold, frankincense, and myrrh to the Child who would become King. Being divinely warned in a dream, they departed in a different way to return to their country. Then, an angel warned Joseph to take Mary and the Child to Egypt (Matthew 2:1–15).

King Herod was a brutal dictator who had ordered his own family to be killed because he feared they might challenge his authority. Realizing the wise men had deceived him, Herod became enraged. Since he couldn't identify this Child whom he presumed posed a potential threat to his throne, Herod ordered all male children aged two and under to be massacred—according to the timeline of the first sighting of the star by the wise men (Matthew 2:16–18). Thus, Herod became Satan's agent to attempt to slaughter the promised Seed, just like the Pharaoh who had tried and failed at the birth of Moses. Shortly afterward, Herod died, and Joseph brought Mary and Jesus back from Egypt to settle in their hometown of Nazareth, fulfilling a number of prophecies from the Old Testament (Matthew 2:19–23).

The eternal light of humility shined brightly. At Jesus' incarnation, Divine nature was joined to human nature *forever* (He ascended to Heaven in glorified flesh—Acts 1:1–11). Laying aside His divine prerogatives and forsaking His independent authority, He became the Servant of the covenant identified in Isaiah's prophetic Servant Songs. Jesus totally submitted Himself to the will of the Father and the leading of the Holy Spirit, and yielded so fully to God that He was filled with the Spirit without limit (John 3:34). He was made in our likeness—assuming human limitations, needs, and weaknesses— yet was without sin (Hebrews 2:17; 4:15). Born as a human baby, He had to grow in wisdom and stature (Luke 2:40).

Jesus was nurtured in his early years by Mary and Joseph, who walked in covenant love and loyalty to the Lord. His *adoptive* father Joseph was a carpenter and is mentioned seven times by name in Scripture—in reference to learning of Mary's miraculous pregnancy, the escape from Bethlehem to Egypt with Mary and Jesus, and their return to Nazareth after Herod's death (Matthew 2:14–15). The final reference to Joseph is when Jesus was age 12 (Luke 2:43). Scripture is silent on the next eighteen years of Christ's life, except to say He worked as a carpenter. Since there is no further mention of Joseph, it is assumed that before Jesus began His public ministry at the age of 30, Joseph died, leaving behind four other sons and more than one daughter—the brothers and sisters of Jesus (Matthew 13:55–56; Mark 6:3).

Mary—the mother of Jesus—is identified six times with certainty in Scripture, and possibly in another three references. Scripture does not venerate Mary, but presents her as a virtuous woman. When Jesus was told His mother and brothers were outside seeking Him, He responded, "Who is My mother and who are My brothers?" Then, stretching His hand toward His disciples, He said, "Here are My mother and My brothers! For whoever does the will of My Father in heaven is My brother and sister and mother" (Matthew 12:48–50; compare Luke 8:19–21).

Jesus' brothers did not believe in Him as the Messiah at first. Scripture implies that it was they who thought He had lost His mind for living such an unconventional lifestyle (John 7:5; Mark 3:21). Therefore, as Mary's first-born Son responsible for her welfare, when she stood in horror near His cross Jesus entrusted her care to His beloved apostle John (John 19:25–27). The last reference to Mary is her presence with the disciples in the upper room on the day of Pentecost (Acts 1:14).

Jesus worked as a carpenter until He was 30 years-old. He was a Master Teacher for three-and-a-half years, often teaching in parables— using common cultural things to illustrate spiritual truths. Astonishing the multitudes, He taught with great authority regarding the kingdom of God that He was ushering in, and about God's requirements of covenant love and loyalty to gain entrance to His kingdom. He opened blind eyes and unstopped deaf ears. He healed diseased bodies, fed the hungry, and raised the dead. He forgave a woman caught in adultery, cast demons out of demoniacs, and transformed fearful disciples into men of faith. Christ came to reveal God's love and show the human race His righteous character and personality.

He was the Son of David—the covenant Son of God—but do you know what Christ's favorite covenant title for Himself was? *Son of Man*—which He used 81 times in the Gospels. Saying, for example: "Foxes have holes and birds of the air have nests, but the Son of Man has nowhere to lay His head" (Matthew 8:20); "For the Son of Man is Lord even of the Sabbath" (Matthew 12:8); "For the Son of Man has come to save that which was lost" (Matthew 18:11); "Just as the Son of Man did not come to be served, but to serve, and to give His life a ransom for many" (Matthew 20:28). Jesus also prophesied that as the Son of Man, He would return in the future in the clouds of heaven with majesty and great power (e.g. Matthew 24:27; Mark 8:38; 13:26).

Significantly, God supplied the same emphasis on Christ's humanity in prophetic vision to Daniel, who saw "One like the Son of Man" who proceeded from the "Ancient of Days" and was given universal authority (Daniel 7:13–14).

CHRIST, THE COVENANT SON OF GOD

Scripture uses the word *begotten* to express two entirely different ideas: 1) it can mean *to sire* or *generate through procreation*; or 2) it is used as a covenant term, whereby _begotten_ means _chosen for a covenant purpose_. God told the nation of Israel He was the Father who had begotten them (Deuteronomy 32:18). Paul wrote that he had *begotten* the Corinthians, and claimed the runaway slave Onesimus as his begotten son (1 Corinthians 4:15; Philemon 1:10). Do you recall what the covenant title _only begotten_ means? It defines a _unique, one-of-a-kind covenant son of promise—the heir of covenant promise_. Abraham sired eight sons, but Isaac was the Lord's promised covenant son and thus was designated as the Patriarch's *only begotten son* (Genesis 17:19; Hebrews 11:17–19).

Who is Jesus? The Apostle John introduces Him as the Word who was with God in the beginning and was God—the Creator God (John 1:1–5). He adds, "the Word became flesh and dwelt among us, and we beheld His glory, the glory as of the **only begotten** of the Father" (v. 14; emphasis added). It was the eternal *Second Person of the Godhead*—the Creator God—who pledged Himself for the purpose of the everlasting covenant before the world began. In anticipation of His incarnation, He was to be the *unique, one-of-a-kind covenant Son of promise*.

Sadly, there are some who do not comprehend covenant language, and mistakenly believe that somehow the One described as the *Second Person of the Godhead* was issued forth from the bosom of the Father, perceiving Him as inferior to the Father. This misguided concept is based on a single Scripture, "The only begotten Son, who is in the bosom of the Father" (John 1:18). The phrase "in the bosom" simply suggests the eternal union of love that exists in the deepest intimacy of continual fellowship between the Person of Jesus Christ and the member of the Godhead who is known as His *Father*. (Other translations, such as the NIV, translate this phrase as "is in closest relationship with the Father" or similar.)

Speaking of Christ, Paul says, "For in Him dwells all the fullness of the Godhead bodily" (Colossians 2:9). He possesses every attribute of God—including His eternal nature. There was never a time when He did not exist, because He is God. The only time He was issued forth or *birthed* was when He came from the womb of Mary.

Let's review the covenant title *firstborn*. Although Scripture uses the word to refer to the actual order of chronological birth, *firstborn* is most often used as a covenant title to refer to *preeminence in position* or *rightful heir*—whether or not a person was birthed first along the timeline. The Lord told Moses to say to Pharaoh, "Thus says the LORD: 'Israel is My son, My firstborn'" (Exodus 4:22). Israel was not the first nation, but God chose them to have superiority in His everlasting covenant plan, and treated them as first in rank.

Who is Jesus? Paul said, "He is the image of the invisible God, the firstborn over all creation. For by Him all things were created that are in heaven and *that* are on earth, visible and invisible. . . . And He is before all things, and in Him all things consist" (Colossians 1:15–17). When God was incarnated as the *Person of Jesus Christ*, He carried the covenant title *firstborn* because, as Creator of all things, He has *preeminence* over all creation. This title emphasizes His honor and dignity. Jesus Christ, who created all things, was not Himself created.

A critical review of the covenant title *son* or *son of God* is now required. Those terms are covenant titles for *human beings who are living in covenant relationship with the Lord* and serve as a channel of covenant promises, chosen to produce the holy seed (lineage) for God's kingdom. The New Testament refers to the first Adam as the *son of God* (Luke 3:38). The Old Testament provides us with a golden chain of covenant sons that links from the first Adam to the last Adam, Jesus Christ. Abraham is the first link. God introduced His covenant in the Garden (Genesis 3:15), and ratified it with Abraham in the *form of a vision* (Genesis 15). Then God renewed the covenant with Isaac and Jacob, who are the second and third links (Genesis 26:3–5; 28:12–15). The fourth link God chose was the entire nation of Israel's twelve tribes as His covenant son (Exodus 4:22–23), and God became identified as their Father (Deuteronomy 32:6).

David is the fifth link in the golden chain of covenant-son successors. Speaking of His servant David, whom the Lord had anointed as king, God said, "He shall cry to Me, 'You are my Father, My God, and the rock of my salvation.' Also I will make him My firstborn, the highest of the kings of the earth. My mercy I will keep for him forever, and My covenant shall stand firm with him. His seed also I will make to endure forever, and his throne as the days of heaven" (Psalm 89:26–29). God chose David's son Solomon as the sixth link, and reaffirmed the covenant with him, saying of Solomon, "He shall build a house for My name, and he shall be My son, and I will be his Father; and I will establish the throne of his kingdom over Israel forever" (1 Chronicles 22:10). What the Lord proclaimed to David and his son Solomon can also be applied to the Son of David, Christ Jesus, as the Messiah that would come from their lineage and establish His throne forever.

Who is Jesus? Immanuel. God with us (Isaiah 7:14; Matthew 1:23). The covenant in the flesh! (Isaiah 42:6; 49:8). He was born a human being to become God's _unique, one-of-a-kind, covenant Son of Promise_ to serve as a channel of covenant promises to all nations, and to produce a line of holy seed (lineage) for God's kingdom. Coming as a human, He walked in perfect covenant relationship with God, and was given the same covenant title _Son of God_ as those who served before Him. When the angel appeared to Mary to announce she would give birth to Jesus, he said, "That Holy One who is to be born _will be called_ the Son of God" (Luke 1:35, emphases added). God declared Himself to be the _Father_ of all His human covenant sons—including the Person of Jesus Christ, who became the human _Son of God_.

WHEN DID GOD BECOME THE SON OF GOD?

In the entire Old Testament, the term _Son of God_ is used only once in reference to the _Messiah-Christ_. It was spoken by the pagan King Nebuchadnezzar, who cast three Hebrews into a fire. Seeing that they were not consumed, the King looked into the fire and was astonished to see the form of a fourth Person, whom he described as being "like the Son of God" (Daniel 3:25). That fiery scene was another pre-incarnate appearance of the Messiah-Christ.

Our study of the progressive unfolding of the everlasting covenant throughout the Old Testament has opened the eyes of our understanding to God's covenant language. This helps us see that the *Second Person of the Godhead* became the *Son of God* by reason of His incarnation, and the *First Person of the Godhead* declared Himself to be Jesus Christ's *Father*. To provide assurance that this interpretation is accurate, we will now turn our attention to the first chapter of Hebrews, which will perfectly reinforce this point of His Story—

God, who at various times and in various ways spoke in time past to the fathers by the prophets, has in these last days spoken to us by His Son, whom He has appointed heir of all things, through whom also He made the worlds; who being the brightness of His glory and the express image of His person, and upholding all things by the word of His power, when He had by Himself purged our sins, sat down at the right hand of the Majesty on high (Hebrews 1:1–3).

Jesus Christ does not merely reflect God's glory, He radiates the glory of God, because He is God. He is the "express image of His person"—the exact representation of God because Jesus shares God's divine nature and essence. He not only created all things, He sustains all things by His powerful Word, and He sits as King on the throne at the right hand of the Father.

For to which of the angels did He ever say: "You are My Son, Today I have begotten You"? And again: "I will be to Him a Father, and He shall be to Me a Son"? (Hebrews 1:5).

Do you realize humans are now temporarily positioned lower than the angels? It's amazing to think our Creator God lowered Himself in humiliation not just to the lower level of His created angels, but to the lowest level of becoming a human. He was begotten of God—chosen to be the human covenant Son, the unique, one-of-a-kind *covenant Son of promise—the Heir of covenant promise.* In anticipation of His incarnation He was considered the covenant Son. The day to which the Father referred when He said, "today I have begotten you," is likely the day Jesus was baptized in the Jordan. The Holy Spirit descended upon Him like a dove, and the voice came from Heaven, saying, "This is My beloved Son, in whom I am well pleased" (Matthew 3:17). Just as God considered Himself as *Father* to all His other *human covenant sons*, so He described His relationship with the *Person of Jesus Christ* as being that of a *Father* and *Son.*

> But when He again brings the firstborn into the world, He says: "Let all the angels of God worship Him.". . . But to the Son He says: "Your throne, O God, is forever and ever; a scepter of righteousness is the scepter of Your Kingdom". . . And: "You, LORD, in the beginning laid the foundation of the earth, and the heavens are the work of Your hands" (Hebrews 1:6, 8, 10; compare Psalm 45:6; 102:25).

In these verses above, God in Heaven is speaking to His *firstborn* human covenant Son on Earth who enjoyed preeminence over all. Let's compare a conversation that Matthew recorded in his Gospel.

Jesus asked the Pharisees whose Son the Messiah would be, and they responded, "The Son of David." Then Jesus asked, "How then does David in the Spirit call Him 'Lord,' saying: 'The LORD said to my Lord', 'Sit at My right hand, till I make Your enemies Your footstool'? If David then calls Him 'Lord,' how is He his Son?'" (Matthew 22:43–45).

Christ's line of reasoning can be applied to the passage we just reviewed from the first chapter of Hebrews. The Father addressed the Son as the Creator God. Since Christ is God, how can He be called God's Son? Because *Son of God* is a *covenant title* assigned to Christ. In anticipation of His incarnation He was eternally considered the promised Messiah-Christ *Son* of the everlasting covenant, but it was when He entered the world through His incarnation that He became the *Son of God.*

Jesus claimed equality with the Father, yet as the human covenant Son He said, "My Father is greater than I" (John 8:58; 10:30; 14:9;

14:28). In His humanity, Christ voluntarily submitted Himself to do the Father's will—through the direction and power of the Holy Spirit—to bring many children to God by faith (John 1:12; Galatians 3:26). He emptied Himself of His glory to become a human, but Jesus prayed before His death that the Father would restore the glory He had before He came to earth (John 17:5). After He bore the judgment and wrath for sin, and was resurrected glorified, He once again shared equal glory with the Father. Paul said the rulers did not recognize who Jesus was, "for had they known, they would not have crucified the Lord of glory" (1 Corinthians 2:8). He will forever retain the covenant title of *Son of God*.

THE REST OF HIS STORY

The rest of *His Story* cannot be fulfilled in this one chapter, but His important covenant roles will now be condensed to a power-packed few pages that help us see Him more clearly.

Who is Jesus? He is our Kinsman Redeemer (a concept explained in the Old Testament, like Boaz in the Book of Ruth). Humanity had to have a human relative to represent and rescue us. Conceived by the Holy Spirit in the virgin Mary's womb, Christ's Divine nature was united with human nature—He was fully God and fully man (Colossians 1:15–23; Hebrews 1:3; 2:14, 17–18). If He had been *Divine only*, He could not have taken our sin upon His perfectly holy being, and His self-existent eternal nature could not have died. If He had been *human only*, He would have had to pay the full penalty of the second death, and perish as the result (Revelation 20:14; 21:8). What qualified Him to stand in as our spotless Substitute? He led a sinless life of perfect obedience and righteousness before God (John 8:29; 2 Corinthians 5:21; Hebrews 4:15; 1 Peter 3:18). If he had sinned, He would have died for His own sins only—sinless perfection was required to die as our Substitute.

Who is Jesus? He is the covenant "Lamb slain from the foundation of the world" (Revelation 13:8). That is the first of two twin pillars that serve as the foundation of the Lord's everlasting covenant and is the heart of the *everlasting gospel* (Revelation 14:6). Before Creation, the Godhead agreed that One of them would come to Earth to pay the penalty of humanity's sins, which could not have been paid by human offenders without perishing in death (Romans 6:23; John 3:16). In anticipation of the crucifixion, He was known by the covenant title *Lamb of God*. As soon as sin entered the world, His death was prophesied to the ancients through the sacrificial system that God instituted immediately, and then pictured clearly in the sanctuary system. He was the Servant-Messiah and "The Lord has laid on Him the iniquity of us all. He was oppressed and He was afflicted, yet He opened not His mouth; He was led as a lamb to the slaughter" (Isaiah 53:6–7).

Who is Jesus? He is Savior and Lord, which introduces the second twin pillar of the everlasting covenant of *righteousness by faith*: "For He made Him who knew no sin *to be* sin for us, that we might become the righteousness of God in Him" (2 Corinthians 5:21). The Lord's goal in the everlasting covenant is to restore humans to righteousness. When we accept Jesus as Savior, His righteousness is *imputed* (credited) to us and we are *justified by faith*—redeemed from the *penalty* of sin, and reconciled to God. When we accept Him as Lord (Master) of our lives, His righteousness is *infused* into us as He lives in our hearts by faith through the Holy Spirit (Ephesians 3:17), and we are *sanctified* by faith—released from the *power* of sin if we are willing to yield to His leading. The Spirit works within us to desire God's will and to empower us to walk in God's will (Philippians 2:13). Jesus came to save us *from* our sins, not *in* our sins (Matthew 1:21). Without doubt, He said only those who do God's will are eligible to enter His kingdom (Matthew 7:21).

Who is Jesus? He is the One who inaugurated and ratified the New Covenant. God had prophesied the day when He would renew the covenant and it would differ from the covenant the unfaithful Israelites continually broke. He said, "I will put My law in their minds, and write it on their hearts; and I will be their God, and they shall be My people . . . for they all shall know Me. . . . For I will forgive their iniquity, and their sin I will remember no more" (Jeremiah 31:33–34). The New Covenant repeats these very words in Hebrews 8:7–11. *New* in the original Greek language means *renewed in quality and form*. The New Covenant is the progressive unfolding of God's everlasting covenant—each stage building on the last through His repeat and enlarge principle of revelation. Three quarters of the New Covenant echo the Abrahamic-Davidic covenants.

The Ten Commandments are at the heart of the New Covenant, just as they were at the heart of the Old. They remain God's Charter of Rights for His government of love. When Jesus delivered His inaugural address of the New Covenant in His Sermon on the Mount (Matthew 5–7), He laid out radically renewed requirements of *righteousness by faith* by magnifying the Ten Commandments, introducing their spiritual principles (e.g. Matthew 5:20–28). James refers to God's "royal law" of love, and calls the Ten Commandments God's "law of liberty," warning that if you break one commandment, you are guilty of all (James 2:8–12).

In the Old Testament, God ratified His everlasting covenant in the *form of a vision* to Abraham (Genesis 15). In the New Testament, Christ ratified the renewal of the everlasting covenant in the *substance of reality* by His own shed blood, identified as "the blood of the everlasting covenant" (Hebrews 13:20).

Who is Jesus? He is the last Adam, the new representative of humanity, who overcame every temptation and conquered His flesh nature, succeeding where Adam failed. Paul said, "And so it is written, 'The first man Adam became a living being.' The **last Adam** became a life-giving spirit" (1 Corinthians 15:45; emphasis added) and "For as in Adam all die, even so in Christ all shall be made alive" (v. 22). When Paul reasoned with pagan philosophers in Athens, he said God "has made from one blood every nation of men" (Acts 17:26). He was referring to Adam as the representative of all humanity. Now God is making a new race of righteous people from the blood of our new representative—the Last Adam, Jesus Christ.

As the Last Adam, Christ regained the authority over the world. In the Garden of Eden the first Adam had not been deceived, but deliberately submitted to Satan (1 Timothy 2:14), forfeiting his God-given rights to rule the operations and jurisprudence of the planet. The New Testament tells us how Jesus was tempted in the wilderness for 40 days, and relates how Satan offered to return authority over Earth to Jesus, if He would only worship the fallen angel (Luke 4:5–7). Christ overcame that temptation, as He did all others. As the Last

Adam, Jesus defeated Satan on the cross, and gained victory over Satan's rule (Colossians 2:15).

Who is Jesus? Christ continues His ministry on our behalf as the High Priest of the New Covenant, who is "seated at the right hand of the throne of the Majesty in the heavens, a Minister of the sanctuary and of the true tabernacle which the Lord erected, and not man" (Hebrews 8:1–2). Some people have been misled to believe that when Christ cried out "It is finished" on the cross His ministry was over. What He had finished was His *earthly* ministry for the first aspect of salvation—*justification by faith*—in which He bore God's wrath of judgment on sin, offering up Himself as the Sacrifice once for all (Hebrews 7:27) and "He became the author of eternal salvation to all who obey Him" (Hebrews 5:9). He now ministers as our High Priest forever in an unchangeable priesthood, so that He can restore righteousness in our character and effect the second aspect of salvation—*sanctification by faith* (Hebrews 7:24, 25).

He was made in our likeness and suffered temptation—yet without sin. His sufferings make Him a sympathetic High Priest who is able to aid us when we are tempted (Hebrews 2:17–18; 4:15–16). Christ invites us to "come boldly to the throne of grace, that we may obtain mercy and find grace to help in time of need" (Hebrews 4:16). Scripture affirms that "He is also able to save to the uttermost those who come to God through Him, since He always lives to make intercession for them" Hebrews 7:25). Only Christ Himself has the character and credentials to intercede for God's covenant people. "There is one God and one Mediator between God and men, the Man Christ Jesus, who gave Himself a ransom for all" (1 Timothy 2:5–6).

Who is Jesus? He is the Surety, or Guarantor, of the New Covenant (Hebrews 7:22). He Himself guarantees our success when we walk in covenant relationship with Him. He is the Guarantor *from God to us*, "For all the promises of God in Him are Yes, and in Him Amen, to the glory of God through us" (2 Corinthians 1:20). No matter how many promises God has made, they find their "yes" answer in Christ. And He is the Guarantor *from us toward God*, for He "works in you both to will and to do His good pleasure" (Philippians 2:13). Jesus promises, "My grace is sufficient for you, for My strength is made perfect in weakness" (2 Corinthians 12:9). That's why Paul could claim, "I can do all things through Christ who strengthens me" (Philippians 4:13). Anyone who is in covenant relationship with Christ can make the same claim.

OUR RESPONSE TO THE BIG REVEAL

May our reaction to the *big reveal* of our Messiah-Christ be the same as His disciple Thomas, who—seeing the scars in the hands of the risen Savior, and reaching his hand to touch Christ's side where He had been pierced by a Roman spear as He hung on the cross— exclaimed in adoration, "My Lord and my God!" (John 20:28).

SUMMARY OF "HIS" STORY
Chapter Twelve

- God's everlasting covenant has always included *justification by faith* and *sanctification by faith*.
- The New Testament narrative picks up where the Old Testament ends—it is the continued unfolding of God's everlasting covenant revelation and the BIG REVEAL of the One who is the covenant.
- The life of Jesus fulfilled 125 Old Testament prophecies of the Messiah—the *principle of probability* makes that completely impossible by chance.
- Jesus claimed to be the eternal "I AM"—the God of history, the present, and the future.
- We can't understand the Person of Jesus Christ or His mission if we don't understand God's covenant language. His identity is revealed through covenant titles.
- Jesus is the *Messiah-Christ*—the *Anointed One*.
- Jesus is the *Seed of the woman*—God miraculously planted the Seed in the womb of a virgin to knit together His divine nature with human nature. Jesus had no biological father.
- Jesus is the *Son of Man*, which was His favorite covenant title used to identify Himself.
- Scripture presents a golden chain of successive *covenant sons* that links Adam to Jesus and includes Abraham, Isaac, Jacob, the nation of Israel, David, and Solomon.

- Jesus is the *Son of God*—a covenant title identifying human beings who are living in covenant relationship with the Lord and serve as a channel of covenant promises.
- The *Second Person of the Godhead* became the *Son of God* by reason of His incarnation.
- The relationship of Jesus to the *First Person of the Godhead* is defined as a Father/Son relationship, just as God defined His relationship to all His other human covenant sons.
- Jesus is the *only begotten*—a covenant title meaning He was a unique, one-of-a-kind covenant Son of promise and heir to God's covenant promises.
- Jesus is the *firstborn* over all creation—a covenant title indicating His preeminence over all, because He created all.
- Jesus is the eternally pledged *Lamb of God*—a covenant title for the Substitute sacrifice who died to pay humanity's sin-debt.
- Jesus is our *Kinsman Redeemer*—He had to have a Divine-human nature to die for us.
- Jesus is the Savior who ratified the everlasting covenant with His own blood, and provides our *justification by faith*.
- Jesus is the *last Adam*—the new Representative of humanity who regained authority over Earth by defeating Satan at the cross.
- Jesus is the new *High Priest*—when His earthly ministry was finished, He began His ministry in Heaven at the right hand of the Father on the throne. Because He was made like humanity in every way and suffered temptation, yet was without sin, He is a sympathetic High Priest who intercedes on our behalf. There is only one Mediator between God and humans—the Man Christ Jesus who gave His life to ransom humans.
- Jesus is *Lord* who became the author of salvation for all who obey, and provides *sanctification by faith*.
- Jesus is the *Surety* or *Guarantor* of the covenant—*from God to us*, because all of God's promises find their "yes" answer in Him; and *from us to God*, because He works in human to desire God's will and empowers them to do God's will.

LIVING IN COVENANT RELATIONSHIP

Chapter Thirteen

In love and compassion, Jesus issued the *great invitation* to the multitudes standing before Him, "Come to Me, all you who labor and are heavy laden, and I will give you rest. Take My yoke upon you and learn from Me, for I am gentle and lowly in heart, and you will find rest for your souls. For My yoke is easy and My burden is light" (Matthew 11:28–30).

Jesus' use of the word *yoke* resonated with the multitude. The Pharisees taught salvation by works, and had weighed believers down with hundreds of tedious religious traditions. The people commonly compared this religious system with a *yoke* frame that was fitted over the neck and shoulders of slaves to carry burdensome loads.

Christ painted a word-picture to help people see His *yoke* differs— it can be compared to the wooden crosspiece yoke that fastens two animals together to pull a cart. His *yoke*, He declared, makes life's burdens bearable. It is the wooden cross of Calvary that *yokes* us to Christ, and when we accept Him as Savior and Lord, He restores our righteousness by faith in Him.

The rest Jesus offers is twofold: 1) a provision of grace to overcome the destruction of sin; and 2) a restoration of peace in the midst of life's storms. Jesus wasn't speaking only to those present that day. Looking down through the ages, He included future generations. He longs for all to come to Him. Do you hear His loving invitation today? Do you need rest from self-imposed burdens caused by lack of self-discipline, or from the inevitable burdens of life that are outside your control?

Jesus addressed the multitudes as the One who was "humble and lowly in heart." He had humbled Himself to be made in our likeness, and laid down His independent authority to totally yield to the Holy Spirit's leading—only doing what the Father showed Him and only speaking what the Father told Him to say (John 5:19; 12:49–50). He announced that "the Son of Man did not come to be served, but to serve, and to give His life a ransom for many," and punctuated the truth of servant-leadership by instructing His disciples to follow Him in self-sacrificing service to others (Mark 10:45; John 13:1–17).

By the example of His life, Jesus showed that self-sacrificing love expressed through humility is the root of righteousness, and the character trait humans most need to develop. Paul calls on Christians to follow Christ's example of humility, having the same attitude and humble mindset that He demonstrated by a life of loving obedience to God (Philippians 2:5–8).

The Bible describes *humility* as total dependence upon God, and *sin* as a refusal to depend on God. The pride and desire to exalt self which initially swelled in Satan's heart is the root of all sin (Isaiah 14:12–14; Ezekiel 28:11–17). Satan certainly proved the Proverb, "Pride goes before destruction, and a haughty spirit before a fall" (Proverbs 16:18). In sharp contrast, because Christ Jesus stooped so low, God exalted Him to the highest place and gave Him the name that is above every name" (Philippians 2:9–11).

GOD LIFTS UP THE HUMBLE

The Lord spoke through His prophet Micah, saying, "What does the LORD require of you but to do justly, to love mercy, and to walk humbly with your God?" (Micah 6:8). The Apostle James echoes this in the New Testament, "'God resists the proud, but gives grace to the humble.'... Humble yourselves in the sight of the Lord, and He will lift you up" (James 4:6, 10).

The God who is described as "the High and Lofty One Who inhabits eternity," is the same up-close-and-personal God who dwells "with him who has a contrite and humble spirit, to revive the spirit of the humble, and to revive the heart of the contrite one" (Isaiah 57:15). There is no barrier between the humble heart on Earth and His humble heart in Heaven. When we are humble before Him, the Lord's heart is moved to help and revive us—changing our attitudes, and renewing our courage and strength.

Jesus explained our great need of humbly depending on God to gain salvation—

"Assuredly, I say to you, unless you are **converted** and **become as little children**, you will by no means enter the kingdom of heaven. Therefore whoever humbles himself as this little child is the greatest in the kingdom of heaven" (Matthew 18:3–4; emphases added).

To be *converted* means to turn—or return—to God. Jesus explained that *conversion* happens as we humble ourselves like a little child who recognizes the great need of a loving parent. Knowing we are helpless to save ourselves and have no spiritual resources of our own, we acknowledge our vulnerability and run into the safety of His loving embrace. Living in covenant relationship with Him requires childlike trust in the promises of His constant presence and provision, and a life of dependence on His grace. Like a child with an open and teachable heart, we learn His lessons of *righteousness by faith*—lessons that prepare us for eternal life. Just as Jesus did, we daily lay down our independent authority and give the Lord permission to lead as we walk hand in hand with Him, following in His footsteps (1 John 1:5–7; 2:6).

Is it difficult to accept that we must fully depend on God? Our culture celebrates independence. We have been trained to think and act independently, while praised for our ability to live without another's support, fueling a sense of pride that hides in a dark chasm of our hearts. Unfortunately, we all suffer the pride of independence to some degree.

God's plan of salvation has always been for humans to depend upon Him. If we don't yield control to our Heavenly Father, Jesus said that we "will by no means enter the kingdom of heaven" (Matthew 18:3). It sounds simple in principle, but it is impossible for us to do unless we allow the Lord to affect this change in our lives. Here is how it begins—

> Repent therefore and be converted, that your sins may be blotted out, so that times of refreshing may come from the presence of the Lord (Acts 3:19).

Repentance brings forgiveness and times of refreshing from the Lord that speed our recovery from the sting of sin, and revive us spiritually. Repentance begins with *recognition* of sin. Examining ourselves in the light of God's Word, we recognize we have fallen short of His righteous requirements. Under the Holy Spirit's convicting power (John 16:8), we begin to think differently, and suddenly sin has a foul smell to it. When we understand God's love and righteousness, and realize how we have sinned against Him, *godly sorrow* seizes our hearts. We regret our sins. This godly sorrow produces a change of heart, which leads us to turn away from sin to embrace His salvation (2 Corinthians 7:10–11).

Confession is the clearinghouse of the conscience, and is our next critical step to demonstrate we have had a change of attitude regarding our sin-sick behavior. Through confession we acknowledge our need for the Savior, and seek forgiveness of our sins. When confession is accompanied with godly sorrow and a sincere desire to change, God is faithful to forgive us and He cleanses us of all unrighteousness (1 John 1:9).

Our challenge is to learn to *receive God's forgiveness* and comfort of grace. While we should examine ourselves and daily confess our sins for the continual process of *sanctification*, if we have already come to Him with a sincere heart full of sorrow for a particular sin, asked for His forgiveness, and have not repeated that sin, we can—by faith— accept that He has cleansed us of that sin. It is done. Let it go. The Lord says, "Forget the former things; do not dwell on the past. See,

I am doing a new thing! Now it springs up; do you not perceive it?" (Isaiah 43:18–19, NIV). This is how we disarm the devil, and are delivered from his trap of condemnation (Romans 8:1).

Now we are ready for a 180-degree turnaround, but we can't achieve this by human will-power alone. It is God who gives us the power to *change our conduct!* Repentance is a gift granted by God to the penitent (Acts 5:31). It is His power working mightily within us that enables us to turn back to Him and do His will (Philippians 2:13).

To sum up this five-step process of repentance: 1) we recognize and think differently about ungodly behavior; 2) godly sorrow causes us to regret our sin; 3) our attitudes are altered and we confess our sins, asking for forgiveness; 4) we receive God's forgiveness, applying His healing balm to our wounded souls; and 5) God empowers us to change our conduct and make a U-turn in the right direction— straight toward Him. Repentance brings joy in His Presence.

God trusts a humble heart. He pours His grace and power into that person to lift them in honor. Humility is *not* weakness. Abraham humbly followed God, not knowing where he was going (Hebrews 11:8). Moses was said to be more humble that all men on the face of the earth (Numbers 12:3). Isaiah's heart was humbled when He saw God high and lifted up—glorious and exalted (Isaiah 6:1–5). God sent an angel to Daniel to say his prayers were heard because he humbled himself before God (Daniel 10:12). When the risen Christ appeared to the self-righteous Saul on the road to Damascus, he was blinded by the eternal light of humility and *converted*, and would become known as the Apostle Paul. He learned God's grace was sufficient (Acts 9:3–19; 2 Corinthians 12:9).

THE HOLY SPIRIT'S ROLE IN SALVATION

The Messiah and the Holy Spirit are introduced and portrayed throughout the Old Testament, but the big reveal for both comes in the New Testament. God provided 58 Scripture passages to offer sufficient proof that the One Sovereign Godhead consists of three Divine Persons. God—the Father, Son, and Holy Spirit. The formula for the Godhead is arrived at through multiplication. $1 \times 1 \times 1 = 1$, otherwise stated as 1^3—or one to the Third power.

The Messiah was called by the Greek title of *Paraclete or Paracletos*, which means He was the Advocate, Counselor, Comforter, Intercessor, and Helper of the people in His earthly ministry. Before His death, Christ announced His soon departure, saying, "Let not your heart be troubled; you believe in God, believe also in Me. In My Father's house are many mansions; if it were not so, I would have told you. I go to prepare a place for you. And if I go and prepare a place for you, I will come again and receive you to Myself; that where I am, there you may be also" (John 14:1–3). Then He delivered His big announcement, saying—

"And I will pray the Father, and He will give you **another Helper** [Greek: *allos Paracletos*], that **He** may abide with you forever" (John 14:16; emphasis added).

Here's a sidebar insert. In the Greek language there are two words for *another*. One is *heteros*, which means *another of a different kind* (like an orange would be another piece of fruit as compared to an apple). The other Greek word is *allos*, meaning *another of the exact kind* (a perfect duplication replacement).

In the Greek, Jesus called the Holy Spirit "allos Paracletos," which meant the Person who would be sent to continue Christ's ministry on earth (after His ascension to Heaven) had the exact same qualities and characteristics as Christ, because the Holy Spirit is part of the Godhead. He is a conscious, intelligent Person, sent to teach, comfort, advise, defend, and intercede for us. There would be no possible comparison of an abstract force to Christ. The Holy Spirit is the perfect duplicate of Christ in His Personhood, power, and purpose.

Jesus identified the Holy Spirit as the "Spirit of truth" and said by the Spirit's coming, "I will come to you" (vv. 17–18). What did Jesus mean by such a promise? When the Holy Spirit dwells in a human, so also does the Father and Son, because the Three are One. Paul prayed—

That He would grant you, according to the riches of His glory, to be *strengthened with might through His Spirit in the inner man,* that **Christ may dwell in your hearts through faith**; that you, being rooted and grounded in love, may be able to comprehend with all the saints what is the width and length and depth and height—to know the love of Christ which passes knowledge; that you may be filled with all the fullness of God" (Ephesians 3:16–19; emphasis added).

The Holy Spirit possesses wisdom and understanding (1 Corinthians 2:10–11). Paul speaks of Him bestowing spiritual gifts, "distributing to each one individually as He wills" (1 Corinthians 12:11). The Holy Spirit exercised authority to choose church leaders, lead in church decisions, and to direct the mission of preaching the Gospel (Acts 13:2; 15:28; 16:6–7). He is endowed with the emotions of a Person: He loves; He can be grieved; He can be insulted (Isaiah 63:10; Romans 15:30; Ephesians 4:30; Hebrews 10:29). He hears what our words testify, and can be lied to and tested—in the sense that He is disturbed (Acts 5:3–4, 9). Endowed with a mind that can formulate thoughts, the Holy Spirit speaks to relay His thoughts (Acts 8:29; 10:19, 20; 1 Timothy 4:1; Hebrews 3:7–9). He helps us with our prayers, interceding for us when all we can do is sigh before the Lord in prayer—

Likewise the Spirit also helps in our weaknesses. For we do not know what we should pray for as we ought, but the Spirit Himself makes intercession for us with groanings which cannot be uttered (Romans 8:26).

Christ's intercession to the Father proves Him to be a distinct Person from the Father and, likewise, the Spirit's intercession proves His distinct Personhood. Some who do not understand Greek make a fuss over the King James Version of Romans 8:26 above, because it was translated "the Spirit *itself*" rather than *Himself*. The Greek word for *spirit* is *pneuma*, which is neuter gender (neither male, nor female). The KJV is grammatically correct to follow *pneuma* with the neuter gender pronoun *itself*. But Jesus used the word *pneuma* to refer to God, saying, "God is Spirit" (John 4:24). Would we ever refer to Him as an *It*?

Christ constantly used the emphatic, masculine personal pronouns *He* or *Him* when referring to the Holy Spirit. Would our Savior employ language that could mislead His disciples? Would we dare accuse Him of such a fearful error? There is no other alternative than to regard the Holy Spirit as another Person of the Godhead. Jesus delivered a sobering message when He said the unpardonable sin was blasphemy against the Holy Spirit (Mark 3:28–30).

The Holy Spirit came to be our Teacher and to bear witness to Christ (John 14:26; 15:26). The disciples didn't grasp all the truths Jesus taught during His earthly ministry, but the Holy Spirit came to enlighten them. He will do the same for you and me. I always pray for the Spirit to guide me in Bible study and lead me in a progressive understanding of truth. He will never speak anything that is contrary to Scripture. When He dwells within our hearts, He bears witness that we are the children of God (Romans 8:16).

Scripture clearly and abundantly affirms that the Holy Spirit possesses attributes of deity peculiar to God. He is holy and described as eternal (Hebrews 9:14). He is omniscient and omnipresent (John 14:26; Psalm 139:7–10). And finally, He is omnipotent. Creation is attributed to Him, no less than the Father or Son. He miraculously formed the incarnate Christ in the womb of Mary, anointed Him for ministry, and His power resurrected Christ (Genesis 1:2; Luke 1:35; Romans 8:11). Who but a Divine Person could have done these things?

Can humans comprehend the co-equal nature of the Three-in-One Persons of the Godhead? God is too wonderful for our comprehension now, but one day we will see Him face-to-face, and enjoy eternity in His Presence to know Him better. What Scripture clearly reveals to us now is that the essential nature of God is self-sacrificing love, and together with His righteous character, this is His eternal light of humility. We glimpse the non-competitive humility that exists among the Three as we see that Christ submitted to the Father's will, the Holy Spirit submits to Jesus' authority, and the Father exalts Jesus to the highest place. In self-sacrificing love and humility, none of the Three clamor for glory.

MY PEOPLE ARE DESTROYED FOR LACK OF KNOWLEDGE

The Lord laments, "My people are destroyed for lack of knowledge" (Hosea 4:6). So many are not taught that He invites us to enter into a covenant where He makes and keeps all His promises to restore our righteousness by faith in Him, or that His expectation of those in covenant relationship with Him is reciprocal actions of love and loyalty to Him.

According to Jesus, we can't be apathetic about our relationship with the Lord and expect to enter into eternal life. He instructs us to "Strive to enter through the narrow gate" (Luke 13:24), and He said, "wide is the gate and broad is the way that leads to destruction, and there are many who go in by it. Because narrow is the gate and difficult is the way which leads to life, and there are few who find it" (Matthew 7:13–14). This was His alarming wakeup call for me—

"Not everyone who says to Me, 'Lord, Lord,' shall enter the kingdom of heaven, but he who **does the will of My Father in heaven**. Many will say to Me in that day, 'Lord, Lord, have we not prophesied in Your name, cast out demons in Your name, and done many wonders in Your name?' And then I will declare to them, 'I never knew you; depart from Me, you who practice lawlessness!'" (Matthew 7:21–23; emphasis added).

Around 1998, as I dutifully read my daily assignment from the Bible, that Scripture lit up like a neon sign, and I wondered, *Do I know the will of the Father in Heaven?* Attending church several times a week, I taught Sunday school and busied myself with Christian service. People told me what a wonderful Christian I was. I carried my Bible everywhere, but I was not engaged in deep study or reflection on the Scriptures. Sometimes I sat on a church pew in muted defeat, wondering where God was, feeling I had hit a wall and didn't know how to get beyond the barrier between us. In a sense, church had become a cultural and social activity. My days were punctuated with prayer, but sadly lacking real intimacy of communion with God.

Worst of all, I had a false sense of security. Jesus' words in Matthew 7:21–23 jarred me. What did He mean by "you who practice lawlessness"? As I began to search the Scriptures, I realized I was not totally yielded to God's plan of salvation by grace, and was not living in covenant relationship with Him. Why not? I didn't know both aspects of His plan of *righteousness by faith*. I had accepted Christ as my Savior whose death *justified* me by faith, but I also needed to accept Him as Lord and Master over my life to be *sanctified* by faith. Knowing what is required is one thing—knowing how to go about it is quite different. I prayed earnestly.

God impressed my heart with three steps that are necessary to enter into covenant relationship with Him: 1) gain knowledge of the Lord's love, wisdom, and power to encourage our trust; 2) stop resisting His love and submit to His authority; and 3) yield to the Holy Spirit's leading as our everyday way of living. These steps equate exactly to what Jesus declared is required to enter the kingdom of heaven—to become His covenant children, we must humble ourselves and become totally dependent upon Him (Matthew 18:3–4).

Let's unpack those three steps.

STEP ONE—KNOW GOD

Jesus said, "This is eternal life, that they may know You, the only true God, and Jesus Christ whom You have sent" (John 17:3). There are two kinds of knowledge—*head* knowledge, and *heart* knowledge. We can read the Bible like a biography of the Lord and know many facts about Him, but that doesn't mean we *know* God personally. The kind of knowledge Jesus referred to for eternal life is the *knowing* of the heart that is learned through intimate personal experience and comes from living in fellowship with God as our Heavenly Father.

God wants us to have heart knowledge of His immeasurable love, His infinite wisdom, and His exceedingly great power so that we can truly trust Him—because trust is the foundation of faith.

As we have dialed in an infinity focus, we have seen the consistency of the Lord's *nature*—"God is love" (1 John 4:8), and the shining light of His righteous *character*—"God is light" (1 John 1:5). He operates by the power of love and humility. He cannot sin, and makes no mistakes. Everything He does is for our eternal benefit. God never changes—His love and justice are the same in both Testaments (Malachi 3:6; Hebrews 13:8). His consistency makes Him trustworthy. He is the covenant Maker and covenant Keeper, who does all within His power to save us.

"God demonstrates His own love toward us, in that while we were still sinners, Christ died for us" (Romans 5:8). What greater love could He have demonstrated toward us? In Ephesians 3:18–19, the Apostle Paul tries to define how limitless and immeasurable the love of God is toward us. The *width* of His love extends to all people; the *length* of His love extends to all time; the depth of His love extends to the lowest condition of human need; and the *height* of His love reaches to the highest heaven. The love of Christ surpasses knowledge, but even a glimpse of it can motivate us to love Him in return. And just think, Paul says the Lord wants to fill our hearts to the brim with all His fullness (Ephesians 3:18–19). **Why wouldn't we trust a love like that?**

God's knowledge is infinite. He knows the end from the beginning (Isaiah 46:10). His intelligence is far superior to ours. His ways and thoughts are exceedingly higher than humans (Isaiah 55:9). Do you know that God wants to be our life coach? Scripture calls on us to "Trust in the LORD with all your heart, and lean not on your own understanding; in all your ways acknowledge Him, and He shall direct your paths" (Proverbs 3:5–6). He has a plan for each of our lives and His plan is better than the lives we are living—we should seek Him with all of our hearts to understand it (Jeremiah 29:11–14). **Why wouldn't we trust His superior knowledge?**

God's great power is limitless, protective, and sustaining (Hebrews 1:3). With God all things are possible—nothing is too difficult for Him (Matthew 19:26; Jeremiah 32:17). Jesus explained that mistaken beliefs are formed when we "do not know the Scriptures nor the power of God" (Mark 12:24). His power is available to us through the Holy Spirit (Ephesians 3:16, 19; 2 Peter 1:3). "He gives power to the weak, and to those who have no might He increases strength" (Isaiah 40:29). He accomplishes His will in every situation and empowers His covenant children to accomplish things we never could on our own (Isaiah 46:10; Ephesians 1:11). He has an inheritance laid up for His children, "who are kept by the power of God through faith for salvation ready to be revealed in the last time" (1 Peter 1:5). **Why wouldn't we trust His power?**

STEP TWO—STOP RESISTING HIS LOVE AND SUBMIT

The Lord created us for a love relationship with Him, and His heart's desire is that we would stop resisting His love. He longs for us to become His covenant children, that He can be our Father to provide for us, bring us peace, fill our hearts with joy, and give us a more abundant life now on this Earth (Romans 15:13; John 10:10), while preparing us for eternal life in His Presence. Once we finally recognize His unconditional love for us, it is difficult just to ignore Him. Love awakens love. The Bible says, "We love Him because He first loved us" (1 John 4:19).

To enter into covenant relationship with Him, the Lord asks us to love Him in return and choose to submit to His authority—His instructions, His direction, and His correction. Because He has given to us the sacred gift of free will, He never forces us to humble ourselves and be dependent upon Him. We must choose to receive His love and enter into covenant with Him by submitting to Him as our Father.

> Therefore He says: "God resists the proud, but gives grace to the humble." Therefore **submit to God**. Resist the devil and he will flee from you. Draw near to God and He will draw near to you. Cleanse your hands, you sinners; and purify your hearts, you double-minded (James 4:6–8; emphasis added).

To *submit* to God requires a conscious decision of our will to yield to His infinite authority as the Sovereign ruler of His kingdom. Submission means to line up under His will, as we purposely determine to follow His leadership and obey His commands, motivated by love. Jesus said, "If you keep My commandments, you will abide in My love, just as I have kept My Father's commandments and abide in His love" (John 15:10).

Consider the first generation of the Israelites whom God redeemed from bondage. As their Savior, the Lord reminded them of His righteous requirements to walk in covenant with Him. However, to them His commandments were just rules, and they refused to remain in a relationship of love and loyalty. Rules without relationship result in rebellion. What happened when they rejected His government of love? They couldn't enter the Promised Land.

To remain in covenant relationship with the Lord we must live in covenant submission to Him, laying down our independent authority. Look at these words of Jesus—

Then He said to them all, "If anyone desires to come after Me, let him deny himself, and take up his cross daily, and follow Me. For whoever desires to save his life will lose it, but whoever loses his life for My sake will save it. For what profit is it to a man if he gains the whole world, and is himself destroyed or lost? For whoever is ashamed of Me and My words, of him the Son of Man will be ashamed when He comes in His own glory, and in His Father's, and of the holy angels" (Luke 9:23–26).

In the day of Jesus, to "take up your cross" meant you were about to be crucified. Jesus is telling us that to follow in His footsteps we must lay down our independent authority, dying to self-will "daily" so that we may gain a better life—eternal life. Denying self isn't appealing at first, but as we are trained in righteousness it becomes easier. And what a trade-off He offers. Jesus promises if we walk in obedience to Him, we will receive the Holy Spirit—

If you love Me, keep My commandments. And I will pray the Father, and He will give you another Helper, that He may abide with you forever—the Spirit of truth . . . (John 14:15–17).

The supreme pleasure of submission is that the Lord gives us the Holy Spirit when we have an obedient attitude (Acts 5:32). When the Holy Spirit dwells in us, we become partakers of the divine nature of God. He provides everything necessary for a life of righteousness, so that we can escape the corruption that fills this old, decaying world (2 Peter 1:3–4). Through the Holy Spirit we have the "exceeding greatness of His power toward us who believe, according to the working of His mighty power" and Christ lives in our hearts by faith (Ephesians 1:19; 3:16–20). The Lord provides the way out of every temptation, and as we take advantage of His power to resist the devil, the devil will flee (1 Corinthians 10:13; James 4:7).

Jesus came to Earth to destroy the works of the devil (1 John 3:8). Accepting Christ as our Savior releases us from the *penalty* of sin and we are *justified by faith*. But Jesus wants to live in our hearts by faith through the indwelling Holy Spirit, so that He can deliver us from the *power* of sin. Thus we will be *sanctified by faith* as we begin to develop and reflect His character. Believers are predestined to become like Jesus, and—like Him—we will delight to do God's will, following His commandments (Romans 8:29; Psalm 40:8). When we heed His authority, He gives us peace that flows like a river, and "righteousness like the waves of the sea" (Isaiah 48:18).

To gain this we must submit our thoughts and motives to the Lord. We can follow King David's example and pray, "Search me, O God, and know my heart; try me, and know my anxieties; and see if there is any wicked way in me, and lead me in the way everlasting. . . . Cause me to hear Your lovingkindness in the morning, for in You do I trust; cause me to know the way in which I should walk, for I lift up my soul to You. . . . Teach me to do Your will, for You are my God; Your Spirit is good. Lead me in the land of uprightness" (Psalm 139:23–24; 143:8, 10). As David did in his famous Psalm of repentance, we also need to cry out, "Create in me a clean heart, O God" (Psalm 51:10).

Here is a sidebar insert of great significance. There are two Hebrew words for create: *bārā'* and *yatzar*. The word *create* that David used in Psalm 51:10 is the same Hebrew word *bārā'* that is used to describe God's creative act in the beginning of time. It means to create something out of nothing and is always used in reference to God alone. In contrast, *yatzar* describes the actions of humans to *generate*, *produce*, or *establish* something from preexisting elements. What significance is that to us? Only God can create a clean heart within us. There is nothing humans can do to accomplish this on our own. Our only chance is to submit to God's power to purify and sanctify our hearts—making us new creations.

We also submit to His correction. Actually, I invite the Lord to correct me and root out my unrighteousness. I do not fear His discipline. He is the perfect Father and His discipline is never done to inflict harm, but to bless us so that we can know righteousness and peace. His discipline is perfect—He knows when we need comfort, and He knows when we need correction. "God disciplines us for our good, that we may share in his holiness. No discipline seems pleasant at the time, but painful. Later on, however, it produces a harvest of righteousness and peace for those who have been trained by it" (Hebrews 12:10–11, NIV).

God guarantees our submission to Him will develop His *righteousness by faith* in our hearts. By the Holy Spirit, He imprints His moral code of love in human hearts once again, that we may fulfill Jesus' commandments to "love the LORD your God with all your heart, with all your soul, with all your mind, and with all your strength" and to "love your neighbor as yourself" (Romans 5:5; Mark 12:30–31).

The Apostle Paul wrote, "may the Lord make you increase and abound in love to one another and to all. . . [for this purpose] so that He may establish your hearts blameless in holiness before our God and Father at the coming of our Lord Jesus Christ" (1 Thessalonians 3:12-13). What is Paul saying? As we grow in love we grow in holiness (separation from sin). God's purpose for our living in submission to Him is that we may "be found by Him in peace, without spot and blameless" at His coming (2 Peter 3:14). We can count on His work in our lives to restore our righteousness by faith—

Now may the God of peace Himself sanctify you completely; and may your whole spirit, soul, and body be preserved blameless at the coming of our Lord Jesus Christ. He who calls you is faithful, who also will do it (1 Thessalonians 5:23–24).

Now may the God of peace who brought up our Lord Jesus from the dead, that great Shepherd of the sheep, through the blood of the everlasting covenant, make you complete in every good work to do His will, working in you what is well pleasing in His sight, through Jesus Christ, to whom be glory forever and ever. Amen (Hebrews 13:20–21).

STEP THREE – YIELD TO THE LEADING OF THE HOLY SPIRIT

The Apostle Paul wrote these amazing words: "Do you not know that to whom you present yourselves slaves to obey, you are that one's slaves whom you obey, whether of sin leading to death, or of obedience leading to righteousness?" (Romans 6:16). What is he saying? We either yield to our own sinful inclinations and let Satan lead us around by his hook in our nose, or we yield to God's plan for our lives and allow Him to lead us by His love.

The concept of *surrendering to God* is really better explained by the word "yield". If we think of the internationally recognized road sign—the *yield sign*—what is its purpose? It establishes who has the right to go first on roadways, and governs how we act at uncontrolled intersections, T-intersections, and school zones. We yield to the authority of that sign to prevent crashes.

In the school of life we daily—even hourly—reach intersections where we need to *yield* to the Holy Spirit and allow Him first access to lead us and prevent us from crashing and burning. The more we *yield* to the Holy Spirit's leading, the more we are emptied of self and become like Christ. If we hunger and thirst for His righteousness, the Lord fills us with His righteousness (Matthew 5:6).

The Holy Spirit opens the eyes of our understanding as we read Scripture, and through our study helps us develop the humble mind of Christ (1 Corinthians 2:13–16; Philippians 2:5). What was the source of Christ's strength? It was obedience to the Word and will of God. He didn't obey to *become* the covenant Son of God. He obeyed because He *was* the covenant Son. His spiritual stamina was fortified because He lived by "every word that proceeds from the mouth of God," and He calls us to do the same (Matthew 4:4). The source of our spiritual strength to remain in covenant relationship with the Lord are His Words of life. Through Scripture, the Holy Spirit increases revelation, gives us wisdom, and helps us to "grow in the grace and knowledge of our Lord and Savior Jesus Christ" (2 Peter 3:18).

Bible study cannot be underestimated in the process of restoring our *righteousness by faith*. Jesus told the parable of the seed, explaining it by saying, "The seed is the word of God" (Luke 8:11). Do you agree that the potential of any harvest is wrapped inside the seed? Plant wheat—harvest wheat. Plant corn—harvest corn. Since the Word of God is the seed, consider this: All of your potential is wrapped inside His Word. Your part is to implant His Word, "which is able to save your souls. But be doers of the word, and not hearers only, deceiving yourselves" (James 1:21–22). Jesus Himself said we are blessed when we "hear the word of God and obey it" (Luke 11:28, NIV).

Obedience is not legalism. Obedience is love, and the highest expression of worship.

Sanctification by faith is the work of God that lasts throughout our lifetime. Development of a righteous, Christ-like character comes a little at a time as we put His Word into practice. The Word of God is alive and active, and contains the power to yield "first the blade, then the head, after that the full grain" (Hebrews 4:12; Mark 4:28). We plant the seed of Scripture in our hearts. It begins to sprout and grow with the power to transform our character.

Covenant relationship requires conversation. Prayer is essential, and the hallmark of humility, because submission requires prayer to seek God's will. God desires that we should "seek His face"—seek His presence through prayer (Psalm 27:8). Paul tells us to "pray without ceasing" (1 Thessalonians 5:17). That happens only as we develop a divine awareness of His constant presence with us, and practice His presence by talking with Him throughout the day, rather than ignoring Him. We simply open our hearts and speak to Him as our loving Father and Friend.

Prayer should be a heart-to-heart, two-way conversation. Since God speaks to us primarily through His Word, I talk with Him as I'm reading the Bible and listen to His Word. Invite the Holy Spirit to guide your prayers—He is our prayer Partner (Romans 8:26).

While there is no question we are saved by grace through faith, and salvation is the "the gift of God, not of works," in the same passage Paul says we were "created in Christ Jesus for good works, which God prepared beforehand that we should walk in them" (Ephesians 2:8–10). Jesus said, "Let your light so shine before men, that they may see your good works and glorify your Father in heaven," and that what we do in service for others, we actually do for Him (Matthew

5:16; 25:40). Walking in covenant relationship requires service for the interests of others (Philippians 2:4). For example, "Pure and undefiled religion before God and the Father is this: to visit orphans and widows in their trouble, and to keep oneself unspotted from the world" (James 1:27).

Finally, walking in covenant relationship with God means we maintain a relationship with His covenant community on Earth. The author of Hebrews wrote, "And let us consider one another in order to stir up love and good works, not forsaking the assembling of ourselves together, as is the manner of some, but exhorting one another, and so much the more as you see the Day approaching" (Hebrews 10:24–25).

We can only be filled with the Holy Spirit to the degree that we are emptied of self. There will be times we sin against the Spirit by resisting Him (Acts 7:51), grieving Him (Ephesians 4:30), or even quenching His influence in our lives (1 Thessalonians 5:19). When we do we should ask for forgiveness. To maintain the vitality of our covenant relationship with God, we should start off each day by praying to be filled afresh with the Holy Spirit, so that we can have the power we need to live in godliness—

> So I say to you, Ask and keep on asking and it shall be given you; seek and keep on seeking and you shall find; knock and keep on knocking and the door shall be opened to you. For everyone who asks and keeps on asking receives; and he who seeks and keeps on seeking finds; and to him who knocks and keeps on knocking, the door shall be opened. . . . If you then, evil as you are, know how to give good gifts [gifts that are to their advantage] to your children, how much more will your heavenly Father give the Holy Spirit to those who ask and continue to ask Him! (Luke 11:9, 10, 13; AMP).

The work of the Holy Spirit is the work of the everlasting covenant—to bring about our *righteousness by faith*. Here is the question on which we should all reflect: What would happen in our lives if we fully surrendered to God's love and yielded to the Holy Spirit's leading?

COVENANT LANGUAGE IS ALSO APPLIED TO NEW COVENANT CHRISTIANS

The Lord Jesus calls on us to "Seek first the kingdom of God and His righteousness," and promised that as many as receive Him as Savior, "to them He gave the right to become children of God, to those who believe in His name" (Matthew 6:33; John 1:12). When we submit to the Lord as Savior we are *born again* by the Spirit (John 3:3, 7). Paul tells us, "if you are Christ's, then you are Abraham's seed, and heirs according to the promise" (Galatians 3:29). And Peter says we are "begotten"—born "not of corruptible seed but incorruptible, through the word of God which lives and abides forever" (1 Peter 1:3, 23).

Did you notice that covenant language is applied to all Christians today who live in covenant relationship with the Lord? We become the *seed* and are *begotten*—we are chosen for God's covenant purpose. As we abide in Christ, we are new creations—old things pass away, and we become new (2 Corinthians 5:17). When our names are registered in heaven, God even describes us by the covenant title *firstborn*—He gives us preeminence and we become the head, not the tail (Hebrews 12:23; Deuteronomy 28:13).

For you are all **sons of God** through faith in Christ Jesus (Galatians 3:26; emphases added).

For as many as are led by the Spirit of God, these are **sons of God**. For you did not receive the spirit of bondage again to fear, but you received the Spirit of adoption by whom we cry out, "Abba, Father." The Spirit Himself bears witness with our spirit that we are children of God, and if children, then heirs— heirs of God and joint heirs with Christ, if indeed we suffer with Him, that we may also be glorified together (Romans 8:14–17; emphasis added).

The covenant title *son of God* that identifies *humans beings who are living in covenant relationship with God and serve as a channel of covenant promises* is applied to New Covenant Christians, just as it was to the ancient people of God and to the Person of Jesus Christ. With the indwelling Holy Spirit we become a *covenant child of God.* The Apostle John spoke in amazement of this, saying, "Behold what manner of love the Father has bestowed on us, that we should be called children of God!" (1 John 3:1).

> What then shall we say to these things? If God is for us, who can be against us? He who did not spare His own Son, but delivered Him up for us all, how shall He not with Him also freely give us all things? (Romans 8:31–32).

Our covenant-making, covenant-keeping God has the very best in mind for us. He asks humans to receive His love, submit to His authority, and yield to the leading of the Holy Spirit. The Lord wants us to hear His voice, and open our hearts wide to Him that He may dwell with us. That is how we enjoy living in covenant relationship.

SUMMARY OF "HIS" STORY
Chapter Thirteen

- Jesus issued the Great Invitation to come to Him to receive: 1) His provision of grace to overcome the destructive influence of sin in our lives; 2) a restoration of peace in the midst of life's storms.
- Jesus said to enter the kingdom of heaven we must become humble like little children.
- Humility is described in the Bible as total dependence upon God.
- Conversion—repentance in turning to God—happens as we humble ourselves.
- Repentance includes five steps: 1) we recognize our ungodly behavior; 2) godly sorrow causes us to regret our sins; 3) with an altered attitude we confess our sins, asking for forgiveness; 4) we receive God's forgiveness; and 5) God empowers us to change our conduct and make a u-turn to return to Him.
- *Pride* and the *desire to exalt self* that swelled in Satan's heart is the root of all sin.

- Jesus walked in humility, laying down His independent authority, delighting to do God's will, and yielding completely to the direction of the Holy Spirit.
- Self-sacrificing love expressed through humility is the root of righteousness and the most-needed character trait for humans to follow in Christ's footsteps.
- The up-close-and-personal God dwells with the humble and lifts them up.
- The Holy Spirit was sent to continue Christ's ministry on Earth—He is our Advocate, Counselor, Comforter, Intercessor, and Helper on Earth.
- God said His people are destroyed for lack of knowledge.
- Jesus said we must *strive to enter* His kingdom through the narrow gate, and do the will of the Father in heaven to enter His kingdom. To remain in covenant relationship with Him, we must walk in loving obedience.
- To enter into covenant relationship with God, three steps are required: 1) we recognize His infinite love, superior knowledge, and great power; 2) we stop resisting His love, and submit to His instructions, directions, and correction; 3) we yield to the leading of the Holy Spirit.
- Jesus said we must daily die to self, and relinquish our independent authority.
- Jesus promised that if we have an obedient attitude, we will receive the Holy Spirit.
- When the Holy Spirit dwells in us, Jesus and the Father live in our hearts by faith.
- The more we yield to the Holy Spirit, the more we become like Christ.
- Jesus received His spiritual stamina from the Word of God, and said we live by every word that proceeds from the mouth of God.
- Spirit-led Bible study cannot be underestimated in the process of restoring righteousness.
- Covenant relationship requires heart-to-heart conversation with our Heavenly Father.
- The Holy Spirit helps us pray.
- Covenant relationship requires that we walk in acts of service toward others, and be a part of a covenant community. The Holy Spirit gifts us to serve.
- When we sin against the Holy Spirit by resisting, grieving, or quenching Him, we should ask for forgiveness for sinning against God.

- To receive much-needed divine power, we should daily pray to be filled with the Holy Spirit.
- The language of God's everlasting covenant is applied to New Testament Christians. We become: the *seed; begotten, firstborn, covenant children of God.*
- What manner of love God has bestowed on us, that we should be called His children.
- God freely gives all things to His covenant children, working all things together for their eternal benefit.
- Living in covenant relationship with God brings joy everlasting.

OUT WITH THE OLD—IN WITH THE NEW

Chapter fourteen

S aul of Tarsus was a religious zealot—a Pharisee of Pharisees, who had intense pride in his Jewish heritage and trusted his self-proclaimed "blameless" adherence to God's law for righteousness (Acts 23:6; Philippians 3:4–6). With preconceived opinions, he had rejected Christ as the Savior-Messiah, and was persecuting the members of the early Christian church (Acts 26:10–11), until he was blinded by the light of eternal humility one day on the road to Damascus.

The risen Christ appeared to commission him to take the gospel to the Gentiles—

> To open their eyes, in order to turn them from darkness to light, and from the power of Satan to God, that they may receive forgiveness of sins and an inheritance among those who are sanctified by faith in Me (Acts 26:18).

In 40 words, Christ summed up all three aspects of salvation through the everlasting covenant of *righteousness by faith* in Him.

First, to receive "forgiveness of sins," we must turn away from sin to Him, believing His substitutionary death on the cross was sufficient to pay our sin-debt. Anyone who accepts Jesus as Savior is *justified by faith* and redeemed from the *penalty* of death. Secondly, those who receive Him as Lord will be *sanctified by faith* and delivered from the power of sin. Finally, the "inheritance" that Christ spoke of is the promise of eternal life—the promise He will deliver when He rescues us from the *presence* of sin. Only those who are "sanctified by faith" in Him receive this inheritance.

Confronted by the risen Lord, Saul came to understand that obedience to any law could not possibly release humans from sin's penalty of death (Acts 9:3). The direction of his life changed immediately. He submitted to the Lord's authority, yielding to the Holy Spirit, who empowered him to make a U-turn and head in the right direction toward God. Saul was his Jewish name, but he was also known by the Roman name of Paul, which he began using on his mission to take the gospel to the Gentiles as God's ambassador of grace (Acts 13:9).

Paul wrote with the voice of experience when he said, "if anyone is in Christ, he is a new creation; old things have passed away; behold, all things have become new" (2 Corinthians 5:17). Out with the old—in with the new! A beautiful promise, but these words can discourage those who have entered into covenant relationship with the Lord and suddenly experience their old sin-nature rearing its ugly head. It can cause us to wonder if we are really "in Christ."

How comforting to know that Paul explained that God "gives life to the dead and calls those things which do not exist as though they did" (Romans 4:17). What does he mean? *Sanctification* is God's work in us throughout our lifetime. God knows our covenant relationship with Him is under construction, but He looks at us with smiling eyes as our loving Heavenly Father. Knowing the end from the beginning, He sees the final results of our restored righteousness as He conforms us to the image of Christ, because "He who has begun a good work in you will complete it until the day of Jesus Christ" (Philippians 1:6).

LIVING "IN CHRIST" IS THE OPPOSITE OF LIVING "IN THE FLESH"

Paul frequently used the term "in Christ" to describe those saved by grace through faith, who live in submission to God's authority and follow the lead of the Holy Spirit. Being *in Christ* means to abide in a day-to-day covenant relationship with Him. This brings not only the hope of the inheritance to come, but hope for the present. *Hope* in the original Greek meant *eager expectation.*

For those *in Christ*, Paul says our hope is this: "We know that all things work together for good to those who love God, to those who are the called according to His purpose" (Romans 8:28). The next verse explains how God works out all things—no matter how distressing or tragic—for our good: "For whom He foreknew, He also predestined to be conformed to the image of His Son" (v. 29). God looked down through history and determined that the destiny of all His covenant children was to be recreated in the image of Jesus.

He brings this about through the process of sanctification as we abide *in Christ*, the true Vine (John 15:1–8). By the power of the Holy Spirit, our hearts overflow with peace and joy, and we abound in hope—eager expectation of the Lord's plan for us (Romans 15:13; Jeremiah 29:11–14). As we abide *in Christ*, we can count on these promises—

And this is the testimony: that God has given us eternal life, and this life is in His Son. He who has the Son has life; he who does not have the Son of God does not have life (1 John 5:11–12).

The LORD your God in your midst, the Mighty One, will save; He will rejoice over you with gladness, He will quiet you with His love, He will rejoice over you with singing (Zephaniah 3:17).

In one power-packed chapter—Romans 8—the Apostle Paul presents the three aspects of God's salvation. He opens the chapter saying there is no condemnation for those who are *in Christ*. He closes the chapter saying we cannot be separated from God as long as we abide *in Christ*. In Romans 8 Paul mentions the Holy Spirit 19 times as our vital life source to remain *in Christ*.

In sharp contrast, Paul describes living "in the flesh" as being "carnally minded," and exactly the opposite of living *in Christ*. So how do we know if we are living *in Christ* or living *in the flesh*? Paul points out the critical difference between these two mindsets and types of existence. In no uncertain terms, he pronounces God's condemnation over a life that is lived "in the flesh"—

> For those who live <u>according to the flesh</u> set their minds on the things of the flesh, but those who live according to the Spirit, the things of the Spirit. <u>For to be carnally minded is death</u>, but to be spiritually minded is life and peace. Because the <u>carnal mind is enmity against God; for it is not subject to the law of God, nor indeed can be. So then, those who are in the flesh cannot please God.</u> But you are not in the flesh but in the Spirit, if indeed the Spirit of God dwells in you. Now if anyone does not have the Spirit of Christ, he is not His. And if Christ is in you, the body is dead because of sin, but the Spirit is life because of righteousness. But if the Spirit of Him who raised Jesus from the dead dwells in you, He who raised Christ from the dead will also give life to your mortal bodies through His Spirit who dwells in you (Romans 8:5–11; emphasis added).

Those who habitually walk *in the flesh* will suffer the penalty of the second death for their sins, as "to be carnally minded is death" (v. 6). The expression *carnal Christian* contains two contradictory and incompatible words. To reject God's instructions for righteousness and gratify the impulses of the fallen sin nature is to express hostility toward God.

> Do not be deceived, God is not mocked; for whatever a man sows, that he will also reap. For he who sows to his flesh will of the flesh reap corruption, but he who sows to the Spirit will of the Spirit reap everlasting life (Galatians 6:7–8).

Paul told the Galatians, "Now the works of the flesh are evident, which are: adultery, fornication, uncleanness, lewdness, idolatry, sorcery, hatred, contentions, jealousies, outbursts of wrath, selfish ambitions, dissensions, heresies, envy, murders, drunkenness, revelries, and the like; of which I tell you beforehand, just as I also told you in time past, that those who practice such things will not inherit the kingdom of God" (Galatians 5:19–21). Those who think they can live like the devil and still be saved by grace are spiritually deluded, and spiritually dead.

Here's the key to understanding how to avoid the works of the flesh—

> For if you live according to the flesh you will die; but if by the Spirit you put to death the deeds of the body, you will live (Romans 8:13).

Do you see that Romans 8:13 defines a cooperative effort? We cannot put to death the deeds of our fallen flesh nature by our own power, and the Holy Spirit will never force us. As we cooperate by taking action to follow His direction, He empowers us to put to death our sinful passions and desires. When we first enter into covenant relationship with the Lord we are all naturally carnally minded, but as we yield to the indwelling Holy Spirit, He circumcises our hearts and we become spiritually minded.

The evidence of the Spirit working within us is that He produces the fruit of love, joy, peace, long-suffering, kindness, goodness, faithfulness, gentleness, and self-control in our lives (Galatians 5:22–25). Developing the humble and righteous thinking of Christ, we are motivated by love to walk in a loyal covenant relationship with Him. As we abide *in Christ*, "Righteousness goes before Him, and makes His footsteps our pathway," and we live as Jesus lived on Earth (Psalm 85:13; 1 John 2:6). We are at peace with God.

Will our old nature occasionally rear its ugly head? Yes, and when it does, we confess our sin to the Lord and He cleanses us of all unrighteousness (1 John 1:9). It's out with the old—in with the new, as we follow the plan of our covenant-making, covenant-keeping Lord.

GOD KEEPS COVENANT WITH THOSE WHO KEEP COVENANT WITH HIM

Our journey through Scripture has provided evidence that God keeps His everlasting covenant of *righteousness by faith* with those who keep covenant with Him, walking in covenant love and loyalty.

He *justified* Abraham by faith because Abraham believed God, then He said, "I am Almighty God; walk before Me and be blameless" (Genesis 15:6; 17:1). Paul echoes this command when he states that we should become "blameless and harmless, children of God without fault in the midst of a crooked and perverse generation, among whom you shine as lights in the world, holding fast the word of life" (Philippians 2:15–16). Of course, Paul first explained how that is accomplished, instructing New Covenant Christians—

Work out (cultivate, carry out to the goal, and fully complete) your own salvation with reverence and awe and trembling (self-distrust, with serious caution, tenderness of conscience, watchfulness against temptation, timidly shrinking from whatever might offend God and discredit the name of Christ). [Not in your own strength] for it is God Who is all the while effectually at work in you [energizing and creating in you the power and desire], both to will and to work for His good pleasure and satisfaction and delight (Philippians 2:12–13, AMP).

Is there a work we must do? Yes—but not in our own strength. It's a work of cooperation with the Holy Spirit. It takes a Spirit-empowered effort to abide in Christ, and to maintain our covenant relationship. Remember, God made all the covenant promises, and He is the One who will faithfully keep us by His power—He is our refuge and strength, and a very up-close-and-personal God to us in times of trouble (Psalm 46:1).

As long as we choose to abide *in Christ*, He promises never to leave or forsake His covenant children (Hebrews 13:5). But we must remember this counsel, "The LORD is with you while you are with Him. If you seek Him, He will be found by you; but if you forsake Him, He will forsake you" (2 Chronicles 15:2). God will never violate our free will. If we choose to forsake Him, He will do everything within His power to humble us and bring us back to Him, but He will not force us to remain in covenant relationship with Him.

Paul's last inspired message was his final farewell letter to Timothy. It included these words: "This is a faithful saying: For if we died with Him, we shall also live with Him. If we endure, we shall also reign with Him. If we deny Him, He also will deny us. If we are faithless, He remains faithful; He cannot deny Himself" (2 Timothy 2:11–13). What does he mean? We all slip in faith, and have to repent, but the faithlessness Paul refers to results in apostasy.

Christ said, "he who endures to the end will be saved" (Matthew 10:22). An apostate doesn't endure to the end, but denies Christ by turning their back on the Lord, sometimes because of the love of the world, but often because of wrong teaching or tribulation. God consistently remains faithful to His Word. He saves those who believe and walk in covenant relationship with Him, and He condemns those who refuse a covenant relationship with Him (John 3:16, 18).

Scripture pictures the outcome of apostasy, but don't turn away disheartened, because it also provides amazing evidence that an apostate can still turn to God for mercy while time remains for salvation. First, the warning—

> For if we sin willfully after we have received the knowledge of the truth, there no longer remains a sacrifice for sins, but a certain fearful expectation of judgment, and fiery indignation which will devour the adversaries. Anyone who has rejected Moses' law dies without mercy on the testimony of two or three witnesses. Of how much worse punishment, do you suppose, will he be thought worthy who has trampled the Son of God underfoot, counted the blood of the covenant by which he was sanctified a common thing, and insulted the Spirit of grace? (Hebrews 10:26–29).

The Greek term for *willfully* carries the idea of *deliberate intention* and *habitual repetition*. If in this manner we reject Christ and His indwelling Spirit, there is no alternative sacrifice in the world to pay for our sins. Under the Old Covenant Law, a provision of sacrifice was made for those who sinned through ignorance, but anyone in the covenant community who deliberately defied God by rejecting His authority and disregarding His commandments was cut off (Numbers 15:27–31). It was the precious blood of our incarnated Lord—the Lamb slain from the foundation of the world—that ratified the New Covenant. Christ's blood that was shed on Calvary was the blood of the everlasting covenant (Revelation 13:8; Hebrews 13:20).

If we willfully, habitually, deliberately sin—not of weakness, but by choice—we trample our Savior underfoot. That is apostasy, and God will judge the person who defies Him. "'The Lord will judge His people.' It is a fearful thing to fall into the hands of the living God" (Hebrews 10: 30, 31). Oh, but praise God for His loving mercy!

One of the greatest pictures of God's mercy and divine grace in the Old Testament is His dealings with wicked King Manasseh (whose history is found in 2 Kings 21, which abruptly breaks off to be resumed in 2 Chronicles 33). Manasseh practiced great evils, introducing the horrifying custom of sacrificing children to Moloch, which God had expressly forbidden. And in further direct violation of God's law, he used witchcraft—consulting spiritists and mediums (Leviticus 19:31; Deuteronomy 18:9–12; 2 Kings 21:3, 6; 2 Chronicles 33:6). Manasseh seduced the people to do more evil than the Canaanite nations whom the Lord had destroyed before them, and shed innocent blood until he had "filled Jerusalem [with blood] from one end to another" (2 Chronicles 33:9; 2 Kings 21:16).

The Lord warned Manasseh through the prophets Isaiah and Micah, but instead of listening, he responded with cruel persecution. Around the twenty-first year of his reign, his unfaithfulness to God led to Judah's ultimate destruction and exile—the result of the Lord's judgment (2 Kings 21:10–16). Captured by the captains of the king of Assyria, Manasseh lost all of his royal dignity when he was carried off in iron bonds and fetters, led by a rope attached to a hook in his nose (2 Chronicles 33:11). Suffering at the cruel hands of his captors, he learned the idols he served were unable to save him. Manasseh's eyes were opened, and he became convinced the Creator was the only true God. In godly sorrow, he humbled himself and cried out to the Lord. The Lord listened and answered his prayers, graciously delivering Manasseh when he entered into covenant with Him (vv. 12–13). The Lord even restored the kingdom of Judah to him.

What an encouragement this is to repentant sinners. When we consider Manasseh's rebellion against God and then the transformation of his character, we see God's long-suffering patience and the renewing power of His grace to subdue the most offensive forms of sin. God delights in mercy and restoration.

ENDURING TO THE END

Returning to Romans 8, Paul explains the *need* and *reward* of enduring to the end, with this amazing promise to God's covenant children, "For you did not receive the spirit of bondage again to fear, but you received the Spirit of adoption by whom we cry out, 'Abba, Father.' The Spirit Himself bears witness with our spirit that we are children of God, and if children, then heirs—heirs of God and joint heirs with Christ, if indeed we suffer with Him, that we may also be glorified together. For I consider that the sufferings of this present time are not worthy to be compared with the glory which shall be revealed in us" (Romans 8:15–18).

Jesus is heir of all things (Hebrews 1:2). God's adopted covenant children inherit the divine right to participate in His inheritance if—and it's a big *if*—"we suffer with Him" (Romans 8:17). We don't often hear that truth preached. The world mocked, ridiculed, and physically persecuted the Person of Jesus Christ, and He said, "'A servant is not greater than his master.' If they persecuted Me, they will also persecute you" (John 15:20). We are called to share in His sufferings. Jesus counsels us, "he who endures to the end will be saved" (Matthew 10:22).

The Apostle Paul endured many persecutions throughout his life (2 Corinthians 11:23–33). He said of himself and his co-workers, "we were burdened beyond measure, above strength, so that we despaired even of life. Yes, we had the sentence of death in ourselves." Paul concluded that God's purpose in *allowing*—not *causing*—these events to happen was "that we should not trust in ourselves but in God who raises the dead, who delivered us from so great a death, and does deliver us; in whom we trust that He will still deliver us" (2 Corinthians 1:8–10).

Paul struggled against the continued presence of his carnal nature, saying he died daily to deny its passions and desires so that he could live by faith in the Son of God (1 Corinthians 15:31; Galatians 2:20). Though his physical body was decaying, he never lost heart, because he recognized God was renewing him inwardly day by day, growing and maturing him in Christ. "For we who are alive are always being given over to death for Jesus' sake, so that his life may be revealed in our mortal body" (2 Corinthians 4:11, NIV).

Paul's perspective on struggles and sufferings was that they were worth the tradeoff. First, he declared that Christ was "revealed in our mortal body" as a witness to the world. Second, mortal life on Earth is temporary, but the inheritance of God is immortality—eternal life in His presence. Paul concluded, "our light and momentary troubles are achieving for us an eternal glory that far outweighs them all. So we fix our eyes not on what is seen, but on what is unseen. For what is seen is temporary, but what is unseen is eternal" (vv. 17–18).

While we await the Second Coming, God uses our trials in this life to strengthen our faith and prepare us to stand through adversity. The furnace of affliction purges the impurities from our heart to make us shine forth like true silver and gold, so that we can reflect the righteousness of Christ (Malachi 3:3; Zechariah 13:9). James counsels us to "count it all joy when you fall into various trials, knowing that the testing of your faith produces patience. But let patience have its perfect work, that you may be perfect and complete, lacking nothing" (James 1:2–4). Peter shares this great hope of suffering, "And after you have suffered a little while, the God of all grace [Who imparts all blessing and favor], Who has called you to His [own] eternal glory in Christ Jesus, will Himself complete and make you what you ought to be, establish and ground you securely, and strengthen, and settle you" (1 Peter 5:10, AMP).

THE SECOND COMING OF CHRIST

"Christ also, having been offered once to bear the sins of many, will appear a second time for salvation without reference to sin, to those

who eagerly await Him" (Hebrews 9:28, NASB). It is critical to understand how Scripture outlines the events of Jesus' Second Coming. The
reason the religious majority missed Christ's First Advent is because
they wrongly interpreted how He would appear. Although the Jewish
nation eagerly anticipated Messiah's arrival, they thought He would
come as a conquering King, not as the Lamb of God who would sacrifice His life for their sins. At His Second Coming, He will not return
in lamblike meekness, but as the King who will tread the "winepress
of the fierceness and wrath of Almighty God" (Revelation 19:15–16).

Scripture clearly depicts the manner of Christ's return. Jesus declared that no one knows the time of His coming, and that the world
will be carrying on as it was before Noah entered the ark and God
flooded Earth (Matthew 24:36–39). But for those who walk in the
light, Paul says this Day should not "overtake you as a thief," because
we should recognize the increasing signs of His coming Day, just as
a pregnant woman recognizes how increased labor pains predict the
coming of her child (1 Thessalonians 5:2–4). Jesus warned that before
He returns many false *prophets* and false *christs* will display false signs
and wonders to try to deceive His covenant people. We need to know
all that He told us in advance to protect us (Mark 13:5–6, 21–23).

Is His Second Coming a secret? The Bible describes it as an
Earth-shattering event. Paul says Christ comes with the Archangel's
loud shout and a loud trumpet (1 Thessalonians 4:16). Jesus said He
would come in a cloud with power and great glory, and the powers
of heaven will be shaken when He returns with His angels (Matthew
24:29–31; Luke 21:26–28). He said His glorious appearing will flash
across the skies from east to west like lightning, and every eye will
see Him (Matthew 24:27; Revelation 1:7). Christ returns ready to
render His rewards to each human according to their works (Matthew
16:27; Revelation. 22:12). The sky will recede "as a scroll" and every
mountain and island will be moved out of its place; Earth's residents
will either run in fear—trying to hide from His face (Revelation
6:14–17)—or they will look upon their Redeemer in joyful anticipation of His reward.

When He shouts with the voice of the Archangel—as Commander
of all the angels—accompanied by trumpet blasts, are we to think

some might sleep through this spectacular event? When the skies recede as a scroll and He circles the globe at lightning speed, with ten thousands upon ten thousands of His holy angels, will some not notice His appearing?

Paul assures us that at Christ's return, the righteous living "will by no means precede those who are asleep" into the presence of the Lord (a sure indication that the dead are not already in His presence), but the "dead in Christ will rise first" and we will all be "caught up together to meet the Lord in the air" (1 Thessalonians 4:15–17). And the Prophet Daniel says, "many of those who sleep in the dust of the earth shall awake" (Daniel 12:2). What do they mean by *sleep*?

Jesus referred to death as a *sleep* (John 11:11–14; Matthew 9:24). Scripture tells us that when we die we are resting in an unconscious state like sleep and know nothing (Ecclesiastes 9:5, 10; Psalm 146:4). We rest peacefully, oblivious to events in heaven or on earth (Psalm 115:17; Job 3:11, 13). Unaware of the lapse of time, the next conscious moment for the righteous dead is at the sound of Christ's voice arousing them from their sleep. Paul shares the great truth with us—

Behold, I tell you a mystery: We shall not all sleep, but **we shall all be changed**—in a moment, in the twinkling of an eye, at the last trumpet. For the trumpet will sound, and the dead will be raised incorruptible, and we shall be changed. For this corruptible must put on incorruption, and **this mortal must put on immortality**. So when this corruptible has put on incorruption, and this mortal has put on immortality, then shall be brought to pass the saying that is written: "Death is swallowed up in victory" (1 Corinthians 15:51–54; emphases added).

Now for an important sidebar insert. Many misinterpret two contrasting statements of Paul in 2 Corinthians 5: "at home in the body we are absent from the Lord"; and "absent from the body and to be present with the Lord" (vv. 6, 8). In context, Paul describes three states of existence: 1) life on earth clothed with our earthly bodies, or *tent*; 2) death described as being unclothed, or naked; and 3) the condition of being further clothed when "mortality is swallowed up by life" (vv. 1–4). Context to Paul's hopeful conclusion is critical. Paul does not here imply we skip the stage of being unclothed in death. This is further proven by everything else he taught on the matter of when the righteous would be further clothed with immortal bodies.

Many believe the righteous are ushered to Heaven immediately after death, based on Christ's comment to the thief on the cross, "I say to you, today you will be with Me in Paradise" (Luke 23:43). Did Christ return to Heaven on Friday? No. On the Sunday morning of His resurrection, He told Mary, "Do not cling to Me, for I have not yet ascended to My Father" (John 20:17). He obviously could not have meant the thief would be with Him in Paradise that very day.

Based on all other scriptural evidence, it suggests that translators who added punctuation to Scripture texts mistakenly placed the comma. How differently it translates to our minds if the comma comes *after today* rather than *before today*: "I say to you today, [comma pause] you will be with me in Paradise." The thief believed in Jesus, and asked the Savior to remember him when He came into His kingdom. That day, Jesus promised that He would remember and resurrect him with the righteous.

At Christ's Second Coming, the righteous who are in their graves will hear His voice and come forward in the first resurrection—the resurrection of life, and He will send His angels to gather all His covenant people who belong to Him (John 5:28–29; Matthew 24:31).

> This is the **first resurrection**. Blessed and holy is he who has part in the first resurrection. <u>Over such the second death has no power</u>, but they shall be priests of God and of Christ, and shall reign with Him a thousand years (Revelation 20:5–6; emphases added).

The righteous "eagerly wait for the Savior, the Lord Jesus Christ, who will transform our lowly body that it may be conformed to His glorious body" (Philippians 3:20–21). Finally, the third aspect of salvation will be completed by the power of the Lord when He gives immortality to His covenant-keeping people and takes them to Heaven for 1,000 years. God will open the Heavenly record books and allow us to review His righteous judgment on who was disqualified from entering His kingdom. God's faithful will praise the Lord for His promise, "He who overcomes shall not be hurt by the second death" (Revelation 2:11).

Will the wicked have a second chance after Christ returns? Paul tells us the light of Christ's countenance will consume evil in "flaming fire" as He takes "vengeance on those who do not know God, and on those who do not obey"—He consumes them with "the breath of His mouth" and destroys them "with the brightness of His coming" (2 Thessalonians 1:7, 8; 2:8). Just as God shut the door to the ark before the flood, at Christ's Second Coming the door on salvation is forever shut. In His parables, Jesus taught that none who are outside His ark of protection at that time will gain entrance to His kingdom (e.g. Luke 13:25–27; Matt. 25:1–13). The dead lie in desolation on Earth during the 1,000 years. The prophet Jeremiah said, "I beheld the earth, and indeed it was without form, and void" (Jeremiah 4:23).

> But the day of the Lord will come as a thief in the night, in which the heavens will pass away with a great noise, and the elements will melt with fervent heat; both the earth and the works that are in it will be burned up. Therefore, since all these things will be dissolved, what manner of persons ought you to be in holy conduct and godliness, looking for and hastening the coming of the day of God, because of which the heavens will be dissolved, being on fire, and the elements will melt with fervent heat? (2 Peter 3:10–12).

THE SECOND DEATH IN THE LAKE OF FIRE

The Bible explains, "the rest of the dead did not live again until the thousand years were finished" (Revelation 20:5). A time will come when all the wicked dead will hear Christ's voice and be raised in the second resurrection of condemnation (John 5:28–29), which occurs at the end of the thousand years. The condemned are raised for the final execution of God's righteous great white throne judgment, and then thrown into the *lake of fire*—to utterly perish in the experience of the second death.

Then I saw a great white throne and Him who sat on it, from whose face the earth and the heaven fled away. And there was found no place for them. And I saw the dead, small and great, standing before God, and books were opened. And another book was opened, which is the Book of Life. And the dead were judged according to their works, by the things which were written in the books. The sea gave up the dead who were in it, and Death and Hades delivered up the dead who were in them. And they were judged, each one according to his works. Then Death and Hades were cast into the lake of fire. This is the **second death**. And anyone not found written in the Book of Life was cast into the lake of fire . . . . The cowardly, unbelieving, abominable, murderers, sexually immoral, sorcerers, idolaters, and all liars shall have their part in the lake which burns with fire and brimstone, which is the **second death** (Revelation 20:11–15, 21:8; emphases added).

Just as God once cleansed the earth with a lake of water, He will for a final time purge all unrighteousness from Earth by turning it into a lake of fire (2 Peter 3:6–7). Remember that Sodom and Gomorrah were "set forth as an example, suffering the vengeance of eternal fire," but they no longer burn today (Jude 7). The word *eternal* is a relative term—it relates to the nature of the thing it describes. When describing mortal humanity or perishable things, it simply means as long as the person or things exists. Earth will become a lake of fire that will not be quenched until it finishes its work. Sin and sinners will be purged—they will perish.

"For behold, the day is coming, burning like an oven, and all the proud, yes, all who do wickedly will be stubble. And the day which is coming shall burn them up . . . that will leave them neither root nor branch. . . . You shall trample the wicked, for they shall be ashes under the soles of your feet on the day that I do this," says the LORD of hosts (Malachi 4:1, 3).

When a righteous God sets out to destroy sin in His execution of justice with fire and brimstone, sinners will be turned to ashes and perish. God's heart of infinite love will be broken on the day He has to do this strange act (Isaiah 28:21). It is not His will that *any* should perish, and He takes no pleasure in the death of the wicked (2 Peter 3:9; Ezekiel 33:11). Yet, He created humans with free will, and He will honor their choice of rejecting Him. These who resisted His love and were unwilling to submit to His government of love on Earth would not enjoy the experience of eternal life in His Presence.

PARADISE RESTORED—HEAVEN ON EARTH

"For the LORD loves justice, and does not forsake His saints; they are preserved forever, but the descendants of the wicked shall be cut off. The righteous shall inherit the land, and dwell in it forever" (Psalm 37:28–29). Jesus promised the humble would be blessed and inherit the earth, but it will not be this old earth that groans under the curse of sin and awaits its redemption (Matthew 5:5; Romans 8:22). It's out with the old, and in with the new heavens and new earth. The Creator will recreate His perfect paradise of pleasure on Earth—a new genesis for those recreated in His image. This is the Promised Land that Abraham awaited (Hebrews 11:10).

The Lord showed the Apostle John what would happen after He destroyed our old Earth. He saw "a new heaven and a new earth, for the first heaven and the first earth had passed away" and "the holy city, New Jerusalem, coming down out of heaven," and heard a loud voice saying, "Behold, the tabernacle of God is with men, and He will dwell with them, and they shall be His people. God Himself will be with them and be their God" (Revelation 21:1–3). The redeemed will see Him face to face—oh, what a day that will be (1 Corinthians 13:12; Revelation 22:4). In the New Jerusalem there will be "no temple in it, for the Lord God Almighty and the Lamb are its temple. The city had no need of the sun or of the moon to shine in it, for the glory of God illuminated it. The Lamb is its light" (Revelation 21:22–23). The new earth will be the Lord's headquarters—Command Central.

God will make all things new, and will "wipe away every tear from their eyes; there shall be no more death, nor sorrow, nor crying. There shall be no more pain, for the former things have passed away"

(v. 4). "Then the kingdom and dominion, and the greatness of the kingdoms under the whole heaven, shall be given to the people, the saints of the Most High. His kingdom is an everlasting kingdom, and all dominions shall serve and obey Him" (Daniel 7:27).

The redeemed will rule and reign the Universe with Christ throughout eternity. "Eye has not seen, nor ear heard, nor have entered into the heart of man the things which God has prepared for those who love Him" (1 Corinthians 2:9). Eternity won't be spent floating around in heaven, strumming a harp. God's covenant family will have a dwelling in the Holy City, as Christ promised, "In My Father's house are many mansions; if it were not so, I would have told you. I go to prepare a place for you" (John 14:2). And they will have a country home, building houses and planting vineyards (Isaiah 65:21). Life in the new earth will be like the one Adam and Eve lived in paradise before the entrance of sin. "The wolf and the lamb shall feed together, the lion shall eat straw like the ox"—and no creature will hurt or destroy another because we will all be vegetarians again (v. 25). In the new earth, the Lord of the Sabbath says, "from one Sabbath to another, all flesh shall come to worship before Me" (Isaiah 66:23).

THE CONCLUSION OF THE MATTER

Why would we hold on to the things of this decaying world system and thereby forfeit eternal life with Him? The God of love and light deserves our unreserved commitment. "Let us hear the conclusion of the whole matter: Fear God and keep His commandments, for this is man's all. For God will bring every work into judgment, including every secret thing, whether good or evil" (Ecclesiastes 12:13–14). The Apostle Peter asks, "Since all these things will be dissolved, what manner of persons ought you to be in holy conduct and godliness?" (2 Peter 3:11). Then he answers the question for us—

We, according to His promise, look for new heavens and a new earth in which righteousness dwells. Therefore, beloved, looking forward to these things, be diligent to be found by Him in peace, without spot and blameless (2 Peter 3:13–14).

The spotless Lamb of God gave Himself for His church "that He might sanctify and cleanse her with the washing of water by the word, that He might present her to Himself a glorious church, not having spot or wrinkle or any such thing, but that she should be holy and without blemish" (Ephesians 5:25–27). He calls us to be righteous, and makes us righteous by our faith in submitting to His authority and yielding to the Holy Spirit's leading. He who calls us is faithful. He will sanctify us completely, shaping us to be what He calls us to be (1 Thessalonians 5:23–24).

To tell *His Story* correctly, we must recognize the unifying theme of all Scripture is that God is a covenant-making, covenant-keeping God. We can count on Him to keep His promises to make us spotless by our faith in Him. All of His promises are fulfilled through Jesus—THE LORD OUR RIGHTEOUSNESS ((2 Corinthians 1:20; Jeremiah 23:6; 1 Corinthians 1:30).

Spotless—the everlasting covenant of *righteousness by faith*. That is His Story.

SUMMARY OF "HIS" STORY
Chapter Fourteen

- In 40 words, Jesus summed up three aspects of salvation: 1) we must turn away from sin to our Savior, believing in His substitutionary death to be *justified by faith*; 2) we must accept Him as our Lord, submitting to His will to be *sanctified by faith*; and 3) only those who are sanctified will receive the inheritance of eternal life and be *glorified by faith*.
- God justified Abraham by faith, then instructed him to "walk before Me and be blameless." God does not change—He requires the same of us today.
- Living "in Christ" is the opposite of living "in the flesh."
- If we abide *in Christ*, we have assurance of salvation by grace through our faith.
- The Holy Spirit empowers us to remain *in Christ*.
- Our hope and our destiny are to be recreated in the image of Jesus.
- Jesus is the true *Vine*—as grafted in branches, humans must remain vitally connected to Him to be saved.

- As long as we abide *in Christ*, God will never leave us or forsake us. But, if we reject Him, He will reject us. He never forces us against our will to remain *in Christ*.
- Those who live "in the flesh" will not inherit the kingdom of God.
- God's dealing with King Manasseh is an Old Testament demonstration of His amazing grace.
- Jesus said we will share in His sufferings and that we must endure to the end.
- Paul experienced being overwhelmed by suffering, and feared for his life.
- Paul thought problems and sufferings were worth the trade off.
- No one knows the time of Christ's Second Coming, but it will be no secret appearing.
- Christ returns with a loud shout, a loud trumpet, and great glory in a spectacular event.
- The skies will recede as a scroll, and He will circle the globe at lightning speed with thousands of His holy angels. Every eye will see Him.
- The dead in Christ will hear His voice and come forward in the first resurrection.
- All the righteous will be changed as He imparts immortality to them and catches them up to meet Him in the air. The *second death* will have no power over them.
- There is no second chance for the wicked. They are destroyed at His coming, and spend the 1,000 years lying dead on the devastated planet.
- The wicked dead will then be resurrected to condemnation, standing before God in the great white throne judgment, and will experience the *second death*.
- God will turn Earth into a lake of fire and burn the wicked to ashes—the second death.
- The Lord takes no pleasure in the death of the wicked. He wants to save all.
- The Lord will create new heavens and a new earth. The New Jerusalem will descend to Earth. God's universal headquarters will be in the new earth.
- God will restore paradise—it will be Heaven on Earth. God will dwell with His people.
- Eternity won't be spent floating around on a cloud, strumming a harp.

- God's people will reign with Him, and life in the new earth will be like the life of Adam and Eve at the Creation.
- Scripture warns that since all things will be dissolved, we should conduct ourselves now in the godly righteousness of Christ.
- To tell *His Story* correctly, we must recognize the unifying theme of Scripture—that our God is a covenant-making, covenant-keeping God.
- All of God's promises are ours through Christ—our Righteousness.

THE END-TIME MESSAGE OF RIGHTEOUSNESS BY FAITH

Epilogue

G*race* and *hesed* are both covenant terms that define the demonstration of God's love toward those who enter into His everlasting covenant of righteousness by faith. The love of God is bestowed in a special manner to those who abide in covenant relationship with Him. He promises His provision, protection, and peace for His children. Moreover, He promises to make Himself known in an intimate manner:

> The person who has My commands and keeps them is the one who [really] loves Me; and whoever [really] loves Me will be loved by My Father, and I [too] will love him and will show (reveal, manifest) Myself to him. [I will let Myself be clearly seen by him and make Myself real to him] (John 14:21, AMP).

Christ reveals Himself through the Spirit and the Word to those who walk in loving obedience to Him. He does not leave His children unaware, but reveals the future through prophecy to provide a greater understanding of what will happen before He returns.

Bible prophecies are not intended to scare us, but to increase our faith. Jesus said, "I have told you before it comes, that when it comes to pass you may believe" (John 14:29). We can have confidence that the Holy Spirit will prepare us for the challenges we will face, and give us the grace to guide our steps as each day requires.

The Bible prophesies that a time of great trouble will come upon the Earth just prior to Christ's Second Coming. Jesus warned about it in Matthew 24. The books of Daniel and Revelation speak of a beastly power that acts to stand in the place of God, and another apostate group who forms an "image" to the beast. These beast powers are interpreted as "kingdoms that will rise from the earth" (Daniel 7:17).

The book of Revelation is all about Jesus Christ (Revelation 1:1). It seems veiled in symbolic language, but the key to understanding the last book of the Bible is that it contains over 500 quotes or allusions from at least 28 Old Testament books. Signs and symbols of Revelation find their meaning as explained in the Old Testament. The Bible interprets itself—"no prophecy of Scripture is of any private interpretation" (2 Peter 1:20).

Just prior to this troubled time, the Lord will illuminate the world with the light of His glory, calling His people out of *spiritual* Babylon—a false system of worship. God has a remnant in every church, and before He passes judgment on spiritual Babylon, the voice from Heaven cries "Come out of her, my people, lest you share in her sins, and lest you receive of her plagues" (Revelation 18:4).

God gives His covenant-keeping children a special end-time message to deliver to the world—the three angels' messages of Revelation 14:6–12. This paradigm-shifting proclamation is meant not only meant to gain the attention of unbelievers, but to call His remnant children to true worship and to warn them of the mark of the beast.

THE FIRST ANGEL'S MESSAGE

Then I saw another angel flying in the midst of heaven, having the everlasting gospel to preach to those who dwell on the earth—to every nation, tribe, tongue, and people—saying with a loud voice, "Fear God and give glory to Him, for the hour of His judgment has come; and worship Him who made heaven and earth, the sea and springs of water" (Revelation 14:6–7).

The first angel is identified as "having the everlasting gospel to preach to all who dwell on the earth (v. 6). The most important message the world needs to hear is God's everlasting covenant of *righteousness by faith* based on the substitutionary death of Christ—the Lamb of God slain from the foundation of the world, and His great exchange of taking our sins that we might become the righteousness of God *in Christ* (Revelation 13:8; 2 Corinthians 5:21).

The everlasting covenant is the foundation of the three angels' messages. The warnings the angels pronounce make no sense to anyone who doesn't understand their need to cultivate a relationship with Christ to receive His *righteousness by faith*, and His power to overcome the wiles of Satan.

This first angel loudly proclaims, "Fear God and give glory to Him, for the hour of His judgment has come; and worship Him who made heaven and earth, the sea and springs of water" (Revelation 14:7). To *fear God* is to hold Him in awe and reverence. This is an invitation to a deeper life of faith, especially in the time of judgment.

Again, I emphasize this point—how can someone respond to this message if they don't know about His everlasting covenant? The Lord offers everything needed for salvation. God says, "let him who glories glory in this, that he understands and knows Me, that I am the LORD, exercising loving kindness, judgment, and righteousness in the earth. For in these I delight" (Jeremiah 9:24). Only by this knowledge can people offer Him the glory due His name for His marvelous works.

The first angel calls the human race to "worship Him" as the Creator who made "heaven and earth, the sea, and the springs of water." This language is lifted directly from the Fourth of the Ten

Commandments—the seventh-day Sabbath commandment which memorializes God as Creator, Redeemer, and the Sanctifier who develops a Christ-like character of righteousness within His people (Exodus 20:8–11; Deuteronomy 5:15; Exodus 31:13).

Here is a critical sidebar insert. God created a 24-hour period of time on the seventh day. He rested, blessed, and sanctified it as a time to celebrate a special relationship with His people, and as a continuing mark of His authority as Creator to establish Earth's periods of time (Genesis 2:2–3). The Lord calls the Sabbath "My holy day" and said He made it for humanity's benefit (Isaiah 58:13; Mark 2:27, 28). Not one single Scripture in the Bible authorizes the transfer of the sacred seventh-day Saturday Sabbath to Sunday.

So why do so many Christian churches celebrate Sunday as the Sabbath? It's no secret. The Catholic Church claims credit for transferring the sacredness of the Sabbath to Sunday. Does the papal system have the power to change God's commandments? Is it true Christians worship on Sunday based on the word of the Pope only? Hundreds of official quotes from Catholic documents could be cited as proof.

Here's one: "Of course the Catholic Church claims that the change was her act. And the act is the mark of her ecclesiastical power and authority in religious matters."[1] This is widely taught in the Catholic catechism and other Church documents. Christians were still worshiping on the Sabbath over three hundred years after Christ's ascension to heaven. The Council of Laodicea, in AD 364, passed a law (Canon XXIX) which decreed, "Christians shall not Judaize and be idle on Saturday but shall work on that day; but the Lord's day [presuming transference of His holy day to Sunday] they shall especially honor, and as being Christians, shall, if possible, do no work on that day. If, however, they are found Judaizing, they shall be shut out from Christ".[2]

In an ironic twist, the Catholic Church chides Protestants who follow their Sunday-keeping tradition. By historic definition, the Protestant Reformation began in protest of the Pope's claim of

---

1. James Cardinal Gibbons, *Faith of our Fathers*, p. 14, quoted from the office of Cardinal Gibbons, through Chancellor H.F. Thomas, November 11, 1895.

2. Charles J. Hefele, *A History of the Christian Councils*, vol. 2, p. 316.

ultimate authority over matters of religious faith. In contrast, Protestants proclaimed *sola Scriptura*—accepting the Bible and the Bible only as the infallible source of God's authority for the practice of the Christian faith.

Catholics respond to Sunday-keeping Protestants, saying: "But since Saturday, not Sunday, is specified [as the Sabbath of the Lord] in the Bible, isn't it curious that non-Catholics who profess to take their religion directly from the Bible and not from the church observe Sunday instead of Saturday? Yes, of course, it is inconsistent, but the change was made about fifteen centuries before Protestantism was born. They [Protestants] have continued to observe custom even though it rests upon the authority of the Catholic Church and not upon an explicit text in the Bible. That observance remains the reminder of the mother church from which non-Catholic sects broke away like a boy running away from his mother but still carrying in his pocket a picture of his mother or a lock of her hair."[3]

THE SECOND ANGEL'S MESSAGE

And another angel followed, saying, "Babylon is fallen, is fallen, that great city, because she has made all nations drink of the wine of the wrath of her fornication" (Revelation 14:8).

Spiritual Babylon—the cryptic title used by first-century Christians for Rome—is denounced by the angel for its fallen state, and for its coercion of others to follow its practices. God's end-time message for the world through the second angel is a warning to avoid false systems of worship and confusion from traditions of men that nullify the Word of God (Mark 7:9, 13).

Paul warns, "Beware lest anyone cheat you through philosophy and empty deceit, according to the tradition of men . . . and not according to Christ" (Colossians 2:8). What is Paul saying? Don't accept counterfeit standards.

People must have knowledge of the Lord's everlasting covenant of *righteousness by faith* to recognize the genuine from the counterfeit.

---

3. Reverend John O'Brien, *The Faith of Millions*, pp. 421, 422.

THE THIRD ANGEL'S MESSAGE

Then a third angel followed them, saying with a loud voice, "If anyone worships the beast and his image, and receives his mark on his forehead or on his hand, he himself shall also drink of the wine of the wrath of God, which is poured out full strength into the cup of His indignation. He shall be tormented with fire and brimstone in the presence of the holy angels and in the presence of the Lamb" (Revelation 14:9–10).

The third angel pronounces an indictment against the beast and his followers, and warns of receiving "the mark of the beast" in the forehead or the hand.

Forehead is symbolic language in Scripture for *mind* (Jeremiah 3:3; Ezekiel 3:9). To receive the *mark of the beast* on the *forehead* means to actually believe what is taught by the *spiritual Babylonian* beast and his image. Whereas, the symbolic interpretation for *hand* is actions (Proverbs 3:27; Matthew 6:3–4). When the *mark of the beast* is finally enforced, those who refuse to receive it will not be able to buy or sell, and will be killed if they refuse to worship (give allegiance to) the image of the beast (Revelation 13:15–17). Some people who know God's truths will still receive the mark in the *hand*, acquiescing to the beast power, and acting accordingly to save their life.

WHAT ARE THESE BEAST POWERS?

The Book of Daniel reveals that a *beast* in prophecy means a *kingdom* (Daniel 7:17). The *beast* described in Revelation 13 mirrors the Daniel 7 description of the *little-horn* power that arose from *national Rome*, speaking pompous words and thinking to change God's "times and law" (Daniel 7:25). The historicists of the Protestant Reformation identified the *papal Rome system* as this *beast* which had combined religious powers with the legal powers of a kingdom. Please note that we are speaking of a *system*—not individual members of the Catholic Church. I know some lovely Catholic Christians. God has a remnant in every church.

The dragon is that "serpent of old, called the Devil and Satan who deceives the whole world" (Revelation 12:9) and he gives "his power, his throne, and great authority" to this beast—no doubt to accomplish his ultimate purpose of receiving worship (Revelation 13:2).

Protestant Reformers saw *papal Rome* as this antichrist power "who opposes and exalts himself above all that is called God or that is worshiped, so that he sits as God in the temple of God, showing himself that he is God" (2 Thessalonians 2:4). The *papal Rome system* claims, "Sunday is our mark of authority. The Church is above the Bible, and this transference of Sabbath observance is proof of the fact."[4]

The image of the beast arises as a lamb-like kingdom with two horns, and speaks like the dragon (Revelation 13:11). All prophetic symbols of this beast point to the United States in prophecy, and foretell a time when the United States will enforce the *mark of the beast* by legislation, echoing the Council of Laodicea in AD 364. Historians report that the penalty for worshiping on the Sabbath was death. Many were martyred. Many more acquiesced to save their lives.

Will history repeat itself? Many believe that when the *mark of the beast* referred to in Revelation is finally established and enforced at the end of time, once again Sunday worship will be demanded, under the threat of death for not keeping it.

God will place His seal in the foreheads of His people—a special truth into the minds of His people to mark them as His (Revelation 7:2–4). This seal will be His sign of protection over His covenant-keeping people. It is the exact opposite of the mark of the beast, which is a symbol of destruction. The Sabbath is God's mark of authority as Creator God, as explained at the beginning of Creation, in the Ten Commandments God wrote on stone, and in the first angel's message.

THE CONCLUSION OF THE THREE ANGELS' MESSAGES

Here is the patience of the saints; here are those who keep the commandments of God and the faith of Jesus (Revelation 14:12).

God will have a commandment-keeping people at the end of time, who walk in covenant relationship with Him. Those who trust in the

---

4. *The Catholic Record of London*, Ontario, Canada, September 1, 1923.

Lord will walk in the victorious faith of Jesus, following His example of loving obedience to God. The Apostle John wrote, "Now by this we know that we know Him, if we keep His commandments. He who says, 'I know Him,' and does not keep His commandments, is a liar, and the truth is not in him" (1 John 2:3–4), and "If you know that He is righteous, you know that everyone who practices righteousness is born of Him" (v. 29).

A time of crisis is coming when the mark of authority over our lives will have eternal consequences. In His abundant grace, God winked at our ignorance in the past. "Truly, these times of ignorance God overlooked, but now commands all men everywhere to repent, because He has appointed a day on which He will judge the world in righteousness by the Man whom He has ordained" (Acts 17:30–31).

That day is rapidly approaching, but religious traditions are once again concealing Bible truths about His Second Coming, and the events that precede His appearing. If we misinterpret the manner of His Second Advent, we will misinterpret the *mark of the beast*. It's clear the *mark* is received before the millennial reign of the saints with Christ.

> Then I saw the souls of those who had been beheaded for their witness to Jesus and for the word of God, who had not worshiped the beast or his image, and had not received his mark on their foreheads or on their hands. And they lived and reigned with Christ for a thousand years (Revelation 20:4).

This time of trouble is the culmination of the cosmic conflict that Satan began in Heaven and brought to Earth. It is Satan's final struggle to steal the worship only due to God. But we need not fear if we walk in loving obedience and covenant loyalty with the Lord. God provided His Ten Commandments as protective boundaries to keep us on His path of everlasting life, and He promises that if we heed His commandments, our peace will be like a river, and our righteousness like the waves of the sea (Isaiah 48:18). "The work of righteousness will be peace, and the effect of righteousness, quietness and assurance forever" (Isaiah 32:17).

The prophet Daniel declares that God's covenant children will not only endure the end times, but "Those who are wise shall shine like the brightness of the firmament, and those who turn many to righteousness like the stars forever and ever" (Daniel 12:3).

SUMMARY OF "HIS" STORY
Epilogue

- God's love is bestowed to and received in a special manner by His covenant children.
- God reveals Himself and the future to those who walk in loving obedience to Him.
- According to Jesus' words in Matthew 24, and the Spirit's warning in the prophecies of Daniel and Revelation, there will be great trouble before the end of time on Earth.
- Revelation contains over 500 quotes or allusions from at least 28 Old Testament books—written in a code of signs and symbols which find their meaning in the Old Testament.
- The Bible interprets itself. There is no private interpretation.
- God gives an end-time message—the three angels' messages—to His people to turn many to His righteousness.
- The foundation of the three angels' messages is the everlasting gospel of the everlasting covenant of righteousness by faith.
- The first angel's message calls us to worship God as our Creator—lifting language directly from the seventh-day Sabbath commandment (the fourth of the Ten Commandments). God blessed and sanctified the day, calling it "My holy day."
- Not one Scripture in the Bible authorizes the transfer of the sacred seventh-day (Saturday) Sabbath to Sunday.
- The Catholic Church made the change, and claim that is their mark of power and authority, saying "The Church is above the Bible, and this transference of Sabbath observance is proof of the fact."
- The Protestant Reformation came about in an effort to turn the church back to the authority of God's Word as the sole basis for faith.
- Catholics chide Sunday-keeping Protestants for following their tradition.

- The second angel's message warns people to avoid the false system of worship and confusion of *spiritual Babylon*. God calls His people out of Babylon.
- The third angel's message warns of receiving the *mark of the beast and his image* in the forehead or hand.
- *Forehead* is symbolic language in Scripture for mind.
- *Hand* is symbolic language in Scripture for actions.
- *Beast* is symbolic language in Scripture for kingdoms.
- The beast described in Revelation 13 mirrors the Daniel 7 description of the *little-horn* power—a religious system that combines church and state, and arose from *national* Rome, speaking pompously and thinking to change God's "times and law."
- Protestant Reformers saw the *papal Rome* system as this beast in prophecy.
- The dragon is the Devil who gives his power, throne, and authority to the beast.
- The *image of the beast* is a kingdom that begins as a lamb-like power with two horns, but ends up speaking like the dragon. All symbols describing this *image of the beast* point to the United States in prophecy.
- The Council of Laodicea in A.D. 364 passed a law that commanded Sunday keeping for the Sabbath, and denounced worshiping on the day prescribed by the Lord. Historians say on the strength of this law, many were put to death.
- Will history repeat itself?
- God will place His seal in the foreheads of His people—a special truth in their minds.
- The Bible prophesies that God will have a commandment-keeping people in the end-time. The *mark of the beast* happens before the millennial reign of the saints with Christ.
- God's people will shine like stars as they hold out the message of *righteousness by faith*.
- The work of righteousness is peace--the effect of righteousness is quietness and assurance.

3ABN

Watch online at **3ABNPlus.tv** or download the free **3ABN+ app** to enjoy live streaming, plus over 2,500 programs On Demand.

 tv **Roku** android tv
android fire tv   iPhone

▶ **YouTube** — On Demand at **3ABNVideos**

dish — Channel 9393: visit **dish.com**
Available upon request.

fios✓ by verizon — Channel 291: visit **verizon.com**

Skitter — Channel 97 on its IPTV HD platform in various cities: visit **skitter.tv**

 Available on over 120 **cable** companies across the US

 Available on over 350 radio stations around the world **3ABNRadio.org**

 **3ABN** ®
Three Angels Broadcasting Network

Info: 618.627.4651 or visit 3ABN.tv